REASSESSING COMMUNITY CARE

(with particular reference to provision for people with mental handicap and for people with mental illness)

Edited by Nigel Malin

CROOM HELM
London • New York • Sydney

Croom Helm Ltd, Provident House, Burrell Row,
Beckenham, Kent, BR3 1AT
Croom Helm Australia, 44-50 Waterloo Road,
North Ryde, 2113, New South Wales
New in paperback 1988

British Library Cataloguing in Publication Data

Reassessing community care: with particular
reference to provision for people with
mental handicap and for people with mental
illness.
1. Mentally ill — Rehabilitation
II. Halfway houses
I. Malin, Nigel
362.2′1 RC439.5

ISBN 0-7099-5523-5

Published in the USA by
Croom Helm
in association with Methuen, Inc.
29 West 35th Street
New York, NY 10001

Library of Congress Cataloging-in-Publication Data

Reassessing community care.

Includes index.
1. Mentally handicapped — Care and treatment.
2. Community mental health services. 3. Mentally handicapped
— services for. I. Malin, Nigel
HV3004.R43 1987 362.2′0425 86-24190
ISBN 0-7099-5523-5

Printed and bound in Great Britain
by Billing & Sons Limited, Worcester.

CONTENTS

LIST OF CONTRIBUTORS

Andy Alaszewski is Senior Lecturer in the Department of Social Policy and Professional Studies at the University of Hull. He has been involved in research on the development of policies and services for mentally handicapped people since 1972. His doctoral thesis (University of Cambridge) was published by Croom Helm (A. Alaszewski (1986) Institutional Care and the Mentally Handicapped). A revised edition of his survey of services for mothers with mentally handicapped children has recently been published (S. Ayer and A. Alaszewski, Community Care and the Mentally Handicapped, 1986, Croom Helm). The research which is reported in this collection is based on a major study funded by the Department of Health and Social Security into the development of an alternative model of care for profoundly handicapped children and a full report is in preparation (A. Alaszewski and B.N. Ong (forthcoming 1987, Residential Care for Mentally Handicapped Children, Croom Helm).

Gina Armstrong studied at the LSE and Oxford University and qualified as a child care officer in 1970. She worked for the West Riding of Yorkshire initially as an action research officer and later as a generic social worker. Between 1973 and 1975 she combined fieldwork and lecturing at Sheffield City Polytechnic. From 1976 to 1979 she worked as a research officer with the Evaluation Research Group looking at services for mentally handicapped people in Sheffield. Her main areas of interest were services to families, provision for children under five and adult training centres. For the past four years she has been employed by Sheffield Family and Community Services establishing a family-based respite care scheme for handicapped children.

Dorothy Atkinson is lecturer in the Health and Social Welfare Department at the Open University. Her background is in social work, and social work education, and includes several years' experience of working with people with mental handicap and their families. Her contribution to this book is based on the findings of a recent research project she undertook in Somerset.

John Cubbon is a Research Assistant at the Nuffield Centre in the Department of Social Policy and Health Services Studies at the University of Leeds working in conjunction with Grimsby Health Authority. He was a student at the University of Cologne in West Germany and then at the University of Oxford where he obtained a BA degree in Philosophy and Politics and a BPhil degree in Philosophy. Since leaving Oxford, he has been involved in social research - first as Research Assistant at Bolton Community Health Council, then as Research Associate at Sheffield City Polytechnic and in his present post. His interests include methods of evaluating health services and the impact of research on social policy.

Larraine Eastwood worked for three-and-a-half years on behalf of the local social services running a group home. Since the home closed in 1982 Larraine has worked at a large Mental Handicap Hospital in the Rehabilitation Unit. She is a strong advocate of 'normalisation' for people with mental handicap and works continuously towards that end. Larraine writes as a lay person with several years' experience at a basic caring level.

Margaret Flynn qualified as a social worker in 1979 following a psychology degree. She has worked at the Hester Adrian Research Centre, University of Manchester, for seven years. Her PhD examined the moral awareness and decision-making skills of adults who are mentally handicapped. Afterwards, as a Research Associate she spent 12 months examining the contribution of Manpower Services Commission (MSC) programmes to the training needs of young persons with disabilities. Since then, as the Project Director of the Community Placement Project

(1983-86) she is studying the lives and circumstances of adults who are mentally handicapped and living in their own homes in the north west.

Nigel Malin has been Senior Lecturer in Health Studies at Sheffield City Polytechnic since 1980, specialising in social policy and research education. Before that he was employed firstly as a social worker and then for seven years as a full-time researcher initially at the University of Strathclyde and then as a member of the Evaluation Research Group at the University of Sheffield. His previous research has been on community and hospital-based residential care for mentally handicapped adults, professional practice and planning within health and local authority services. His publications include two books: Services for the Mentally Handicapped in Britain (co-author, Croom Helm, 1980) and Group Homes for Mentally Handicapped People (HMSO, 1983) along with a large number of articles. At present he is director of a post-qualification programme in mental handicap studies that emphasises social policy, normalisation and evaluation. He is currently engaged in research on employment and disability.

Sheila Manning qualified as a radiographer in 1970 working for three-and-a-half years at Pilgrim Hospital, Boston, Lincolnshire. She recommenced her career with the national health service in the administrative and clerical field involved in statistical and medical records. In 1981 she was appointed as administrator to commission a residential unit and day centre for the Mental Handicap Services. Since this time she has contributed towards the development of services for people with mental handicaps in South Lincolnshire. At present she is commissioning officer for the development of 12 bungalows and associated day centres and support services in Spalding, Grantham and Bourne. This project is running in conjunction with the eventual closure of institutional buildings within the area, and in partnership with the development of group homes by the social services.

Malcolm May began his career in the field of general nursing followed by further training in psychiatric nursing at the Maudsley Hospital, London. He left nursing in 1963 to become a mental welfare officer for the old West Riding County Council where he worked until 1974. During this period he studied for his CQSW. He was appointed Principal Adviser (Mental Health) for Leeds Social Services Department in 1974 and he has held this post since. In this post he has a wide range of advisory, development, training and liaison functions in the field of mental handicap and mental illness. He enjoys running, swimming and music and has run a Gateway Club for the past 16 years.

Jim Monach is Senior Lecturer in Social Work at Sheffield City Polytechnic, and Chair of Sheffield MIND. After a sociology degree, he spent a time as a psychiatric nurse before becoming a psychiatric social worker. Having qualified, he worked in generic and specialist roles in local authority social services. His interest in mental health issues is pursued via teaching, research, MIND, and membership of various other bodies including Sheffield's Family Practitioner Committee and Joint Consultative Committee.

Bie Nio Ong is a Research Fellow in the Department of Social Policy and Professional Studies at the University of Hull, and Honorary Research Fellow in the Department of Sociology at the University of Liverpool.

David Race graduated in Management Sciences from UMIST. After two years in industry he entered social services research first as a joint research fellow with Berkshire Social Services and Reading University and then as a member of the Evaluation Research Group at Sheffield University. During this time his research gradually focused on services for people with mental handicap and he was awarded a PhD in 1977 for a thesis on this subject. Then, after four years as a lecturer at the University of Hong Kong he joined the Church of England Children's Society as a Consultant (Handicap). He has published widely in the field of mental handicap.

Val Reed is a psychologist with a nursing background and extensive experience in professional and continuing education for nurses and multidisciplinary health care staff. A registered nurse tutor and first class honours graduate in education, he was a nurse educator for some years before obtaining a master's degree in educational psychology and a PhD for research into learning problems of handicapped youngsters. While DHSS Research Fellow at Nottingham University, he gained extensive experience in assessmental and clinical work with children, teachers and parents in community contexts. For seven years he lectured in communication studies and mental handicap studies to student CPNs/CMHNs at Sheffield Polytechnic. He is now a freelance writer, research consultant and scientific advisor to the DHSS Nursing Research Liaison Group.

Phil Thomas has been a social worker in Sheffield since 1975, and has held a specialist post working with the mentally ill in the community since 1979. He has had both an academic interest, and grassroot involvement in the area of residential and accommodation services for those with mental health problems, having completed a research project and been involved in the development of different types of residential schemes. Recently he has moved from fieldwork to take up a post as principal in a hostel for mentally ill people.

Kevin Teasdale is Senior Tutor for In-Service Training and Post-Basic Nurse Education in South Lincolnshire Health Authority. He has experience of working as a nurse in daycare settings for the adult mentally ill. He has also completed research projects on clients' perceptions of the value of a day service, and of the nature of stigma in daycare settings.

Alan Tyne was a teacher and then a teacher trainer for ten years, followed by several years researching social policy and services for people with mental handicaps. He lives at Wivenhoe in Essex and is director of the Community and Mental Handicap Educational and Research Association, an independent limited company and registered charity, whose work is described in his chapter.

Linda Ward is Research Fellow in the Department of Mental Health, University of Bristol, where she is engaged in research on the development of local services for adults with severe learning difficulties. She is currently seconded part-time as lecturer in the Department of Health and Social Welfare at the Open University, where she is involved in the production of the forthcoming Mencap/OU Course for parents and staff 'Mental Handicap: Patterns for Living'.

PREFACE

This book is an attempt to bring together many of the relevant issues surrounding the policy of community care. Its title, Reassessing Community Care, highlights the topicality of this subject and the vast amount of words that have been expressed upon it. The intention of this volume, however, is to appraise its current status - its content and its future implications. There is, at the time of writing, a serious dearth of evaluative material on this subject despite its importance. This book aims to be useful both as a course book to students - for example, in social work, nursing, social policy and health studies - and to planners and professionals who have an interest in the current 'state of the art'. Some of the predominant themes are as follows and these are put under close scrutiny: Community care needs to be properly resourced and to be supported by central Government; the aims of community care need to be articulated clearly and practice needs to be client-centred; partnerships need to be formed between consumers and providers of services; community care has major implications for the quality of staff performance and staff training; the means of providing practical and emotional support to people living in the community requires imagination and innovation.

Finally, an underlying theme is for the need to forge links between theory and professional practice. Several of the chapters that comprise this book are based on case-study material showing the circumstances and problems surrounding individual schemes and individual people as they experience living in the community. It is by drawing lessons from practical experiment and achievement that real progress can be made. The development of community-based services for people with mental handicap or with mental illness depends not only upon political will and initiative but also upon the commitment of individual professional people to being open-minded, honest and purposeful. It is hoped that this book will make some contribution towards creating an informed climate among those concerned with the interests of disadvantaged people.

I would like to acknowledge my students who have helped develop my ideas on community care.

Nigel A. Malin

For Charlotte

Chapter One

COMMUNITY CARE: PRINCIPLES, POLICY AND PRACTICE

Nigel Malin

INTRODUCTION

'Community care' as a phrase now means very little (House of Commons Second Report from the Social Services Committee Session 1984-85 Community Care (with special reference to adult mentally ill and mentally handicapped people) Vol. 1 para. 8 - subsequently to be referred to as HCSC).

Historically it began with concern over the 'function' of hospital care for people with long-term needs: studies of the 1960s and early 1970s, for example Tizard (1964) DHSS (1969); Morris (1969); King, Raynes and Tizard (1971) reaffirmed criticisms of existing institutions and pleaded for more stimulating environments within which care should be provided. The phrase gradually came to mean an 'alternative' to hospital care: living in the community. In the early 1970s the predominant view was that services for clients needing long-term care should be either in hospital or in the community - the community was not appropriate for all. More recently the view has arisen that it is not only a question of one's needs but also of one's rights to live in the community - people have a right to live in the community regardless of their disability, behaviour or other incapacity (although some writers, such as Angus (1984) and Spencer (1985) have argued that it may not be in their interests). Community care has become well-accepted; its meaning is still open to debate but there is consensus among most if not all interested parties that it is a 'good thing'. Is the problem then simply one of deciding on the means? Community care has become confusing (to interested students) owing to the lack of political commitment at both the wider government and the professional levels. All parties must take the blame for both the difficulties that have arisen in recent years and the ensuing piecemeal approaches.

The chapters in this book consider the effects of the many approaches that have emerged to provide community care for client groups, principally mentally handicapped and mentally ill people. The case studies have much to say both in a wider political context and towards the provision of services for other client groups. By concentrating on administrative, professional and client-centred interests, it can be argued that community care has done little to affect the overall quality of life of people dependent on health and welfare services. At the same time there is hope that as many ideas and practical schemes offer excellent care and potential for development there is the means for a way forward beyond much of the present conflict, confusion and demoralisation among professionals.

The policy of community care can be traced back to the Royal Commission on Mental Illness and Mental Deficiency of 1954-57 which considered the problem of outdated mental hospitals and recommended the 'development of community care' as a duty of local authorities in relation to section 28 of the National Health Service Act. The Mental Health Act 1959 emphasised the importance of providing services alternative to hospitals within the community, and the subsequent years saw a gradual build-up of new forms of provision. The shaping and effects of this policy are the subject of this chapter.

It is claimed that the policy has made relatively little progress since these early days, owing to several major factors. The impact of 'community care', has, it is argued, been influenced by four particular concerns:

(1) In order to take effect a policy needs to be properly resourced; ambiguity over the respective roles of responsible agencies along with increasing resource constraints have had a serious impact on the outcome of policy.
(2) The competing interests of professional and other groups have served to shape and inhibit progress.
(3) The policies of central government - seen as a principal agent in determining the character and direction of overall policy - have themselves changed.
(4) The actual meaning of community care has changed both at the planning and professional service delivery level; the <u>new definitions</u> have had

major implications for developing new types of services. This tendency towards innovation has called for new skills and new talents among both those planning and delivering care. These issues are presented for closer examination; at various times their interdependence is clear. Jointly, it may be argued, they have had the effect of shaping community care as a policy and of determining current priorities.

Certain writers (Brown, 1983; Ayer and Alaszewski, 1984; Graham, 1985) have seen during the 1970s a breakdown of political consensus. In the early 1960s it appeared that there was broad agreement about social ends and that social means were increasingly practical matters subject to rational decision-making processes. This is now no longer the case - a clear difference of interests exists at the political level: for the political right community care may mean hospital closure and savings on welfare services; for the political left it may mean both a chance to increase the quality of life of people and to redistribute welfare to better ends. The 1970s has seen an increased concern both with evaluation in social policy and alternative methods - how other countries tackle social issues, for example; - more recently there has been considerable emphasis on policy-based case studies - those explicit in their conceptual framework that pay attention to the political context of change and how ideas become shaped (Hall et al., 1975; Loney, Boswell and Clarke, 1983).

While the tradition of social investigation is still an active part of modern social administration, methods of social research have been refined and developed. The concern for a sound empirical base has remained constant, yet political pressure has made the distribution of welfare the art of the possible. Limited and increasing cutbacks in resources have had the effect of transforming good ideas into bad ones.

Current discussion centres on whether or not the welfare state is still alive; while professionals and planners debate the client ends up getting very little benefit. The client takes up a position of competitor for resources as professionals become managers of priority need, being forced by limited resource availability to decide upon priorities when many more than the bare minimum of clients deserve the services. In a climate of stifled development within welfare is it no surprise that clients are the main losers?

The real question about community care then becomes: whose interests are being served by this policy and is it a policy at all? Starting with a description of welfare state provision may inhibit the development of an unprejudiced approach to both explanations of social problems and alternative welfare strategies. One reason for this is the fact that health and social services are becoming increasingly unable to provide services for those in need. Many of the real interests of clients become overlooked, and professional views of client interests dominate instead. During the last few years the government has pulled back on public expenditure to make it difficult if not impossible to consolidate any proper plans for clients - the law of priorities within priorities. There are many examples of how authorities have developed 'showpiece' schemes to adhere to government and professional thinking - an advocacy project, a set of ordinary houses serving very dependent clients, an elderly persons support unit, a homemaker scheme - although there is a widening gap between such schemes and patchy underfunded services for the majority (Day, 1985). This is the very 'tip of the iceberg', and although useful in an experimental sense there is no guarantee that public sector services will respond to tested 'good' practice.

There is currently a move for clients to 'buy in' services from the private sector. If people are forced to leave long-stay hospitals and become dependent on social security payments then they may choose (and sometimes there is no choice) to spend money on private sector care. At the time of writing there is no great body of knowledge on the experience of the private sector in providing for clients who require long-term care. LeGrand and Robertson (1984) state 'Privatisation is too complex an issue to be dealt with adequately in terms of the simple for/against, public/private dichotomies in which it is often discussed', and consequently make the case for needing theoretical and empirical evidence.

Laming (1985) raised the following important question 'how can the element of chance which typifies the private sector both in terms of availability and in terms of quality be reduced and a system of monitoring and control which affords assurance of minimum standards but which does not crush the entrepreneurial spirit be established?'

Current research at the Centre for the Analysis of Social Policy at the University of Bath (see, for example, Bartlett and Challis, 1985) into the growth of private nursing homes has shown primarily that these are vastly different in many respects, operating on very individual bases with differing priorities and operational policies; this shows that demand for nursing home places appears to outstrip supply, thus limiting the possibilities of real consumer choice, and that the nursing home population at present is very elderly and highly dependent.

With the increase in demand on the health and social services and the changing status of the British economy it will be increasingly difficult to pursue policies that ignore other means of funding activities in the field of social welfare. It has been predicted that around the mid-1990s a real economic problem will arise about the financing of public expenditure caused by, for instance, the decline and eventual disappearance of North Sea oil revenues, and by the expected increases in the number of old people.

Rees (1985, p.250) presents one interpretation of recent government policy as a 'prolonged exercise in the spreading of blame ... the British economy has failed to respond sufficiently to the medicines which have been administered so both responsibilities and problems have been exported from the central government to local authorities, private companies, voluntary organizations or individuals'. According to this view 'privatisation' becomes not only a way of providing opportunities for profit, but also a matter of the transfer of costs and risks. However, the same author highlights anomalies in the outcome of such a policy, giving the example of the decision in 1980 to permit supplementary benefit monies to be used freely for board and lodgings charges in residential rest homes and fees in private nursing homes: 'This represented a shift from cash-limited local authority expenditure on old people's homes and domiciliary services like home help to non cash-limited "demand-led" central government expenditure. The result was that rest homes mushroomed, and the bill borne by the public purse escalated even faster' (Rees, 1985).

As increased charges are thought to bear no relation to the quality of the service provided, privatisation has brought with it an increased need for regulation by public authorities. There seems little doubt that private agencies will continue to grow and prosper as more people have index-linked pensions and home ownership increases. The number of elderly residents in private old people's homes has more than doubled since 1979 from around 34000 to over 70000. Whereas privatisation may well offer greater choice to consumers a practical outcome may be that such choice becomes only available to those who can afford the service rather than to those who actually need it.

Returning to the central issue of community care, it is clear that the term can mean different things to different groups of people, a meaning defined both by the perspective of those using the phrase and by the context in which it is used. Any discussion of the phrase centres on what community care actually means in practice - who is doing the caring? Is it a means of the government evading its responsibility to ensure that vulnerable members of society are properly cared for, or is it a liberation of people from dependency on monolithic welfare bureaucracies?

In his evidence to the House of Commons Select Committee on Social Services into Community Care (HCSC) Chris Heginbotham of MIND stated quite simply, 'There is no alternative to the government making available substantial extra resources each year to district health authorities and local authorities for the next seven to ten years, for a co-ordinated programme of community care provision'. This is not the kind of message the present government may wish to hear, committed as it is to the ideological task of weaning us off the state and cutting public expenditure. It prefers to consider community care as a potential resource saving and a boost to self-help values.

THE HCSC REPORT

The HCSC Report makes interesting reading, but as Bosanquet (1985), for example argues, it fails to deal with the central question: can the system actually be tuned to deliver community care? Some of the main recommendations are as follows:

(1) The committee supports a policy for community care for mentally disabled people which cannot be drawn up overnight nor on the cheap.
(2) The pace of the removal of hospital facilities has far outrun the provision of services in the community to replace them - hospital provision should not be reduced without 'demonstrably adequate services being provided beforehand'.
(3) Nobody should be discharged from hospital without a practical individual care plan

devised by all concerned, and communicated to all those responsible for its implementation.

(4) The existing mental disability service is underfunded and understaffed in both its hospital and social aspects. The government should accept that the policy is only achievable with some real increase over a period of years in expenditure on services - joint finance as a means of transferring further responsibilities from the NHS to local authorities 'is now virtually played out'. The DHSS should create central bridging monies to assist in developing alternative services.

(5) The government should promote a positive programme designed to gain a greater acceptance by the public of community care.

(6) Greater attention should be paid to the housing and employment needs of mentally disabled people.

(7) The considerable number of social security problems arising from community care has 'not always been fully appreciated by those responsible for the formation of social security policy'.

(8) The DHSS should give specific guidance on (a) the future care of so called 'old longstay patients'; (b) the care of homeless, mentally ill people; and (c) the role of DGH psychiatric units. Clear lines of responsibility as to who provides services should be given.

(9) In the long term all social care mental handicap facilities should be provided by local authorities. For most adults this should be in the form of ordinary housing within the community. The long-term separation of health and social services for mentally disabled people is 'illogical and inimical to joint services', and some means of eventually bringing together the two services is desirable.

(10) The DHSS 'is not in every respect living up to its duties of central management'.

The Report comments on the lack of cases in which there has been a radical shift of focus from hospital-based to community-based services. It could be said that the Committee has failed to tackle the issue of deperpetuating hospital care: there is a 'low productivity' of the funds currently being spent on hospitals (approximately £1.5 billion); there is the disproportionate influence of professional monopolies - not least that of medical consultants in both mental handicap and mental illness; maintenance costs on hospitals and costs per capita are likely to rise without higher admission rates and longer stays. The point that community care requires an initial investment, but in the long run the costs of greater independence are likely to be much lower, has not been fully realised. In addition the House of Commons Committee failed to grasp the nettle of structural change, despite recognising that the separation of services continues to be a major factor in achieving effective community-based services for mentally ill, mentally handicapped and elderly people. As community care increasingly becomes the norm, and hospital care is reduced as a proportion of the NHS, new opportunities exist for the various professional groups concerned.

The Report highlighted the sad state of collaboration between health and social services in most areas of the country, but was ambivalent regarding the options of how resources could be transferred and how services could in practice become more integrated or unified. Financial resources are restricted in local government, and many local authorities can no longer take on the long-term financial commitment of existing joint finance schemes.

Parker and Etherington (1985), for example, have supported the transfer of adult care to the NHS indicating that politically it is much more difficult to cut health services than it is the more nebulous local authorities. This would leave the latter to deal with the wider interests of children. The issue of integrating health and welfare services (or hospital and community services) is one deserving of far greater attention than can be provided here. The government consultative document <u>Care in the Community</u> (DHSS, 1981d) has succeeded in reopening the debate on both how resources might be transferred at local level from health to local authority services and on the need to 'separate off' individual services from the 'mainstream'. In the current political climate it does not seem feasible to make major gains in the latter area or even to 'earmark' funds for the benefit of specific client groups. Nevertheless it seems probable that in future there will be a greater emphasis on separating hospital services from the broad gamut of community services, giving local authorities far more client-group-based responsibilities - a reversal to the pre-Seebohm era. There are indications, for example, of more integration between community nursing and social work taking effect in the future (DHSS, 1985a). Although no political party has made integration official party policy, the increasing anxiety of public sector unions over the potential transfer of resources, and the unrelenting financial constraints faced by local authorities will, however, ensure its place on the political agenda in the not too distant future.

THE OBJECTIVES OF COMMUNITY CARE

The objectives of community care are confused by the range of interest groups involved.

It has been stated that 'the outlines of the post-war (Welfare State) settlement, though more and more insistently questioned from a variety of standpoints remains very much in place.' (Rees, 1985). Nonetheless, a degree of consensus is now breaking down and community care is a good example of a policy fitting this mould. From the 1959 Mental Health Act to the present day, successive pieces of legislation, White Papers and government policy statements have been based on assumptions that caring for patients in the community is both more humane and more effective than allowing them to remain in long-stay hospitals. Further, the assumption has also been made that community care could be less costly. These and other assumptions are now under challenge, for example, from trade unions who see job prospects threatened by large-scale closures, from relatives of patients who see community care as a poorly resourced alternative, and from economists who question the reality of savings to be realised from such policies.

Before the 1946 NHS Act local authorities had a dual responsibility towards both mentally ill and mentally handicapped people for residential and day care. In 1948 their 'colonies' became 'hospitals' serving both groups of people within the NHS, so that when in 1959 the wider local authority role was re-emphasised, the local authorities started almost from the beginning to build up an alternative residential care system. At about the same time voluntary groups were being established which also helped to challenge traditional assumptions and provide practical alternatives.

In the case of services for mentally handicapped people the development of policies may be traced back beyond the 1971 White Paper to the Royal Commission which sat from 1954-57 and the provision of the 1959 Mental Health Act which stemmed from its report; yet the 1971 White Paper provided for the first time ever a planned strategy. Local and health authorities could now debate the content of services for mentally handicapped people in operational terms. The overall concern of the White Paper was with the movement of people from hospital into the community and with increasing the support given to families. It set targets for local authorities to achieve in the number and range of services they should provide, and presented an overall 20-year plan.

During the 1970s groups were formed or set up, such as the National Development Group, the Warnock Committee that reported in favour of taking more positive action to integrate mentally handicapped people within the community; this was an era of positive policy discrimination towards services for mentally handicapped people, yet in practice few real alternatives to institutions, such as hospitals, hostels, training centres, special schools, were offered (Malin, Race and Jones 1980). Between 1945 and 1960 the manifestoes of neither main political party made mention of anything that might be done specifically to help disabled or handicapped people. Between 1959 and 1964 there was not one single debate on disability in the House of Commons, although there was a growing interest in different client groups in both policy and academic circles.

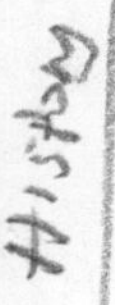

Other major events in the early 1970s included reorganisation of both health and local authorities which provided opportunities to revise structures in line with current needs. The Local Authority Social Services Act 1970 paved the way for a strengthened social services effort assisted by both the White Paper (1971) and the Chronically Sick and Disabled Persons Act 1970 which initiated concern over the rights of disabled people and over identifying and measuring their need for services. The Education Act 1970, by providing entitlement to education for all children regardless of handicap, set off a movement concerned with the closer integration of special education with ordinary school education.

The measures begun in 1975 by the then Labour Government to strengthen interest and concern for mentally handicapped people were central to the development of a policy of positive discrimination. Of these the National Development Team - a national body set up to assist at local level with the formation of community units and support teams comprising, in the main, psychology, social work and nursing professionals - survives today despite increasing controversy in recent years over the confidentiality of its work and concern over its actual influence on bringing about changes in services.

Another of these measures led to the setting up of the Committee to investigate the pattern of training appropriate to caring for mentally handicapped people which reported in 1979 (the Jay Committee, 1979, vol. I). Its recommendations in many ways surpassed its basic remit - a new 'model of care' was proposed which emphasised the need for a service geared to enhancing the social status of mentally handicapped people. These recommendations have had far-reaching effects both in deciding the nature of appropriate staff training and considering the quality of care to be provided.

The years since Jay have witnessed the highlighting of strong divisional interests within professional groups that has served to sharpen the debate over the aims of agencies serving the particular client-group. While one might conclude that the topic of mental handicap currently has little or no interest at the broader political level (despite an announcement in November 1985 that a Labour Member of Parliament would be supporting a private members bill to achieve more resources for this group (Guardian, 1985) within the professions themselves clear right and left centres of opinion have emerged.

POLITICAL DIVISIONS

Right-wing Policies

Before discussing these divisions some reference needs to be made to the political background within which such professional interests have emerged and have been fostered. Both right and left thinking are evident in the manner and style by which welfare policies have become articulated at party political level. There has for example been a marked revival in ideological modes of thinking, such as left-wing radicalism more penetrated by Marxist assumptions, than ever before in Britain.

However, since 1979 when the Conservative Government first took office, a new right pattern of thinking has dominated policy employing arguments like:

(1) the state is increasingly led to do things

which, although perhaps good in themselves, could be more efficiently done in other ways;

(2) that its undertakings are often extravagant and wasteful for reasons that are inherent in the nature of public action;

(3) that public employees at all levels are as self-interested as any other groups of economic actors and see this self-interest as being best advanced through the inflation of their programme budgets;

(4) that the goods and services known as 'welfare' are no different in principle from any other bundle of goods and services;

(5) that the market is a more sensitive register of preferences than are elections, and that social policies are no more than a subcategory of economic policies, and certainly in times of economic and financial stress the lines of demarcation between the two are no longer so clearcut.

If some of these ideas are translated to a more practical and specific level they may be shown to have implications as follows: the government supports:

(1) a greater role for voluntary organisations in the delivery of care;

(2) the closure of long-stay institutions where services have become concentrated and self-perpetuating;

(3) a policy of more self-care through the support of family networks;

(4) more choice by the consumer over services offered, and a consequent incentive to the expansion of private care as opposed to monolithic state provision;

(5) pressure on both NHS and local authority agencies through cutbacks in public expenditure.

The then Social Services Secretary, Norman Fowler, in a speech at the Joint Social Services Conference in 1984 made it clear that he saw the future role of local authority social services departments as a strategic one, taking into account all the resources available (private, voluntary, informal as well as statutory) in the department's area and recognising that the direct provision of services may not always be the most effective way of the social services department ensuring that needs are met. He told delegates:

> I recognise that for some this approach will represent a difficult change from a position where authorities have seen themselves as almost exclusively service-providing agencies ... calling for a wider conception of social services, directed to the well-being of the whole of the community and not only of social casualties and seeing the community it serves as the basis of its authority, resources and effectiveness.

Probably the most important elements of this contribution concern: the call to consider the needs of the whole community; the stress on using all the resources of the locality so that links can be established to blur the distinction between the helpers and the helped; and that local authorities should see themselves not only as a provider of services but also as fulfilling a role of enabling, facilitating and planning.

However, in recent years there has been widespread concern that the present government's references to mobilising and co-ordinating community resources have little to do with enlightened pluralism and much more to do with cutting back resources for local authority spending. No local government initiative at present can be seen in isolation from the government's overall strategy for cutting spending, rate-capping and abolishing the metropolitan county councils. Opponents of government policy argue that given this context of reduced central government funding and lost local autonomy any talk of reducing the service role of social services departments cannot mean anything but cuts in the level and quality of service provision.

It has been forecast that the government intention to switch the role of social services departments to 'enabling authorities' with a main role in contracting out their services to charities and private businesses will bring substantial staff reductions in the present £2.3 billion budgets, curtail trade union influence, and save ratepayers' and taxpayers' money by eventually allowing a reduction in rate support grants (Guardian, 1985).

The example of the Green Paper on Social Security published in 1985 further underlines the fact that the present government sees public expenditure as a problem and privatisation as a solution. Its purported objectives were to design a social security system capable of meeting genuine need, simple to understand and easy to administer, that fits in with the government's overall objectives for the economy. In effect, its renewed emphasis on means-testing will make it more difficult for people to receive the support they need.

Evidence for the intended cutback on services can be gathered from the regional health authorities 10-year strategic plans which show, for example, between 15 and 40% fewer hospital beds for the elderly being made available against the background of an increasing aged population. If health planning shows a shift to community care without provision of adequate facilities the effect, according to some critics, will be that the burden will fall on families and that means women. 'Today there are already more women at home looking after disabled and elderly relatives than are looking after children.' (Meacher, 1985).

Left-wing Policies

In contrast the position of the left offers a more committed defence of welfare state provision through increased state support and maintaining levels of public expenditure. Some complications arising from this include the ordering of priorities within statutory services, and determining standards for and methods of providing care. Broadly, the socialist position is for greater resources to be provided to local health and social services authorities and for a greater overall state role in the delivery of care; and greater provision of services to a minimum standard through granting local authorities mandatory powers. Harriet Harman, opposition spokeswoman on social services, stated in an article her belief that 'there has got to be a mobilisation in defence on basic provision' (Community Care, Murray, 1985b).

Critics of this view might claim that determining an acceptable level of basic provision becomes an almost impossible task as both demand and expectations increase in line with provision. There is also the view that an increase in public expenditure needs to be matched by a plurality of production in order for it to have a positive material outcome. Bosanquet (1985) has argued cogently that a lack of planning on the supply side automatically leads to demand-led change, which may in fact be wholly inappropriate. This may imply the need for an effective local planning framework, considering consumers and services on the basis of individual client need. He goes on to state that 'tax financing does not necessarily mean tenured posts in local government nor public monopoly but can mean encouraging the diversity which gives consumers choice'. In this sense the state-led alternative is seen as consistent with the use of a wide range of service-providing agencies contracted by and accountable to statutory funders.

In addition, the left supports pressure groups that are heavily trades union-based, for example, the nurses' pressure group represented by the Confederation of Health Service Employees (COHSE). A report published in 1985 (HSSJ, 30 May 1985) showed COHSE's condemnation of plans by Sheffield's district health authority and city council to move mentally handicapped people into the community without making provision for care by properly qualified nurses. COHSE maintained that the care of mentally handicapped people would be put in the hand of unskilled people with disastrous consequences, and emphasised its concern over deprofessionalisation and the fall in demand for qualified nurses as fewer mentally handicapped people are kept in hospitals.

This point indicates the quite serious complications that can emerge in planning circles where, for example, a council committed as it is to developing care within the community for a particular client group can be forced to back-pedal on such an issue in deference to its political masters. In _As of Right - Labour's Call for Citizenship for all Disabled People_ (Meacher _et al_., 1985) the authors (a group of MPs) support the view that

> the rights to properly paid, fulfilling work, to proper housing and appropriate health care, to education and recreation, are not special privileges for a lucky minority but fundamental rights ... many disabled people experience hurtful and damaging discrimination (not least in employment, education and housing) against which, unlike other oppressed groups, they are unprotected by legislation.

This report endorses the need for legislation to tackle discrimination: 'legislation (that would) affect people's attitudes and behaviour through education, persuasion and example'. It calls for such measures as a comprehensive disability-income scheme, enforcement of the quota system in employment, and more suitable housing to enable handicapped and disabled people to live independently in the community. The Labour view attacks the poor implementation of the Chronically Sick and Disabled Persons Act (1970) and the Education Act (1981) as, it is argued, both require a substantial injection of resources to be effective; the latter followed the recommendations of the Warnock Report (1978) supporting the integration of children with 'special needs' into ordinary schools.

Finally 'As of Right' calls for more representation of disabled people in decision-making machinery - more policy proposals reflecting the wishes and aspirations of clients themselves; 'self-advocacy and citizen advocacy for mentally handicapped people is an exciting and important example of what can be achieved by and from them'.

Service Provision in Mental Handicap - Political Views

In the area of actual service provision, taking the field of mental handicap as an example, both right and left-wing views again provide a useful focus for understanding trends that have emerged in recent years.

Professional groups have taken sides on community care and their views reflect the diverse range of ideas associated with this concept. Planning the care of mentally handicapped people has involved, for instance, taking into account the interests of the medical profession, nurses and social workers, as well as the clients themselves and their parents. It would be far too simplistic to interpret events as merely the outcome of a battle between interested parties; there are divisions within the parties themselves and other factors are important such as the increased control of central government over local authority budgets.

The relative power of professional monopolies has influence over the outcomes of care, but for convenience purposes the right view can be characterised with maintaining the status quo and rather less concerned with experimenting with new forms of care, and the left view as an alternative to this, one that sees professional monopoly as a hindrance to achieving a better overall level of care. Both see the meeting of client needs on an individual basis as of importance although the contribution offered by the different approaches towards this objective provides a principal source of dispute.

Right-wing views. In the area of mental handicap, then, the right (represented in part by such organisations as the Royal College of Psychiatrists (RCP) and COHSE) takes the following line: clients need a protective environment; hospitals are needed to provide asylum to people who need protection from pressures of community living; local authorities have a poor track record in community provision and are still unclear about their direction after 20 or so years; local authorities lack properly trained staff; many people 'living in the community' are exploited, left to idle around and their quality of life is not enhanced. 'As the focus of attention leaves the large hospitals and is diffused into a variety of directions in the community, there is a danger that the overall care of the patient will become fragmented' (RCP, 1985).

This view is often consistent with the need for professional specialists in mental handicap to be in charge of the service, also that different services are needed for different client dependencies, and that the NHS role in mental handicap should be maintained. In his minority report to the Jay Committee, David Williams (now general secretary of COHSE) challenged the prevalent view that local authorities would provide a better base for community care deploying the above arguments and others - such as that local authority priorities are determined by ratepayers' priorities, both mental handicap and mental illness will never be a high priority, and that the administrative upheaval would be to the detriment of care to each client: 'the poor quality of local authority services is the basis of criticisms from patients and their relatives ... the lack of respite care and provision and family support services are the greatest areas of deficiency' (Bamford, 1984). There is some evidence (for example, Mencap, 1984; Drummond, 1984) to suggest that parents do not want their handicapped relative to live independently and that their primary concern is that they should be cared for in a protected environment.

Left-wing Views. The left-wing view in mental handicap is expressed very clearly, for example, in publications by the Campaign for Mentally Handicapped People (CMH), that stress the significance of interpreting properly the principle of normalisation (Tyne and O'Brien, 1981), and of developing services based upon this principle. The first statement of the normalisation principle is taken from Wolf Wolfensberger (1972): 'The utilization of culturally valued means in order to establish and/or maintain personal behaviours, experiences, and characteristics that are culturally normative or valued'.

Tyne and O'Brien restate the principle as follows: 'The use of means which are valued in our society in order to develop and support personal behaviour experiences and characteristics which are likewise valued'. They state that the normalisation principle applies very widely to groups of people who are at least at risk in our society of being thought 'less valuable' than others: 'people who have mental handicaps, people who are elderly, or have physical handicaps, people who have a mental illness, children who have been in trouble (and so on)'. This view calls for services that enhance the social status and self-image of mentally handicapped people, that seek to integrate them within the life of the community and that provide the means for greater client involvement in planning services than exists at present. This implies, for example, the use of residential provision based on ordinary housing and daytime provision based on employment and education services (use of ordinary schools, adult and further education colleges).

There is, furthermore, a call for much greater consumer involvement in the planning of services. The All Wales Strategy (AWS) (Welsh Office, 1983) is a very good example of a current project where participation of clients themselves - in this case, mentally handicapped people - is of prime concern. Here the Welsh Office has committed up to £26 million of recurring revenue over 10 years to the development of comprehensive community and related hospital services, this money being additional to allocations planned by health and social services authorities. Although this financial provision has been influential in forcing authorities together to draw up integrated plans, the Strategy has made quite explicit its desire to see planning systems evolve which are based upon principles of participatory democracy. This goes far and beyond conventional notions of joint planning between health and social services authorities (Grant, 1985).

Overview

Naturally there are various gradations of opinion lying between right and left and the plans for services outlined in local policy documents represent in many respects a compromise of these extremes. The views of parent groups, of organisations such as Mencap and other local agencies, 'take on board' ideas of the need to provide community-based services, of meeting individual client need, and acknowledging the important contribution of different professional groups to the overall provision of care.

Nevertheless, the argument is that (a) the relative status of individual groups both national and locally, and (b) the substantive differences in both philosophies of care and the means through which care should be achieved, have complicated the outcome in a manner not always beneficial to the quality of services clients may receive. It can be said that the principal influence of government policies discharged wthin an arena of expenditure cuts to state services, and a general demand for quality control, has been to reinforce these difficulties by making it much harder to achieve any acceptable consensus among groups involved.

DHSS POLICY FROM 1971 TO THE PRESENT DAY

From 1971 to the present, DHSS policy on providing community-based services has changed in substance. There have been specific changes in, for example, the emphasis on the role of long-term care in hospital. The 1971 White Paper Better Services for the Mentally Handicapped (DHSS, 1971) recommended the provision of suitable substitute homes (for both children and adults who had to leave the family home) which would either be a hospital if the person had 'physical handicaps or behavioural problems that require(d) special medical, nursing or other skills', or a local authority establishment 'for all others' (para. 158).

In the 1980 review of progress the DHSS claimed instead that 'large hospitals of any kind do not provide a favourable environment for a child to grow up in' (para 2.39) that the White Paper target for hospital places for children was excessive and that 'it (was) likely that the White Paper overestimated the number of hospital places for adults' (para 2.47). The following year Care in the Community: (DHSS, 1981d) estimated that 'about 15000 mentally handicapped people at present in hospital could be discharged immediately if appropriate services in the community were available' (para 3.1), and furthermore that most people needing long-term care 'should be looked after in the community' (para 1.1). Since 1981, DHSS policy has been to support the planned closure of most long-stay hospitals and provide a range of suitable alternative care within the community commensurate with individual client needs.

The evidence for the above rests upon several factors, most of which have a fairly recent origin.

(1) Some of the 1971 White Paper targets have been dropped.
(2) The way ahead now seems more in terms of the build-up of local services through much closer co-operation between health and local authorities.
(3) A greater role is being played by the voluntary sector in terms of service provision.
(4) Specific earmarked grants to facilitate local developments have been made.
(5) Greater emphasis is now put on the role of the local authority as service-initiator.
(6) Service planners and providers have become more sensitive and aware of the values and principles that underpin services clients receive.

In this section specific changes in services, the majority of which are set against broader issues of social policy, are referred to. Clearly, ideological considerations have a part to play in determining such policies, but there is also evidence that government budgets during this period have been somewhat insensitive to the political preferences or prejudices of particular administrations (Alt and Chrystal, 1983). For example, public spending was brought down from 46.3 per cent (of the British gross domestic product) in 1974-75 to 42.5 per cent in 1978-79 but was back to 44 per cent by 1983-84. While it can be argued that social security spending has grown sharply in response to the increase in the numbers of unemployed and pensioners, the NHS and the personal social services, have also grown during the overall period. Since 1983-84 however, state-provided welfare services have been deliberately cut, and their effects have been exaggerated through, for example, the passing of legislation such as the Education Act 1981 and the Mental Health Act 1983, both of which demanded extra funds to implement that were not made available. Let us take each of the above points in turn.

Dropping Targets

The role of hospitals in providing care for mentally handicapped people has diminished since 1971, when the White Paper envisaged a future need for district-based 200-bedded units for adults, but this aim was dropped 10 years later. The DHSS (1980) review of services no longer saw this as a priority and instead considered that few districts needed more than 150 health care places and that these need not be on the same site.

In addition the aim of providing long-term care in hospital for mentally handicapped children was dropped (DHSS 1981a, 1983b); however, targets set in 1971 for the provision of local authority residential care for both children and adults, along with those for daycare provision, remained.

For mentally ill people, since the social services reorganisation in 1971, there have been real achievements in service development. The number of places in homes and hostels has doubled, while the number of daycare places has increased by 50 per cent.

The increase in places available for mentally handicapped people has been of a similar order, yet even this advance lags behind need. Figures from the House of Commons Second Report from the Social Services Committee (HCSC, 1985) show that expenditure on residential care for mentally ill people rose three times as rapidly as the average overall increase on all social services spending between 1975 and 1981, that on daycare for mentally ill people was four times the average, that on residential care for mentally handicapped people five times the average and even expenditure on ATCs twice the average. This is a relative improvement, however, and does not show that the overall level of resources is sufficient to match presenting needs. Instead ways are required for deploying resources to the end of providing community care through transferring money out of hospitals, making joint planning far more effective than it is at present, and encouraging local authorities to concentrate on 'flexible packages' of services commensurate with individual needs rather than upon the creation of alternative institution-based schemes. The issue of changing the objective from maintaining the hospital service to running it down dramatically has in some recorded cases placed exceptional burdens on the families of mentally handicapped relatives. While regional health authorities are refusing hospital admissions, clients are often given no alternative but to stay at home, when support has been requested.

On the mental illness front despite plans - often of 20 years standing - to close long-stay hospitals, at the time of writing not one has been shut down. The DHSS pilot scheme to test the problems of community care (the Worcester Development Project) became fully operational in 1978. This envisaged the closure of a hospital and the establishment of networks of health and social services such as psychiatric departments in general hospitals, day hospitals, community psychiatric services, local authority residential services, daycare facilities and social work support services. Although the number of hospital patients has been reduced, there are still local disputes over the nature of alternative services - for example the size and shape of core and cluster homes, the need for continued provision of asylum. Contrary to the remark of the House of Commons Committee that 'any fool can close a hospital' it would instead seem not to be an easy course of action.

Build-up of Services

The way ahead seems now more in terms of the build-up of local services through the encouragement of closer partnerships between health and local authority services, emphasising the outcome of joint planning and delivery, of services as opposed to over-concentration on distinguishing their separate roles and responsibilities (see for example, DHSS 1981 a and d). Towell (1985) comments on the lack of leadership within local authorities in the formulation of community services and in taking over responsibility for providing alternative services. Current regional health authority strategies to replace institutional provision have the potential of placing 'several hundred million pounds' of recurring revenue available for the creation of local services. Towell's point is that efforts need to be made in tackling the weaknesses in the present operation of health and social services as these affect reform in long-term care. One weakness is certainly that the 'topdown' preoccupation with relocating resources from the large hospitals seems typically to have underestimated the sophistication and sensitivity of the strategies required for change and, therefore, of the managerial and professional leadership necessary in creating alternative patterns of community-based services responsive to local needs (Korman and Glennerster 1985). 'The existing distribution of resources has put the NHS in the "driving seat" for reform, often with local authorities trailing along in a subordinate role, but the NHS, particularly at Regional level, is still in many respects a hospital service, poorly equipped to develop community-based provision' (Towell, 1985).

Glennerster (1983) refers to the use of gross planning methodologies endemic in both health and local authorities that may have the effect of being counterproductive in achieving a service based on individual client need. These are:

(1) grouping clients into categories which fail to reflect individual diversity;
(2) concentrating on disabilities rather than abilities;
(3) defining needs in terms of the way services are currently provided rather than in functional terms by the assistance actually required;
(4) divorcing planning from the experience of the staff mainly responsible for implementation.

The consequent emphasis is on planning buildings as opposed to services. A transfer of focus from hospital-based to community-based care requires sophisticated management, financial and personnel policies that can be executed at a senior administrative level across health and local authority boundaries. This requires equivalent senior management representation from the social services departments at regional level in order that policies can be properly agreed and taken forward to the action stage. While on the one hand local authority social services departments are moving towards more decentralised provision, on the other hand the issue of developing an appropriate and realistic management structure to assume control for community services becomes exceptionally important. The National Development Team for Mentally Handicapped People (NDT, 1980) in its fourth report covering the period 1981-84 criticised the fact that there were some health service managers who allowed friction between personalities to thwart effective development of services. It was claimed that poor communication between various tiers of management had in many instances hampered the development of locally based provision. This is a matter of increasing importance and one which the NHS is currently tackling with fervent abandon (see DHSS, 1983).

Nevertheless on paper there has been a huge growth in NHS/local authority collaborative machinery over the past decade. By 1982 almost every district health authority had established both a joint consultative committee and a joint care planning team, and a total of 21 JCC subcommittees and 302 JCPT subgroups was also reported. It is not clear how successful individual subgroups have been in pursuing joint planning, but a report by the Campaign for Mentally Handicapped People (1984) does shed some light. Its survey was based on 79 district health authorities showing an apparently promising picture of 88 per cent of DHAs reporting the existence of such local planning groups, but disparities in function and range of membership are wide. Over a third of the groups were quite openly concerned only with health service provision; 21 per cent embraced health and social services; and 29 per cent claimed additionally to involve education representatives.

Two important points were raised by this report: (a) very few districts saw themselves as being involved in the planning of comprehensive local services; and (b) the survey indicated that joint planning for mentally handicapped people remained dominated by health professionals with the likely, though not inescapable, implication that a medical model of mental handicap remained influential. This again is an extremely important issue in the context of planning future services and, as one might observe, wholly in contravention of the Jay Report proposals.

On the positive side there are some very interesting attempts to develop local services (in populations of around 30000-50000) that innovatively cut through current administrative and professional arrangements. The Wells Road Service in Bristol, for example, supplies services for mentally handicapped people covering a catchment population of 35000. It comprises two main elements: community and residential support (three community workers co-ordinate networks of support for clients living at home with their families or in homes of their own) (Ward, 1985). The training for staff for this project began from scratch as it was reported 'existing training programmes were geared either to nursing staff, working mainly in hospital settings, or to social services staff, working in hostels or "homes"'. Some useful training materials have been developed for this purpose relevant to staff supporting clients in ordinary housing accommodation (Felce et al., 1982; Shearer, 1983; Ward, 1984) and for whom no traditional hierarchy of staff support has been available. The training needs of staff operating in a 'locally based service' is something to which we shall return later in this section.

Role of the Voluntary Sector

Central to the implementation of community care is the role of the voluntary sector in terms of individual voluntary effort and voluntary organisations as advocates/supporters of carers or actual providers. A far greater role for the voluntary sector has been envisaged since 1979, outlined specifically in DHSS (1981), and made public knowledge in policy documents that stress the need to increase support to relatives looking after handicapped, disabled and elderly people at home.

This move has led to a general questioning of the dominant role of voluntary bodies - for example, are voluntary organisations being asked to take over state provision as opposed to maintaining their distinctive role as advocates, innovators and partners to statutory providers? Increasingly, government money has become available for the support of community care projects led by the voluntary sector, for example, the Barnado's Liverpool scheme to house severely mentally handicapped children. The parallel 'holding back' of statutory services has had the effect of diverting professional energy into defensive activities and causing staff demoralisation within the public sector.

A wealth of literature has recently become available on the effects of informal caring showing, by and large, that carers are supporting their dependent relative at great costs to themselves (Equal Opportunities Commission, 1980; Levin, Sinclair and Gorbach, 1981; Nissel and Bonnerjea, 1982; Buckle, 1984; Jones, 1985). This literature does not support the view that carers wish to give up their role of caring, but rather that they would like their load to be lightened and the caring to be shared. Giving support to this type of voluntary activity would appear to be the present government's espoused policy, yet evidence shows that at a practical level there is still a long way to go.

Grants for Local Developments

It has been said that the voluntary sector has benefited from specific earmarked funds to facilitate local developments. In addition, such funds have become available for use by other agencies, such as health and local authorities. Government policy has been to put money aside for particular causes, usually relatively small sums for developing community schemes. Each initiative has been advertised and agencies have put in proposals to obtain 'some of the cake'. The following are the main examples since 1980:

(1) one million pounds available over four years to help voluntary organisations provide homelike care for mentally handicapped children;
(2) nine million pounds over three years to health authorities for similar purposes;
(3) other grants for general purposes or specific projects have been made to voluntary bodies active in developing mental handicap services, for example £566000 in 1982-83;
(4) under the 'care in the community' heading, joint finance (first introduced in 1976) has been extended in range to cover education and housing as well as social services provision, made more flexible and increased in duration (94 million pounds was allocated for joint finance in 1983-84, of which more than one-third was spent on mental handicap services);
(5) between 1984 and 1988 some 15 million pounds of joint finance has been reserved to support a programme of pilot projects to promote the 'Care in the Community' initiative for transferring patients and resources from hospital to community care - approximately one-half of these projects have been for mental handicap services.

Critics have argued that these resource transfers are 'small beer' for dealing with the large-scale issues in question: some projects are being formally evaluated although no evidence is yet available on their outcomes; in addition the provision of funds to support community schemes for small numbers of hospital residents has had little real impact (at least up to the present) on hospital closure plans.

The series of centrally funded pilot projects announced in 1983 and 1985 provides the clearest evidence of a national initiative to develop and monitor community-based schemes; 13 projects were announced in 1984 and a further 15 in 1985. The schemes are aimed at enabling mentally ill and handicapped people to move from hospital into the community; they include a home support scheme for the elderly in Darlington which will enable 60 people to leave hospital, and the Calderdale project providing hostel accommodation or shared homes for 32 mentally handicapped people who were previously in hospital.

The projects are being evaluated by a team based at the Personal Social Services Research Unit, University of Kent with the main objective of 'to provide policy guidance about the circumstances in which cost-effective community services can be provided to meet the needs of particular groups of long-stay hospital patients' (PSSRU, 1985). The stated aims of the evaluation are to look at service outcomes, costs, the service in practice - the quality of care provided etc., and process issues, including management, accountability, assessment and selection of clients.

Two other major schemes have received wide publicity: the NIMROD (New Ideas for Mentally Retarded in Ordinary Dwellings) service in Cardiff and the All Wales Strategy for the Development of Services for Mentally Handicapped People. Both are examples of specially funded schemes aimed to create better community services, and both are innovative and have external monitoring built in.

The NIMROD service was set up in 1979, following the submission of a report of a joint working party on the provision of a community-based mental handicap service in South Glamorgan. The aims of the project were to set up/evaluate and document a community-based service to those mentally handicapped people and their families from a defined geographical catchment area of approximately 60000 total population. 'The service (would) provide access to the full range of existing, health, social and other services together with a wide range of specialist advice, help and support provided on an individual basis' (NIMROD, 1978, Volume 1). The total catchment area was to be divided into four subcatchment areas and provision made for each area in turn, based upon the 'use of individual programme plans (IPPs) and training schemes for clients, fostering and lodgings, planned residential care in "normal" houses, short-term care, sitting-in services and an advice, information and resource centre. A wide range of existing services will be made use of and links will be fostered with voluntary agencies and parent groups. (JWPR, 1978). The Mental Handicap in Wales-Applied Research Unit (MHW-ARU) was established in 1975 with a brief 'to examine ways in which services might be developed in order to improve both the personal ability of the handicapped and the adaptation of their families to that handicap' (MHW-ARU, 1984). The following is quoted from this Report to illustrate the ways in which service evaluation has developed. NIMROD is a good example of a relatively small-scale project concerning the development of community services involving external funding, and one to which much attention has been drawn in recent years. DHSS policy has been to support specific projects from which it is expected lessons may be drawn for the development of broader national initiatives:

> Early work (in the MHW-ARU) encompassed aspects of domiciliary, day and residential service provision. This included the development and evaluation of the Portage service for pre-school children (Revill and Blunden, 1979); a series of projects examining ways in which staff might work with profoundly handicapped adults in day settings (see, for example, Porterfield, Blunden and Blewitt, 1980). This was followed by a series of projects in hospital and other residential settings which examined the development of staff roles and the effect of these upon clients (Coles and Blunden, 1981; Jones, Evans and Blunden, 1984; Porterfield, Evans and Blunden, 1984).
>
> This programme of research suggested two broad conclusions. Firstly, the projects demonstrated that positive outcomes can be achieved for mentally handicapped people by modifying the activities of those (staff or parents) who work with them. Thus parents can be helped to teach new skills to pre-school handicapped children; staff in day and residential settings can increase clients' levels of engagement with activities and materials, and can introduce opportunities for learning new skills. Whilst much previous research had concentrated on broad issues such as the need for attitude change, policy changes and the development of new forms of service provision, our work indicated that attention can also usefully be given to the detailed organisation of service provision and staff roles.

This research also demonstrated the limitations of traditional forms of service provision. The opportunities for handicapped people and their families to enjoy the experiences of everyday life was often severely restricted by the nature of the services provided. In particular, day and residential services limited their clients' opportunities by virtue of their remote location and the extent to which large groups of handicapped people were segregated from their non-handicapped peers. The organisational constraints imposed by institutional environments created difficulties in changing staff routines and in maintaining staff behaviour.

Later research in the Unit has therefore been concerned with developments within community-based service systems, where some of the constraints of institutional provision are absent. NIMROD (1978) provided an opportunity for researchers to participate in the design of a community-based service which would attempt to maximise the opportunties for handicapped people and their families to participate in the activities of everyday life. The All-Wales Strategy (Welsh Office, 1983) provides a further opportunity for the development of community-based services.

These policy initiatives provide exciting opportunities for the development of research materials (Blunden, 1984). They make possible new forms of intervention, such as domiciliary support services and alternative forms of residential provision. They also create the need for new forms of measurement and experimental design. Measuring the extent to which community-based services meet their client-related aims is no simple exercise. It is not possible to define a single, easily measurable outcome variable such as the absence of particular clinical conditions in some medical research. Instead it is necessary to measure a range of client outcomes, some having general applicability (such as measures of 'quality of life') and others relating to the solution of specific individual problems (such as securing accommodation or learning a new skill). The research on NIMROD (Humphreys, Lowe and Blunden, 1983) provided one opportunity to develop such measures and further work in this direction will take place in connection with the

All-Wales Strategy (Blunden, 1985).

How care should be evaluated is not the principal subject of this book, although subsequent chapters do raise evaluation issues and do refer to evaluation approaches. It is extremely important when considering current policies in this area to take account of the increasingly valuable role of monitoring and evaluation. The setting-up of national and local pilot projects is now followed often by external evaluation; internal evaluation has been furthered through the compilation of checklists for use by planners and practitioners (see, for example, NDG, 1980; Centre for Policy on Ageing, 1984; NSMHC, 1977). DHSS policy smacks of 'wait and see' - wait until the results of major studies have become available before making a commitment to change. It has become common practice for governments to demand evaluation of any scheme they support and that applicants for 'Care in the Community' monies have needed to give priority to this in constructing their proposals. On the ground, this creates anxiety among professional staff who are left unsure as to the future outcomes of 'new policies', and to the DHSS's real intentions when it comes to planning of services.

Local Authority Services

Since the 1962 Hospital Plan (HMSO, 1962) and the subsequent Community Care Blue Book (Ministry of Health, 1963) the policy of community care has meant increased provision of local authority care and support services. The last two-and-a-half decades have seen the build-up of local authority services albeit, as some critics state, at 'a snail's pace'.

Today the issue is as crucial as it has ever been: policy documents consistently support community services as an appropriate framework in which a whole range of care should be provided. As the responsibilities and obligations of local authorities grow, funding relative to that received by other public sector agencies has diminished making it harder for them to respond; in addition, the relationship between central and local government has given much cause for insecurity and concern (central government has not granted special funding to local authorities to enable them to respond to new policy directions). Between 1970 and 1982 the number of mentally handicapped people in hospitals has fallen from 56000 to 42000, and the number of children from 7000 to 1500; in Care in the Community (1981) the DHSS estimated that 15000 mentally handicapped people living in hospitals, about one-third of the total, could be discharged immediately if services were available. It is likely to take some time before this aim is achieved. The emphasis on the need for local authority provision is in 1986 much stronger than it was ten or indeed five years ago and comprises an actual shift in the substance of policy. This can only foreshadow radical change in the method of assessing need, and in the respective role and function of statutory service providers. In the field of long-term care the real alternatives to institutional provision may mean more fragmentation of services, the development of poorly resourced specialisms and much sharper contrasts in the variety and calibre of services available based upon both statutory and non-statutory bodies.

Value-based Services

All services provided to people are value-based; their aims and the methods used to achieve such aims either overtly or covertly say something about how service-providers view the clients concerned. For example, it is claimed that the grouping-together of handicapped people and their segregation from society at large (in old-fashioned mental asylums) manifests the negative view society takes of them as people: they are 'unfit' to live in the community, they need to be isolated for their own good, and so on.

More recently, thinking about services has in planning terms at least conveyed the notion that the goal of integrating people (previously hospitalised) into the community calls for sensitive and sophisticated approaches concerned with enhancing the image of those individuals. Such plans and programmes for community-based services have stressed the need to articulate their principles for action which has in practice meant an initial statement or series of statements setting out what the authors believe to be the rights of the client group concerned - both human rights and rights to services and support. This has focused valuable attention on the deficiencies of service provision and on creating a kind of administrative consensus albeit at a theoretical level. In mental handicap, the Kings Fund's series of publications around the theme of 'an ordinary life' (Towell, 1985), and in mental illness, the recent MIND manifesto 'Common

Concern' (Mind, 1984) are further examples of how the planning of services should proceed on the basis of preset principles, formed around the idea of granting more social status to the clients in question. The Jay Committee (1979) was a forerunner in making explicit the principles that underpin the new philosophies of service provision. Whereas the principles outlined in the 1971 White Paper and in the 'Declaration of the Rights of Mentally Handicapped Persons' (United Nations General Assembly, 1972) adopted by the United Nations Organisation in 1971 indicated a growing national and international consensus about the rights of mentally handicapped people and the need to take positive action, the Jay Committee went further in stipulating what such rights should mean in practice. The Committee identified three broad sets of principles:

(1) Mentally handicapped people have a right to enjoy normal patterns of life within the community.
(2) Mentally handicapped people have a right to be treated as individuals.
(3) Mentally handicapped people will require additional help from the communities in which they live and from professional services if they are to develop to their maximum potential as individuals.

(para 89)

'Living like others within the community' implied being able to live with a family, to leave the family home if one so wishes, to live as a member of a small group, or with one's peers who are not mentally handicapped, and so forth. Personal rights embrace the main concept of the right to be treated as an individual - the right to live, learn and work in the 'least restrictive environment appropriate', and the right to make or be involved in decisions that affect oneself.

Whereas many local policy documents have become sensitised to promoting positive policies concerning mentally handicapped people; for instance, it is not always clear whether such positive thinking has been brought down to the practice level when programmes actually become implemented.

THE MEANING OF COMMUNITY CARE

The actual meaning of community care has changed

considerably; such changes in definition have called for developing new services and innovating within traditional ones.

The HCSC (1985) noted this and presented its own definition which underlay the basic principle of community care:

> Appropriate care should be provided for individuals in such a way as to enable them to lead as normal an existence as possible given their particular disabilities and to minimise disruption of life within their community.
>
> (para 11)

During the last 20 or more years the phrase 'community care' has changed from meaning simply a service outside hospital to one concerning the improvement of the quality of life of individuals based in a community (ordinary life) context. The HCSC (1985) sets out four useful principles to indicate the current direction in providing community care:

> (i) a preference for home life over 'institutional' care;
> (ii) the pursuit of the ideal of normalisation and integration and avoidance so far as possible of separate provision, segregation and restriction (i.e. the least restrictive alternative)
> (iii) a preference for small over large;
> (iv) a preference for local services over distant ones.
>
> (para 10)

It noted a changed emphasis towards providing a range of services 'in the community' that prevent people being hospitalised. Services should have the function of enabling people to remain at home wherever possible by giving support to carers, by providing relief and day care and by planning services in a way that is commensurate with the needs and wishes of individual clients. Emphasis is also on getting good value for money, on justifying the outlay of resources in a framework where (a) the interests of the client remain paramount, and (b) every alternative method of providing care is assessed and evaluated. As further emphasis is on the skilful integration of available resources to this end, those professionals and others involved need to be aware of what is available in a person's 'community' and of ways in which a person's needs might be met.

This calls for an enterprising approach towards care and support deploying the resources of statutory agencies, voluntary agencies and neighbourhood facilities. It may involve, for instance, approaching individuals who live locally to seek advice and knowledge of available amenities. The fact that the meaning of community care has changed in substance has caused confusion among those operating a service, and some measure of cynicism on the part of such staff towards political masters and planners. When operational policies are both unclear and subject to fluctuation those responsible for implementing policies may lose commitment, and the dynamism needed to effect policies wanes. DHSS evidence to the HCSC (Volume II, 1985) stated that the current concept of community care needs to stress the following key characteristics: a network of services (within the client's 'community'); co-ordination of service planning; information and delivery of care; a balance of services, meaning a 'local mix' relevant to specific local client needs; services that are accessible to clients and flexible in their operation, that offer a choice to clients, and that can be held to account for themselves. This relatively new emphasis on integrated services geared towards specific individual needs represents both a challenge to would-be service providers and a sharp contrast to past notions of 'institution-based' services where units were planned, built and served merely to occupy clients or provide custody.

The change from 'institution' to 'individual' based care has presented a need both for new <u>types</u> of services and <u>adaptations</u> in existing forms of services. This has had the effect of 'slowing down' development in some areas. While new practices are being tested and experimented with, the policy machine enters a 'freeze' phase. Until procedures for identifying need become established such as the setting up of registers, the direction of services often becomes unclear and some complacency sets in. Models of social work intervention proposed firstly by Seebohm (1968) and later by Barclay (1982) are examples of revisionist thinking towards delivering community care. Neither supported unequivocally a new form of practice, but both espoused a 'community' approach directed towards meeting individual need through the support and enabling of local networks of formal and informal relationships.

Seebohm set a trend for the 1970s with the theme

of encouraging good neighbourliness and played a crucial part in transposing the meaning of community care as care <u>in</u> the community (as described in the original government White Paper - Health and Welfare: the Development of Community Care (Ministry of Health, 1963) to care <u>by</u> the community, provided primarily by the dependent person's family. The 'community approach' adopted by the Seebohm Committee never really proved successful owing to the bureaucratic tendency of local authorities and to the heavy resource consequences of this mode of operation.

The Barclay Committee, reporting in 1982, underlined the need for this approach stressing that social workers should help to set up, maintain and advise existing 'caring networks'. To do this properly, it was argued, new forms of organisational arrangements were needed - 'which placed social workers in localities, where they would be better attuned to local needs and practices and more directly accountable to the local community that they seek to serve' (Derricourt, 1983). The report called for a change in the unit populations served by area teams - from 50000 to 100000 as recommended by Seebohm (1968) to 20000 to 30000 with a number of subteams within each; and for social worker attachment (for example, basing social workers in patch teams, resource centres, hospitals, general practice centres and schools). In all, this new proposed working model required expansion of social services staff. Critics of Barclay argued that decentralisation, as such, was emasculating to social work as a profession as it called upon social workers to play an ever-increasing part in prevention without providing administrative back-up or the scope needed to influence other agencies. In addition, this was to be enacted against a background of cuts being made to local authority services. Attempts to test the efficacy of 'localised' services have been carried out in several areas such as Normanton (Hadley and McGrath, 1984) and Dinnington (Bayley and Parker, 1980). These and other studies have shown what can be achieved, albeit in the short term, by using small groups of staff who become involved in relatively small neighbourhoods, with the aim of activating forms of self-help and increasing sensitivity to background factors affecting individual and community needs.

At the time of writing, the move towards decentralised practice continues on a much wider scale, while there is evidence of some conflict arising over the commensurate objective of local authorities, for example, to plan and set up specialist services for certain client groups. The relative impact of new forms of care upon policy development can be measured in terms of both awareness and commitment on the part of planners and providers of services. Much external advice has had the effect of increasing disparity in professional attitudes and separating planning on paper from practice issues, owing to the vagueness around which certain goals have become formulated.

ADAPTATIONS IN EXISTING PROVISION

Four examples are given here where policy changes (towards increased community care) have demanded corresponding changes in other areas and systems of service provision; these are income maintenance, housing, daycare/employment and staff training. In each of these areas the development of community services has called for an alteration in the contribution and structure of provision in order to match the requirements of modern approaches to 'care'.

Income Maintenance

Social security benefits are crucial to the implementation of care in the community; they are also important both as a means of assisting families to maintain care and in providing scope for 'buying' care from the private sector. At present all attempts to move people from hospital into the community depend to some extent for their revenue on client's statutory benefits. Without adequate income there would be no possibility of clients 'buying' all the services and facilities that were freely available to them in the hospital. For policy-makers, too, the existence of welfare benefits was originally a major consideration in the development of community care. The Care in the Community projects (PSSRU, 1985) have already shown social security benefits to be an unstable source of income - 'rates of benefit can fluctuate, they can be withdrawn and they are client-related'.

The research team state that this can endanger the integrity of a project and any future changes in benefit regulations even more so. They give examples of different schemes where dependence on social security payments has caused problems; for instance:

> the continuing costs of the ... hostel for mentally ill people ... will be met from boarding out allowances, but there have been delays in building works. Clients were unable to leave hospital as planned, but staff had been appointed to schedule. As board and lodging payments were to pay staff salaries there was a temporary financial shortfall.

Furthermore, the issue of registration stemming from the Health and Social Services and Social Security Adjudications Act (1983) and the arrival of the 1984 Registered Homes Act has provided a financial incentive to register a community facility with all the regulations that this involves - a registered home can claim a higher rate of board and lodgings payments from the DHSS - yet it has been suggested (for example, Churchill, 1985) that this process in itself can encourage institutionalised models of care.

Another relevant but separate matter concerns the employment of clients living in domestic housing within the community. High levels of benefit may be payable for people who need staff support - enough benefit, indeed, to pay for that staff. If, however, such people work even part-time, benefit may be substantially reduced. The PSSRU pamphlet argues that this places a project in a very difficult position. 'On the one hand it is dependent on maximum benefit for its existence, and therefore needs to discourage a resident from seeking paid employment. On the other hand, the point of its existence is to ensure that a client leads as full a life as possible.' The authors recommend 'special solutions' to this employment disincentive for disabled people.

The HCSC (1985) report stressed the need to include within national, regional and local plans for community care 'explicit reference to the role of social security entitlements' and the implications of such plans for public expenditure. The report stated that the intended future emphasis on social security as the major source of financing community-based schemes had not been 'widely appreciated' by central government nor by local authorities. It was thought important that any long-term pressures to reduce the social security budget should not make people being discharged into the community vulnerable. Plainly this issue needs to be examined as many current plans imply that the revenue consequences of schemes should be met through a 'bottomless' social security budget. In addition the consequences of increased board and lodgings allowances payable to the owners of private homes have been (at least in the view of the Association of Directors of Social Services) to place discharged hospital patients 'in private homes or cheap lodging houses with little concern for their longer-term welfare'. This has led to a trend away from statutory authorities actually sponsoring people in private care to a situation where increasing numbers of mentally disabled residents are not 'placed' in a private home by anybody other than themselves, their relatives and the owners of the homes who accept them. The anomalies in this area, if not resolved, will lead eventually to a number of possible outcomes: thwarted plans to implement community services, the latter 'on the cheap', the unsupervised hegemony of private sector care and discrepancies in client entitlement to welfare benefit. Current policies call for early action to be taken on the subject of income maintenance.

Housing

Community care policies mean collaboration by health and social service departments with local authority housing departments and with other housing agencies such as the Housing Corporation and the private sector. Many current 'projects' to place mentally ill or mentally handicapped people, for example, in domestic housing are based on very flexible planning programmes but nonetheless programmes that require much attention to staffing support and other servicing, administrative considerations and community 'integration'. Housing plans are determined by factors such as the local stock of available housing - which varies geographically; and the extent to which use is made of both local authority and private housing - which is influenced partly by the political environment. Much current evidence shows that 'the true capital cost of care in the community has not been recognised' (PSSRU, 1985) and points to a need for funds to be made available both to convert existing housing stock and to put up new buildings where necessary. A system of care based upon individual needs will require major capital investment in housing in order to rebuild existing infrastructures.

A search conducted during 1981 of existing housing schemes* for mentally ill or mentally

---

* A scheme was defined as a unit or set of units

handicapped people revealed a total of 1048 schemes throughout England and Wales (Ritchie, Keegan and Bosanquet, 1983). Of these 662 (63 per cent) were for mentally ill, 355 (34 per cent) were for mentally handicapped people, and 31 (3 per cent) were intended for both groups. The schemes identified were providing accommodation for just over 3300 mentally ill, and just under 2000 mentally handicapped people. Approximately two-thirds (65 per cent) of the provision was based in housing department properties, 28 per cent in housing association properties and 6 per cent in properties belonging to voluntary organisations.

The role of housing associations in the area of special needs provision has since increased substantially. The Housing Corporation's Shared Housing Supplement to the Schemework Procedure Guide (Department of the Environment, 1983) endorses and updates the methods for approval of shared housing projects allowing schemes to receive housing association grants if they concur with cost and standards criteria, which include appropriate management and planning arrangements. The Department of Environment (1983) report went on to observe that unstaffed group homes formed the major part of domestic housing provision, offering an average of four places per scheme; that 90 per cent of schemes were based in existing or renovated properties and 10 per cent were newly built for the purpose; and that approximately half the schemes provided direct tenancies or licences to the residents, the other half offering subtenancies through the support agencies.

These findings indicate a rising contribution made by housing authorities to social welfare provision. The authors, however, state that 'with one exception, local authority housing departments saw no difficulty in providing the number of houses required, mainly because they did not think the demand would ever be that great'. Since then demand has risen sizably and schemes for hospital closure are placing enormous strains on the availability of suitable housing stock such as to halt, albeit temporarily, the transfer of certain clients into the community. The HCSC (1985) report has also seen this

---

based within one building, offering housing accommodation for mentally ill or mentally handicapped people. The term should not suggest a specialised form of accommodation since in most cases it is ordinary housing which is involved.

as a problem, and while commending the role played by housing associations, called for further incentives to be offered to the Housing Corporation and housing associations to provide housing for mentally disabled people, and to remove any existing disincentives.

Apart from ensuring the availability of housing, there is an issue of acknowledging fire, planning, registration and safety regulations appertaining to the use of domestic housing for 'care' purposes. Source material (Heginbotham, 1981; Malin, 1983; PSSRU, 1985) has indicated how certain regulations can actually work against the objective of client independence, where the philosophy of care involves an element of risk to the client. For example, fire extinguishers can be obtrusive and prevent the creation of a homely atmosphere, and some facilities would prefer to do without them.

The Registered Homes Act provides for regulating the standard of residential provision and the accompanying document (Centre for Policy on Ageing, 1984) constitutes a checklist on practical details. Following this advice, however, several examples have arisen of variations in local inspection criteria causing some private proprietors to consider taking legal action against local authorities (Churchill, 1985). The importance of monitoring the standard of residential care in the community is axiomatic, but there are indications that the new legislation will encourage the imposition of institutional or overstrict standards. The CPA guidelines apply to homes across the board although a warning is given against a blanket application of rules when consideration of individual client needs should be the fundamental concern. Whereas the document states approval of 'normalisation' and ideas like trying to lead an ordinary life, the array of rules and regulations (218 recommendations in all) do make it difficult to be normal in a registered home. The interpretation of these standards can become a matter of individual discretion on the part of local officers. This is an area where good precedents need to be set and partnerships forged at local level in order for the system to operate beneficially. Time alone will show how far such local arrangements can prove successful. The goals of professional workers can so easily come into conflict with administrative criteria, and standards set for the pursuit of good practice can result in stifling the development of client independence.

Housing-based models of care require attention being given to support methods, community networks and living arrangements (Malin, 1983; Atkinson, 1984; Flynn, 1985). Flynn reviewed the circumstances of 41 mentally handicapped adults living in their own homes, with particular reference to social work objectives, and concluded that the management of money and the development of social networks were the major preoccupations. The literature contains an array of descriptive accounts of individual housing-based schemes, but relatively little evaluation or hard data that might be used for future planning (McKnight, 1981). During the 1970s studies of non-institutional residential care have covered size, physical design and location (Dalgleish, 1979; Felce et al., 1978; King, Raynes and Tizard, 1971; McCormick, Balla and Zigler, 1975; Raynes, Pratt and Roses, 1979; and Tyne, 1977; 1978), staffing issues (Baker, Seltzer and Seltzer, 1977; Davies, 1977; Jay Committee, 1979, Vol. II; Malin and Race, 1978; and Mulhern, 1975) and community integration (Dalgleish and Matthews, 1979; Locker, Rao and Weddell, 1979; Pushkin, 1976a, 1976b and Willms, 1979). McKnight (1981) in an official DHSS review of this literature (on non-instutitional care) summarised some of the main 'findings' as follows:

> ... the size of living unit is more important than the size of facility, small living units being associated with a higher quality of care; an enriched environment has positive effects on resident development compared to an impoverished environment; there are indications that unit location in a catchment area with good transport facilities is favourable. Staff training background is not seen as a significant factor in care but the numbers of trained staff are low; decentralisation, less rigid rules and the involvement of staff at all levels may improve care; there is a need for more communication among staff and the development of a clear, shared policy; the need for separate unit-based staff accommodation has been questioned; residential staff lack support from outside professionals. There is hardly any evidence on the appropriate ability, sex and age mix of residents. Community attitudes are important in the setting up and continuing success of a community residence, initial resistance coming from a minority of the local community; understanding of mental handicap is related to

> opinion of and opposition to a residence; opposition diminishes and acceptance increases with contact as the home is in operation.

Several of these issues continue to vex planners and service providers in establishing care and support schemes based upon ordinary housing.

Daycare/employment

Planned provision of community-based services demands attention to daycare in its broadest sense. The Campaign for People with Mental Handicaps (CMH) in its evidence to the HCSC pointed out 'There are unfortunate precedents in the 60s and 70s where people leaving long-stay hospitals have been found a place to live but offered no further support' (Volume II, p.184, 41). Daycare services are complementary to residential services and fundamental to providing a comprehensive community service. Several sources have noted with concern the current need to review daycare (for example, PSSRU, 1985; HCSC, 1985; Independent Development Council, 1985) extending its definition beyond nine-to-five provision during weekdays and developing its emphasis towards employment and further education as opposed to an institutional and occupational function.

Historically the development of day services has been accorded very low priority, yet with hospital closures imminent it is important that substitutes are found in the community for the whole range of hospital living: social life, evening and weekend activities, opportunities to contribute to the everyday work of the institution. The HCSC recommended expansion of daycare in adult training centres (ATCS) (sometimes known as social education centres or SEC), while at the same time making training more purposeful and educational and less repetitive:

> We recommend that ATCs be the centres for a network of daytime activities, including sheltered employment, social education and training and recreation (HCSC, Volume I. para.86).

This theme is consistent with proposals in the National Development Group's Pamphlet 5 (NDG, 1977) to use day centres as multipurpose resource centres that provide both a variety of activity and opportunities for personal development within activities themselves. However, in practice too little consideration has been given to this issue. Some interesting employment developments have occurred (for example, the Pathway Employment Service, the Shaw Trust scheme), and some schemes based upon joint finance or special grants have emerged (for example, the Rural Training Scheme attached to the Bolton Neighbourhood Network), yet overwhelmingly the system has failed to show signs of adapting to the needs of providing for increasing numbers of people living in the community in both a practical and a developmental sense.

On another front, the emergence of mental health centres (or drop-in centres) provides possibly a new focus for delivering support to individuals suffering from, recovering from, or liable to recurrence of mental illness. The growth of such centres throughout the United Kingdom has become the basis for an interest in monitoring community-sited day provision not least in order to identify the individual and overall contribution made by the various centres and day facilities. While there is an agreement to expand the broad level of such provision on the part of both health and local authorities, there is little evidence that either agency sees it as yet a major priority; hence there is a danger that people will be left to 'idle around' in the community unless an attempt is made to co-ordinate meaningfully the disparate elements of services available.

The PSSRU reports (1985 a and b) of the DHSS Care in the Community initiative have stated that by and large local facilities for daycare have been found to be inadequate for the projects.

> ATCs, SECs and day centres seem to be all things to all people and the terms seem to be used interchangeably for a range of different types of facility. The SEC's are not suitable for certain client groups, such as the elderly and those in employment, and many ATCs are institutionalised themselves run by staff who feel threatened by the move towards community care (PSSRU, 1985).

The authors make recommendations to co-ordinate residential and daycare more closely, and to review and examine what goes on in day centres - 'to in effect consider the quality of service not just the quantity'.

There has always been some interest in job creation and employment services for handicapped people not least within the context of reviewing the role and function of the day centre (see, for example, Whelan and Speake, 1977, 1981; DHSS, 1980). Yet with high unemployment the possibilities seem bleak. There have been creative moves to find jobs for handicapped and disabled people on the part of voluntary and private trusts often using monies from the Manpower Services Commission, but little has been done by the statutory sector. Some staff and parents reinforce the low expectations that many mentally handicapped people have about obtaining a job (Lane, 1980; CMH, 1985). Such people, however, should not be thought of as having fewer rights than non-handicapped people, and the gross imbalance in the way jobs are distributed needs to be considered (Kings Fund Centre, 1984; Porterfield and Gathercole, 1985). For example the national unemployment rate in December 1984 was 13.4 per cent, whereas unemployment among people who have been labelled severely mentally handicapped is estimated to be greater than 95 per cent; government figures, however, do not include mentally handicapped people and hence understate the problem of unemployment. Recent work (Porterfield and Gathercole, 1985; Turner, 1985, personal communication concerning evaluation of Welsh Initiative for Sheltered Employment (WISE)) has been concerned over the issue of mentally disabled people becoming contributing members of society and ceasing to be dependent on state services. There is an argument that employment changes a person's image away from the dependency role and towards one that enhances their self-image and evokes a more positive response on the part of others towards them.

Overall the issue of daycare and its constituent parts is an urgent one if care within the community is to become a reality. The DHSS is currently conducting studies of 'daytime activity', yet the message at the present time is one of advocating a range of facilities that need to be provided - leisure, employment, social skills, further education and so on. On employment in particular the government response to the HCSC states:

> Mentally disordered people are very much among the intended beneficiaries of the current efforts by Government, voluntary bodies, employers and trades unions to improve work opportunities for disabled people generally and to improve practice within industry and commerce in giving them fair opportunities for

> employment and for advancement within employment (para.59).

A clearly formulated set of goals is needed in this area for this policy to be put into practice.

Staff Training

Changes in the direction of services have reached a point where staff training is a key issue. There is a need for training at all levels (basic, post-basic and inservice) to help staff contribute effectively to 'the new service'. Bell (1985) outlines four different types of training needs (arising from care in the community initiatives):

(1) training to meet the changing needs of clients, or to meet the needs of new client groups;
(2) training staff to adopt new ways of working and to change their attitudes towards the needs of the client and the ways in which they work to meet those needs;
(3) multidisciplinary and interagency training;
(4) management training.

She states that these are not discrete owing to the fact that the effective introduction of any new policy contributing towards care in the community may necessitate training of staff in any number of the areas. Training is required both by those who are professionally qualified and by those who have not had previous professional training.

> Policies which seek to support extremely frail and dependent elderly people in their own house, when they would have previously been taken into residential or hospital accommodation; home policies which can, if required provide 24-hour care for clients discharged from hospital or provide respite care for the informal carers of elderly and mentally confused people, have considerable training implications for the people who provide the basic care for these clients (Bell, 1985).

This refers not only to the changing needs of clients but also to the need for staff attitude change: staff who have moved out from a hospital environment to working with (say) mentally handicapped people in the community are likely to need to reorientate their whole approach to care.

Instead of working for or on behalf of clients staff need to work with them, as advocates, facilitators, or aides.

The need for joint training between professionals employed by different agencies is a major requirement and prerequisite if joint working arrangements are to be forged. The joint ENB-CCETSW initiative to develop qualifying and inservice training (ENB-CCETSW, 1982, 1983) has been a significant beginning, but as yet had little real impact on local developments. In mental handicap further publications by CCETSW in 1984 and 1985(a) have emphasised: the need to promote staff development and relevant training; to facilitate informal and formal co-operation locally, regionally and centrally between services; and the need to explore post-qualification studies in the context of management development.

Community nurse training is the subject of a current major DHSS review aimed at evaluating the various contributions of nursing in a community context including the interface with social work and other functions. Clearly the objective both centrally and at the professional level is to re-examine the match between training and tasks (Kratz, 1985) with the expectation that both policy demands and current recommendations to change basic training (see, for example, ENB, 1985; CCETSW, 1985) will have a materially significant impact on future developments.

In spite of attempts by some authorities to adopt corporate management, the reality is that departmental boundaries are closely guarded and training is very rarely able to cross. Bell (1985) reports very little evidence indeed of joint training between housing and social services or the latter and health services 'despite the obvious need to develop common philosophies and approaches to care, e.g. in methods of assessment and the development of care plans'. The National Health Service Training Authority and the Local Government Training Board have recently set up a joint working group to develop and pilot joint training initiatives, whereas it has also been reported (Health and Social Services Journal, 1986) that the former body along with the DES is on the point of promoting a scheme aimed at co-ordinating nationally inservice training for nine professions working in the NHS, including nurses, midwives, clinical psychologists and paramedical staff. There is this clear concern for taking stock of recent innovations in training and clear acknowledgement of the changing basis of service development.

The Jay Committee (1979) provided an initial incentive to explore the roots of training but very little advice on training content. This is probably the weakest dimension in this area: the process of building up relevant training packages that both respect new philosophies of care and are practicable and attractive to staff in terms of professional development. It is a challenging area that calls for innovation and systematic planning.

Finally, of major concern is the inherent task of management reorientation; if policies are to succeed then the complex activity of managing the various agencies involved needs to be adequately recognised. Community care implies an increase in the number of different staff, agencies and organisations that contribute and the task of co-ordination puts an inevitable extra pressure on managers. The DHSS in a recent circular (1985) saw this area as a priority and its own role as one of working closely with the professional bodies to achieve 'retraining' of staff at all levels, and stated that 'it is clearly not good enough to identify the problem while doing nothing to solve it'.

The above areas indicate some of the ways in which services are altering their focus and their expertise base.

NEW TYPES OF PROVISION

We now turn to examples of new types of provision that have recently come to the fore within the wider initiative to move services 'into the community'. Modern care philosophies call for the more effective use of some resources - housing and educational, for example - that already exist. However, there are other instances where the drive to 'place the client first' has supported clear innovations in service provision that cut across some of the traditional methods of delivering services and indeed call for substantively new types of professional expertise and modus operandi. Such new methods draw into question the actual role of services within clients' lives and focus on the more primary question of 'to what extent are services trying to withdraw from people's lives?' Two examples will be considered: client advocacy and community teams.

Client Advocacy

A rich literature exists on the subject of consumer participation in planning social welfare provision (see, for example, Rose, 1975; Hadley and Hatch, 1981; Smith and Jones, 1981; Richardson, 1983). Many recent initiatives in social policy have included attempts to promote a participative approach to involve consumers and users in planning services. Advocacy, however, is an important additional thread and is described as

> a process of pleading the cause and/or acting on behalf of mentally ill or mentally handicapped people, to secure the services they require and the enjoyment of their full rights. Advocates may be consumers, volunteers or professionals who act independently. As agents of people with handicaps, they owe them a duty of loyalty, confidentiality and zeal in promoting their cause (Gostin, 1984).

The United Nations Declaration on the Rights of Mentally Retarded Persons, adopted in 1971, embodies the principles of equality, integration, individualised habilitation, periodic review and natural justice. The International League of Societies for Persons with Mental Handicap published guidelines on the implementation of the 1971 Declaration, identifying three forms of advocacy: self-advocacy, legal, and lay advocacy.

Self-advocacy involves persons with handicaps asserting their own rights, expressing their needs and concerns and assuming the duties of citizenship to the extent of their capabilities. Self-advocates often form groups which assist members to acquire the necessary training, skills and experience to participate more fully in their communities.

Legal advocacy describes the broad range of methods and activities by which lawyers and other skilled individuals help mentally ill and mentally handicapped people to defend their rights. This can include reform or creation of new laws, as well as formal representation (for example at mental health review or supplementary benefit tribunals) and information to publicise the cause.

Lay advocacy also known as citizen advocacy refers to the persuasive and supportive activities of trained, selected and co-ordinated people, who, working on a one-to-one or group basis, attempt to foster respect for human rights and dignity. This may involve giving voice to the individual's personal concerns and aspirations, seeing that everyday social, recreational, health and related services are provided, and practical and emotional support.

The Advocacy Alliance in Britain is organised in this way. It was formed in 1982 by five voluntary associations (Mind, Mencap, One-to-One, the Spastics Society and the Leonard Cheshire Foundation) as a pioneering project to create a one-to-one scheme of friendship, protection and representation for many isolated people living in long-stay mental handicap hospitals. The DHSS (1980) review of services stated that many of these disadvantaged people needed more than friendship:

> ... the most important factor in safeguarding the position of vulnerable patients and ensuring that their rights are upheld is personal contact between the patient and someone whose job it is to explain the position from the patient's point of view.

This need was highlighted by the discussions about the DHSS (1981a) paper on patients' money. In its response to this consultation document, Mencap argued that if mentally handicapped people are to manage their own affairs, including welfare benefits and savings, then 'independent advocates' should be appointed to protect their interests (Sang and O'Brien, 1984). Sang's detailed account of the setting up of Advocacy Alliance (Sang and O'Brien, 1984) provides an important insight into the problems and issues that need to be faced. He considers the 'preparatory period' where agreements and working relationships with the relevant authorities and management were made and an ethical code for advocates established. This was followed by the 'creating advocates' phase involving recruiting and selecting volunteers from the community to befriend individual clients and represent their interests. The advocates had a role in helping to meet both the 'instrumental' needs of the client (accommodation, welfare benefits, transport, leisure and recreation facilities, voting rights and so on) and the 'expressive' needs (friendship, companionship, warmth, affection, love and so on).

Sang concludes that 'advocacy is a difficult concept for people to accept and assimilate (but that) it offers the possibility for intervention across the whole spectrum of health and welfare services'. For this reason he argues that advocacy programmes should seek independence from the agencies that provide for people who are dependent on some form of care. This is a radical step and the experience of Advocacy Alliance, and the more recent experience of setting up an advocacy service in Sheffield (Sheffield Advocacy Project, 1985), serve to show the immense difficulties in developing an approach that does not fit comfortably within the current services structure. These developments rely for their success on committed individuals within the health and social services who are able - in many cases - to set themselves apart from professional self-interest and judge the longer-term benefits of such a cause.

Community Teams

In mental handicap community teams have recently emerged as a resource for serving clients living in the community. The concept of the community mental handicap team (CMHT) was developed by the National Development Team (DT) and has gained popularity across the country. The variation in style and function of teams was highlighted in a study by Plank (1982) showing that some areas had both CMHTs and a district handicap team, some had neither, and some had one or the other. The main variation related to core membership, function, client group served, bases, referral policies and key worker systems. The Development Team suggested that for districts with very little in the way of mental handicap services the appointment of community mental handicap nurses to form, with a social worker, the core of a team is a good starting point - one team serving a population of 60000-80000 depending on local factors. These core team members should have, as a named resource, other members from various disciplines upon whom they can call - notably consultant psychiatrists, clinical psychologists, physiotherapists, and occupational and speech therapists.

Since Hall and Russell's (1979) survey of community nurses there has been some concern over their role and function. Hall and Russell concluded that although there is evidence of the emergence of a 'new' professional role 'there is still a need for both community nurses and social workers to occupy roles as key workers in CMHTs as they represent two parallel sets of resources which may both be needed by mentally handicapped people and their families' (Hall and Russell, 1982, p.23).

The HCSC (1984-85) in its report restated the problem of task definition recommending that in the case of community mental handicap nurses 'the Department (should) gather information on the tasks of (nurses) and produce an agreed statement of their role and functions' (Vol. 1, para 198). Although the main evidence (Plank, 1982) shows a health service bias within CMHTs there is more recent evidence that this is changing (Cotmore et al., 1985). The long-term research programme begun at Loughborough University aims to monitor the impact of CMHTs both within a local context (Nottinghamshire) and at a wider national level. The Nottinghamshire CMHT experiment, in this instance, involves exploring the use of CMHTs as service developers as opposed to a client-centred service. The study intends to monitor the impact of this role upon the uptake of services within Nottinghamshire, to examine the relationship of CMHTs with informal caring systems, and to look at their overall impact on families and service consumers.

The Development Team considered a CMHT to have two main functions, both primarily oriented towards direct work with individuals and their families:

(1) to provide advice and help, through counselling and support for parents, and specialist advice on day-to-day management problems;
(2) to act as front-line co-ordinators of services to mentally handicapped people and their families.

Nottinghamshire Social Services Department (SSD) considered these objectives too static (Cotmore et al., 1985) feeling that while co-ordination of services was a laudable objective, the first priority was to establish services on the ground: 'For example, counselling and support may help a family, but what they may really need is a residential place for their mentally handicapped member. Hence Nottinghamshire SSD gave the CMHTs an explicit development role' (Cotmore et al., 1985). The incentive in this case was the absence of actual services on the ground, and hence CMHTs have become the vehicle for creating, for example, cost-effective community-based alternatives to traditional residential provision, such as unstaffed group homes, adult fostering and lodging schemes.

Much has been written of the expectations of CMHTs - a sign of the range of demands made of them. They can engage the community, especially if they have an open referral system and a system of organisation based on key workers (Ferlie, Pahl and

Quine, 1984). It is also clear, from experiments trying to devolve more managerial and budgetary responsibility onto social services teams or their individual members, that frontline workers are capable of rising to the challenge and working in creative and effective ways (Challis and Davies, 1981; Hadley and McGrath, 1984).

The success of a grassroots participative approach may be dependent on administrative and managerial sensitivity to, and support of, what CMHTs are saying, and on an ability to resolve tensions about delegating sufficient authority to teams to enable them to get on with the job while also ensuring that service providers are held to account (Grant, 1985). While teamwork constitutes one trend, the success in establishing interagency teamwork has in real terms proved to be minimal. Interagency teams do exist, but the prevailing trend is more in the direction of community social work (as in Nottinghamshire) or community nurse teams. The lessons to emerge from the Loughborough studies may well show the considerable impact of community development organised primarily from within the local authority; yet as many district health authorities develop their plans for hospital closures, in reality what is emerging from the NHS side is a prolonged covert commitment to using NHS-based services to provide community care, and one of the key components is the development of community nurse teams. Overall community teams have been set up more or less nationally; their composition and function vary considerably - some are still in embryonic form. The original concept of, for example, the community mental handicap team was based on a joint-agency partnership and upon joint working in practice (in the main between health and social services staff). What form they will take in the longer-term future is unclear as their destiny is set against a background of agency and professional control.

This chapter has sought to raise a number of issues concerning both the feasibility and present practice of community care. It has tried to argue that several factors have been responsible for the development and implementation of this policy initiative such as resource constraints, agency role confusion, the interests of competing professional groups, government 'shifts' in approach and new styles of service delivery. If community care is to be a serious future strategy or not, as Walker (1982) claimed '(a policy) based on often unacceptable assumptions about the duty, willingness and ability of families, and women in particular, to care for dependents', then central government initiative is required. A strong sense of commitment and leadership asserted against vested institutional interests may well result in real progress. Unless government takes this lead, services on the ground are fated to flounder and a further spell of indifference will set in. There are many impressive ideas being developed around the country but good faith alone is not enough to effect change. Community care needs to be properly resourced and co-ordinated at both national and local level. This calls for both structural change in the organisation of welfare services and for a high degree of professionalism among those employed within the services. Only then will individual consumers of services be able to benefit in a positive way - towards more personal fulfilment and independence as opposed to being possible victims of an alternative system of provision that offers restricted choice and limited opportunity for growth, and the establishment of personal identity.

REFERENCES

Alt, J.E. and Chrystal, A.K. (1983) Political Economics (Wheatsheaf Books, Brighton)

Angus, P. (1984) 'Sheffield: Step Forward or Back', Nursing Times, 12 December

Atkinson, D. (1984) 'The Use of Participant Observation and Respondent Diaries in a Study of Ordinary Living', British Journal of Mental Subnormality, 33(2), no.59

Ayer, S. and Alaszewski, A. (1984) Community Care and the Mentally Handicapped: Services for Mothers and Their Mentally Handicapped Children (Croom Helm, London)

Baker, B.L., Seltzer, G.B. and Seltzer, M.M. (1977) As Close as Possible: Community Residences for Retarded Adults (Little, Brown and Co., Boston)

Bamford, T. (1984) 'The Mirage of Community Care', Community Care, 15 November

Barclay Committee (1982) Social Workers: Their Role and Tasks, Appendix B (Bedford Square Press, London)

Bartlett, H. and Challis, L. (1985) 'Surveying the Boom in Private Nursing Homes', Health and Social Service Journal, 3 June

Bayley, M. and Parker, P. (1980) 'Dinnington: An Experiment in Health and Welfare Co-operation', in R. Hadley and M. McGrath (eds) Going Local (Bedford Square Press, London)

Bell, L. (1985) 'Training Initiatives', Community Care, 16 May

Blunden, R. (1984) 'Behaviour Analysis and the Design and Evaluation of Services for Mentally Handicapped People', in Breuning, S., Matson, J. and Bennett, R. (eds) Advances in Mental Retardation and Developmental Disabilities, Vol. 2 (Greenwich, Connecticut, JAI Press)

Blunden, R. (1985) Annual Report for 1984 (MHW-ARU, Cardiff)

Bosanquet, N. (1985) 'Failure to Identify Opportunities, Health and Social Service Journal, 18 April

Brown, M. (1983) 'The Development of Social Administration', in Loney, M., Boswell, D. and Clarke, J. (eds) Social Policy and Social Welfare (Open University Press, Milton Keynes)

Buckle, J. (1984) Mental Handicap Costs More (DIG Charitable Trust)

CCETSW (1984) Paper 5.2 Initiatives in In-service Training (Helping staff to care for mentally handicapped people in the community), October

CCETSW (1985a) Paper 5.3 Mental Handicap (Progress and prospects in staff training) September

CCETSW (1985b) Policies for Qualifying Training in Social Work. The Councils Propositions. Paper 20.3

Centre for Policy on Ageing (1984) Home Life: A Code of Practice of Residential Care. Report on a Working Party sponsored by DHSS, and convened by CPA

Campaign for People with Mental Handicaps (CMH) (1985) Going to work: Employment opportunities for people with mental

handicaps in Washington State, USA
CMH (1984) A Survey of District Health Authorities Planning Groups for Services to People with a Mental Handicap, 12a Maddox Street, London W1R 9PL
Challis, D. and Davies, B. (1981) 'A New Approach to Community Care of the Elderly', British Journal of Social Work, 10(1), 1-18
Churchill, J. (1985) 'Restricted by Red Tape', Community Care, 29 August
Coles, E. and Blunden, R. (1981). 'Maintaining New Procedures Using Feedback to Staff, a Hierarchical Reporting System and a Multi-disciplinary Management Group', Journal of Organisational Behaviour Management, 3, 19-33
Cotmore, R., Sinclair, R., Webb, A. and Watson, G. (1985) 'Five Faces of Care', Community Care, 27 June
Dalgleish, M. and Matthews, R. (1979) Community Reaction to Local Buildings: Pilot Study. (Sheffield Development Project for Mentally Handicapped People Report 3), Mental Health Buildings Evaluation (DHSS, London)
Dalgleish, M. (1979) Children's Residential Accommodation: Policies and User Reaction (Sheffield Development Project for Mentally Handicapped People Report 2) Mental Health Buildings Evaluation (DHSS, London)
Davies, T.S. (1977) 'Hospital-based Community Service for the Mentally Subnormal', British Medical Journal, 1, 1156
Day, K. (1985) 'Care in the Community is "Clapped Out"', Health and Social Service Journal, 19/26 December
Department of the Environment (1983) Housing Corporation's Shared Housing Supplement to the Schemework Procedure Guide, (HMSO, London)
DHSS (1969) Report of the Committee of Inquiry into Allegations of Ill-Treatment of Patients and Other Irregularities at the Ely Hospital, Cardiff. (HMSO, London)
DHSS (1971) Better Services for the Mentally Handicapped. Cmnd 4683. (HMSO, London)
DHSS (1980) Mental Handicap: Progress, Problems and Priorities (HMSO, London)
DHSS (1981a) Patient's Money: Accumulation of Balances in Longstay Hospitals (HMSO, London)
DHSS (1981b) Care in Action: A Handbook of Policies and Priorities for the Health and Personal Social Services in England (HMSO, London)
DHSS (1981c) Helping to Get Mentally Handicapped Children out of Hospital, £1 Million for £1 Million Scheme (HC (81) 13) (HMSO, London)
DHSS (1981d) Care in the Community: A Consultative Document on Moving Resources for Care in England (HMSO, London)
DHSS (1983a) NHS Management Inquiry Report (HMSO, London)
DHSS (1983b) Helping to Get Mentally Handicapped Children out of Mental Handicap Hospitals (HC (83) 21) (HMSO, London)
DHSS (1985) Government Response to the Second Report from the

Social Services Committee, 1984-85 Session. Community Care, (HMSO, London)
Derricourt, N. (1983) 'Strategies of Community Care', in Loney, M. et al. (eds) Social Policy and Social Welfare (Open University Press, Milton Keynes)
Drummond, P. (1984) 'One Step Forward and Two Back', Health and Social Service Journal, 6 September
ENB (1985) Professional Education/Training Courses. Consultation Paper.
ENB-CCETSW (1982, 1983) Co-operation in Training. The Report of the GNCs (now ENB)/CCETSW Joint Working Group, Part 1 - Qualifying Training 1982; Part 2 - In-Service Training, 1983
Equal Opportunities Commission (1980) The Experience of Caring for Elderly and Handicapped Dependents. Survey Report
Felce, D., Kushlick, A., Lunt, B. and Mansell, J. (1978) Evaluation of Locally Based Hospital Units for the Mentally Handicapped in Wessex: The recruitment and allocation of staff to, and maintenance of staff continuity in, established posts in five Wessex locally-based hospital units and in five villas on a traditional hospital campus (Research Report 140). (Health Care Evaluation Research Team, Winchester)
Felce, D., Jenkins, J., Mansell, J., De Kock, U., Toogood, S. and Pomfrey, A. (1982) Staff Induction, Training. (Health Care Evaluation Research Team, University of Southampton)
Ferlie, E., Pahl, J. and Quine, L. (1984) 'Professional Collaboration in Services for Mentally Handicapped People', Journal of Social Policy, 13 (2), 185-202
Flynn, M. (1985) 'Objectives and Prognoses Recorded in the Case Records of Mentally Handicapped Adults Living in Their Own Homes', British Journal of Social Work, 15, 519-524
Glennerster, H. (1983) Planning for Priority Groups (Martin Robertson, Oxford)
Gostin, L. (1984) Foreword, in Sang, B. and O'Brien, J. Advocacy. Kings Fund Centre Project Paper No. 51
Graham, H. (1985) 'Health and Welfare', in R. Oakley (ed.) Issues in Sociology Series (Macmillan Education, London)
Grant, G. (1985) 'Towards Participation in the All Wales Strategy: Issues and Processes', Mental Handicap, 13
Guardian (1985) 'Move to Switch Care Services Worries Charities', Guardian, 6 June
Hadley, R. and Hatch, S. (1981) Social Welfare and the Failure of the State: Centralised Social Services and Participatory Alternatives (Allen and Unwin, London)
Hadley, R. and McGrath, M. (1984) When Services are Local: The Normanton Experience (Allen and Unwin, London)
Hall, P., Land, H., Parker, R. and Webb, A. (1975) Change, Choice and Conflict in Social Policy (Heinemann, London)
Hall, V. and Russell, O. (1979) A National Survey of Community Nursing Services for the Mentally Handicapped. Research

Report No. 10 (Department of Mental Health, University of Bristol)
Hall, V. and Russell, O. (1982) Mental Handicap and Health Care Organisation. Final Report (Department of Mental Health, University of Bristol)
Hampson, R., Judge, K. and Renshaw, J. (1985) 'Caught in the Turbulence', Community Care, 9 May
Health and Social Service Journal (1986) 'Education Programme Launched', news item, 20 February
Heginbotham, C. (1981) Housing Projects for Mentally Handicapped People CEH (Centre on Environment for the Handicapped, London)
Heginbotham, C. (1985) 'What Future for Community Care', Health and Social Service Journal, 14 March
HMSO (1962) A Hospital Plan for England and Wales, Cmnd 1604 (HMSO, London) (Centre on Environment for the Handicapped, London)
House of Commons Second Report from the Social Services Committee Session (1984-85) Community Care - with Special Reference to Adult Mentally Ill and Mentally Handicapped People. Vols I-III, (HMSO, London)
Humphreys, S., Lowe, K. and Blunden, R. (1983) 'Long-term Evaluation of Services for Mentally Handicapped People in Cardiff', Research Methodology
Independent Development Council for People with Mental Handicap (1985). Living Like Other People - Next Steps in Day Services for People with Mental Handicap (IDC, London)
Jay Committee (1979) Report of the Committee of Enquiry into Mental Handicap Nursing and Care, Vol 1. Cmnd 7468 (HMSO, London)
Jones, A.A., Evans, G. and Blunden, R. (1984) 'Introducing a General Prompting and Recording System: Its Effect on client and Staff Behaviour in an Institutional Ward. Applied Research in Mental Retardation, 5, 125-136
Jones, D. (1985) 'A Carer's Work is Never Done. Community Care, 4 July
King, R., Raynes, N. and Tizard, J. (1971) Patterns of Residential Care: Sociological Studies in Institutions for Handicapped Children (Routledge and Kegan Paul, London)
King's Fund Centre (1984) An Ordinary Working Life (Vocational Services for People with Mental Handicap) Project Paper No. 50 (King's Fund Publishing Office, London)
Korman, N. and Glennerster (1985) Closing a Hospital: The Darenth Park Project (Bedford Square Press, London)
Kratz, C. (1985) 'The Tip of the Iceberg', Nursing Times, 12 June
Laming, H. (1985) 'Building a New Welfare State', Community Care, 19 September
Lane, D. (1980) The Work Needs of Mentally Handicapped Adults (Disability Alliance, London)
LeGrand, J. and Robertson, D. (1984) Privatisation and the

Welfare State (Allen and Unwin, London)
Levin, E., Sinclair, I. and Gorbach, P. (1981) The Supporters of Confused Elderly Persons at Home (National Institute for Social Work Research Unit, London)
Locker, D., Rao, B. and Weddell, J.M. (1979) 'Knowledge of and Attitudes Towards Mental Handicap: Their Implications for Community Care', Community Medicine 1(2), 127-136
Loney, M., Boswell, D. and Clarke, J. (eds) (1983) Social Policy and Social Welfare (Open University Press, Milton Keynes)
McCormick, M., Balla, D. and Zigler, E. (1975) 'Resident-care Practices in Institutions for Retarded Persons: A Cross-institutional, Cross-cultural Study'. American Journal of Mental Deficiency, 80, 1-17
McKnight, D. (1981) Review of Literature on Non-Institutional Care, (HMSO, London)
Malin, N. and Race, D. (1978) Voluntary Services for the Mentally Handicapped. ERG Reports No. 3. Evaluation Research Group (Department of Psychology, University of Sheffield)
Malin, N., Race, D. and Jones, G. (1980) Services for the Mentally Handicapped in Britain, (Croom Helm, London)
Malin, N. (1983) Group Homes for Mentally Handicapped People (HMSO, London)
Meacher, M. et al. (1985) As of Right: Labour's Call for Full Citizenship for all Disabled People (House of Commons, London)
Meacher, M. (1985) 'Lack of Services "Overburdens" Families', Nursing Times, 13 February
Mencap (1984) 'A Home from Home', Parents Voice, Journal of the Royal Society for Mentally Handicapped Children and Adults, 34 (11), 12
Mental Handicap in Wales - Applied Research Unit (1985) Annual Report for 1984, MHW-ARU, Cardiff CF1 9DU
Mind (1984) Common Concern (MIND, London)
Ministry of Health (1963) Health and Welfare: The Development of Community Care. Cmnd 1973 (HMSO, London)
Morris, P. (1969) Put Away: A Sociological Study of Institutions for the Mentally Retarded (Routledge and Kegan Paul, London)
Mulhern, T. (1975) 'Survey of Reported Sexual Behaviour and Policies Characterising Residential Facilities for Retarded Citizens', American Journal of Mental Deficiency, 79(6), 670-673
Murray, N. (1985a) 'Voluntary Organisations', Community Care, 17 January
Murray, N. (1985b) 'Mr Fowler's Future', Community Care, 6 June
National Development Group for the Mentally Handicapped (1977) Day Services for Mentally Handicapped Adults, July
National Development Group for the Mentally Handicapped (1980) Improving the Quality of Services for Mentally Handicapped

People: a checklist of standards (DHSS, London)
National Society for Mentally Handicapped Children (NSMHC) (1977) STAMINA: Local Action for Services (NSMHC, London)
NIMROD (1978) Report of a Joint Working Party on the Provision of a Community based Mental Handicap Service in South Glamorgan. Vol. 1: The Working Party Report
Nissel, M. and Bonnerjea, L. (1982) Family Care of the Handicapped Elderly: Who Pays? Policy Studies Institute No. 602
Parker, C. and Etherington, S. (1985) 'Health and Social Needs: Bridging the False Divide', Health and Social Service Journal, 11 April
PSSRU (1985a) Care in the Community, Summer (The University of Kent, Canterbury)
PSSRU (1985b) Care in the Community: Housing and Support Services, Winter (The University of Kent, Canterbury)
Plank, M. (1982) An Enquiry into Joint Planning of Services for Mentally Handicapped People (CMH, London)
Porterfield, J., Evans, G. and Blunden, R. (1984) 'Working Together for Change: Involving Clients, Families and Staff in Planning Improvements in Mental Handicap Services', Mental Handicap, 12(2), 67-69
Porterfield, J. and Gathercole, C. (1985) The Employment of People with Mental Handicap. Kings Fund Centre Project Paper No. 55 (Kings Fund Centre, London)
Porterfield, J., Blunden, R. and Blewitt, E. (1980) 'Improving Environments for Profoundly Handicapped Adults: Using Prompts and Social Attention to Maintain High Group Engagements', Behaviour Modification, 4, 225-241
Pushkin, R. (1976a) 'Community Confusion over Abnormality Needs a Remedy', Health and Social Service Journal, 86, 1856-57
Pushkin, R. (1976b) Lay Criteria for Defining and Recognising Mental Subnormality (Department of Community Medicine, University of Manchester)
Raynes, N., Pratt, M. and Roses, S. (1977) 'Aides' Involvement in Decision-making and the Quality of Care in Institutional Settings', American Journal of Mental Deficiency, 81 (6), 570-577
Rees, A.M. (1985) T.H. Marshall's Social Policy, 5th edn (Hutchinson, London)
Revill, S. and Blunden, R. (1979) 'A Home Training Service for Pre-School Developmentally Handicapped Children', Behaviour Research and Therapy, 17, 207-214
Richardson, A. (1983) Participation (Routledge and Kegan Paul, London)
Ritchie, J., Keegan, J. and Bosanquet, N. (1983) Housing for Mentally Ill and Mentally Handicapped People (HMSO, London)
Rose, H. (1975) 'Participation: The Icing on the Welfare Cake', In Jones, K. (ed.) The Yearbook of Social Policy, 1975 (Routledge and Kegan Paul, London)

Royal College of Psychiatrists (1985) Evidence to the House of Commons Second Report from the Social Services Committee, Session 1984-84, Community Care (with special reference to adult mentally ill and mentally handicapped people) Vol. II, p.108

Sang, B. and O'Brien, J. (1984) Advocacy - UK and US Experiences. Kings Fund Centre Project Paper No. 51 (Kings Fund Centre, London)

Seebohm Committee on Local Authority and Allied Personal Social Services (1968) Report cmnd 2703. (HMSO, London)

Shearer, A. (ed.) (1983) An Ordinary Life. Issues and Strategies for Training Staff for Community Mental Handicap Services. (Kings Fund Centre, London)

Sheffield Advocacy Project (1985) Annual Report 1984-85 (Sheffield Advocacy Project, Sheffield)

Smith, L. and Jones, D. (eds) (1981) Deprivation, Participation and Community Action (Routledge and Kegan Paul, London)

Spencer, D. (1985) 'NHS Provision for Mental Handicap - The Clinical Experience/Political Dogma Dilemma', British Society for the Study of Mental Subnormality Newsletter, 11 (1 and 2), July and November

Tizard, J. (1964) Community Services for the Mentally Handicapped (Oxford University Press, Oxford)

Towell, D. (1985) 'Health and Social Services Relationships in the Reform of Long Term Care', British Journal of Social Work, 15, 451-456

Tyne, A. (1977) Residential Provision for Adults who are Mentally Handicapped (Enquiry Paper 5) (CMH, London)

Tyne, A. (1978) Looking at Life - in Hospitals, Hostels, Homes and Units for Adults who are Mentally Handicapped (Enquiry Paper 7) (CMH, London)

Tyne, A. and O'Brien, J. (1981) The Principle of Normalisation: A Foundation for Effective Services (CMH Publications, London)

United Nations General Assembly (1972) Declaration on the Rights of Mentally Retarded Persons. Resolution 2856, 26th Session, para 88

Walker, A. (ed.) (1982) Community Care: The Family, the State and Social Policy (Blackwell and Robertson, Oxford)

Ward, L.M. (1984) Planning for People. Developing a Local Service for People with Mental Handicap. Recruiting and Training Staff (Kings Fund Centre, London)

Ward, L. (1985) 'Training Staff for "An Ordinary Life". Experiences in a Community Service in South Bristol', British Journal of Mental Subnormality, Vol. 34, Part 1

Warnock Committee (1978) 'Special Educational Needs', Report of the Committee of Enquiry into the Education of Handicapped People. Cmnd 7212. May (HMSO, London)

Welsh Office (1983) All-Wales Strategy for the Development of Services for Mentally Handicapped People (Welsh Office, Cardiff)

Whelan, E. and Speake, B. (1977) Adult Training Centre in England and Wales: Report of the First National Survey. (National Association of Teachers of the Mentally Handicapped, Manchester)

Whelan, E. and Speake, B. (1981) Getting to Work. Human Horizons Series (Souvenir Press, London)

Willms, J. (1979) Retarded Adults in Community-based residences: an investigation of neighbourhood attitudes and concerns, Paper presented at IASSMD conference Jerusalem, August 1979

Wolfensberger, W. (1972) The Principle of Normalisation in Human Services (Toronto, NIMR)

Chapter Two

NORMALISATION: THEORY AND PRACTICE

David Race

INTRODUCTION

In many ways, writing this chapter provokes considerable anxiety in the author - not least in the fact that much of the apprehension lies in the very nature of the principles of normalisation themselves. Normalisation is a set of ideas, relating to services for people, which unfortunately have been represented by many as being simply a series of statements of the obvious. Many practitioners, if questioned, respond with three points:

(1) They understand all there is to know about normalisation - because after all it is only 'applied commonsense';
(2) They are applying, and have always applied these principles in their practice except where they become:
(3) Too idealistic - 'the real world' whatever that may be, prevents normalisation being fully implemented, sometimes to the extent of denying the principles themselves as 'idealistic' or 'impossible'.

Nearly all these statements are, however, based on a very brief exposure to the full complexity of normalisation ideas, and it is for this reason that apprehension comes. It may be that this chapter will contribute to that lack of depth, by readers imagining that once it is absorbed they need think no further on the matter.

Given the reality of the situation - in other words, that the ideas around normalisation are far more deep-rooted and complex than people imagine - what can this chapter attempt to do? In essence, it can do no more than present an overview of the ideas, point the reader towards the sources of those ideas and the currently available ways of exploring them further, while indicating on the way some examples of non-application and misapplication of the ideas in the practice of services for devalued people, particularly those with mental handicaps.

SOURCES

No doubt a student somewhere is already writing a thesis on the development of the principles of normalisation, from their beginnings in Scandinavia, through the major developmental work of Wolfensberger and his colleagues in America, and as applied to the English scene by such as the Community and Mental Handicap Evaluation and Research Association (CMHERA). While we await the production of that thesis, however, this section will briefly indicate the major sources for interested readers to pursue. It should also be noted that these are, perhaps obviously, the sources of the material in this chapter.

Wolfensberger's original text (1972) still remains the basic starting point for any serious student of normalisation, though perhaps an easier route, particularly for English readers, would be to begin with the booklet of Tyne and O'Brien (1981) and then go on to Wolfensberger's work. For a more immediate and, one would suggest, powerful impact workshops on PASS (Wolfensberger and Glenn, 1978) and PASSING (Wolfensberger and Thomas, 1983) run by CMHERA in various parts of the country are highly recommended.(1) The PASSING manual, in fact, also provides the most up-to-date version of Wolfensberger's formulation of the themes of normalisation, and it is this famework that will be used in this chapter. The framework, referred to as the seven 'themes' of normalisation, has also been the basis of a number of normalisation workshops particularly those run by Wolfensberger's Training Institute. (2)

THE SEVEN CORE THEMES

In an age when more and more technological solutions are being offered to solve human problems it is perhaps inevitable that eager students should be seeking the 'key' to normalisation and that even an abbreviation to seven core themes is met with demands to supply the 'most important' theme, or at least some form of ordering of the themes. In resisting such demands, and pointing out that the coherence of the principles depends on an interaction of the various themes, one is still left with the simple logistical problem of where to start. Partly, therefore, because the first theme is often the one omitted (because it is difficult to come to terms with, especially for 'professionals'), and partly for the simpler reason of starting somewhere, we begin with the role of (un)consciousness in human services.

The Role (Un)consciousness in Human Services

One does not need to be a Freudian or, indeed, any other sort of psychologist to be aware of how much of our lives function with a high degree of unconsciousness. If readers had to answer why they chose to do most things in their everyday life, for example: Why do you eat what you eat, wear what you wear, live where you live, work where you work, work how you work, have the friends you have, treat them the way you do? They would probably after some thought and much soul-searching come up with a more or less convincing justification for each one.

But of course people do not go through this performance each time they make these sorts of choices - a huge amount of unconscious processing is taking place.

Given the above, what has this to do with normalisation? The argument runs as follows. If the above is true, then it is highly likely that human services and human service organisations being run by ordinary people like the readers of this chapter will also operate with a high level of unconsciousness, and particularly will push into unconsciousness the negative aspects of the various levels of its work replacing them with outwardly positive ones. Table 2.1 (Thomas, 1984) lists a number of observed features of human services that are usually expressed if they are positive, or not mentioned much, if they are negative.

Readers are invited to examine those services with which they are familiar and consider the expressed ideologies, functions and actual events that happen in these services, as compared to negative ideologies, functions and things that are actually happening to the people who use the services. This is not to suggest, and it is a point that needs to be emphasised time and again when discussing normalisation, that any sort of 'evil

Table 2.1: Consciousness and Unconsciousness in Human Services

	Positive - usually expressed	Negative - usually repressed
Ideologies that control how services are rendered	Christianity Humanism Measurement of worth by membership of humanity	Materialism Racism Measurement of worth by economic value membership of ethnic group intellectual level
Functions that services are intended to fulfil	Care Meeting clients needs Rehabilitation Integration Independence	Control Rejection Meeting others needs, including server's needs for employment and organisations need for survival Segregation Dependence
What goes on in services	Love Family life Development Fulfilling potential Rewarding experiences Restoring value to people	Degradation Institutional life Low expectation - low effort Segregated and limited experience Devaluing people

intent' is being carried out by services, or that 'bad' people are running them. The whole notion of the first theme is that many human activities have negative aspects to them, some of which dominate the activities, others of which are merely the price to be paid for the positive aspects. It is not the case that normalisation goes from the observation that such negative aspects exist to condemn the individuals who work in and run such services. Its importance is to make conscious what, for entirely understandable and almost universally occurring reasons, currently remains unconscious.

Normalisation is explicit in its efforts to look at what you are doing and why you are doing it in a conscious way - to dig out the hidden negatives and look at ways of overcoming them; in other words, to break into the vicious circle which is at the heart of the next theme.

Role Expectancy and Role Circularity

Once again, this is something apparently obvious: something we all feel we know about, but something which is addressed directly by normalisation - the imposition of social roles by people on one another, and the resultant reinforcement of stereotyped behaviour in that role.

Feminist readers may well find a familiar ring to all this - as well they should, representing the largest devalued group in society. For other devalued people, however, roles typically ascribed to them by others are even more negative.

The observation of how social roles were ascribed to devalued, and especially handicapped, people formed one of the major planks on which Wolfensberger developed the principles of normalisation, and this is discussed at length in his book. The limitations of space in this chapter confines us to listing some of these historical roles and to link these roles to the media by which they have been, and still are, conveyed to the non-handicapped world. Society's perceptions are increasingly based around images conveyed through what they see and hear at a very superficial and, as the earlier theme discussed, unconscious level. These perceptions are heightened by an individual's response to them, and that response can be transmitted not only by what people say, but what they do, where they do it, and who else is there with them. (Table 2.2, adapted from slides used in Thomas, 1984.)

Table 2.2: Historical Roles of Devalued People and the Media Through Which They are Conveyed

Roles Ascribed	Media of Role Expectancy
Menace	Physical environment
Subhuman	People associated with
animal	Behaviours expected /demanded
vegetable	Language
thing	
Unspeakable objects of dread	
Objects of ridicule	
Objects of pity	
Burden of charity	
Holy innocent	
Children	
eternal	
once again	
Sick people	

Looking at all the aspects of a service by which messages are conveyed, therefore, and not just what actually goes on in direct work with users, an overwhelming array of role ascriptions can result. Some examples are given in Table 2.3 but again readers are invited to examine the services with which they are familiar.

With the last part of Table 2.3 in mind, readers might care to reflect on their own use of language, not just in their professional lives, but in their ordinary conversation. How do they describe people with handicaps, or other devalued groups?

As with consciousness, normalisation is not seeking to blame people for using language which ascribes social roles, or for providing services in environments and in ways which produce these roles but, more importantly, to break into the circle of role ascription: (a) by realising it is there; (b) by altering the circumstances which perpetuate it.

Here, of course, simply altering one part (for example, not using devaluing language, or providing a residential service in ordinary houses) does not alter the whole. Normalisation suggests that attention needs to be given to all the ways in which messages are conveyed about devalued people. This leads on to the next theme.

Positive Compensation

At this point in the seven themes, Wolfensberger

Table 2.3: Examples of Roles Conveyed by Various Aspects of Human Services

Media	Examples	Roles Suggested
Physical environment	Locks, bars on places where people live	Menace
	Herding together groups of devalued people in one place - moving them about in groups	Animal
	Public display via signs on homes, minibuses etc.	Object of pity, ridicule
	Decor of internal environment - posters, childlike images	Eternal child
People associated with	More devalued people	'A race apart' - another species
	Putting handicapped people in excessive contact with animals	Subhuman - animal
	Adults and children all together	Eternal child
Behaviours expected/ demanded	No risks - excessive protection	Children, holy innocent
	Non-serious work selling goods 'made by handicapped people'	Objects of pity
	Excessive contact with plants, gardens	Vegetable
Language	Too many examples to list - many simply naming the role, such as 'subnormal', 'low grade', 'eternal children', 'the handicapped' 'cabbage'	Subhuman Vegetable Eternal children Separate species Vegetable

Table 2.4: Examples of the Reinforcing Effect of Devaluation

1. Physical Appearance		
Valued people can have	casual clothes long or unkempt hair some physical stigmata:	But for devalued people this would reinforce 'difference', 'unnaturalness'
2. Behaviour in Public	Without causing much comment	and raise the comment
Valued people can	get drunk sing songs produce mildly antisocial behaviour: Without causing much comment	'What do you expect'

introduces a rather difficult phrase in an English context, the 'conservative corollary', to the principles of normalisation - an easier alternative might be positive compensation. This is not the same thing as affirmative action, or positive discrimination - what it is addressing is the fact that for devalued people, activities, styles of dress and other outward appearances which would not in themselves cause comment if exhibited by valued people, can combine to reinforce the devalued state - it could be called the 'what do you expect' aspect of devaluation (Table 2.4).

Providing positive compensation for this state of affairs means to address oneself more to the issues than would be the case for someone not at risk of devaluation and try for:

(1) the best physical appearance,
(2) greater opportunities for valued behaviour,
(3) generally veering to the 'conservative' side of appearance and behaviour.

This is an area of some controversy, particularly to people who have a gut reaction to the word 'conservative', but at the heart of it is the continuous message of normalisation - 'don't devalue people'; so even if it is regarded as a sad state of affairs that appearances should be so important - putting oneself in a devalued person's place and thinking how one would feel if people started remarking on how 'typically' one looked and behaved and 'what can you expect from your sort of people' can be a salutory experience.

Let us now move on to the major positive voice of normalisation, the developmental model.

The Developmental Model

Once again this is a familiar almost trite phrase (Table 2.5, adapted from slides used in Thomas, 1984).

Table 2.5: The Developmental Assumption

Assumptions	Key Factors
People can grow	Relevance of how you help to real needs of individual
People can become more competent	Power of your help Skills are not the only thing in life

The idea of 'developing potential' is perhaps the most commonly voiced objective of services for handicapped people - almost to the extent of overshadowing other aspects which are as important in the devaluing process. The points that normalisation makes on this theme are:

(1) Make sure you really identify what peoples' needs are, not just those that fit some scale or chart, or some service defined need.
(2) Recognise the importance of experiences other than skill learning as contributors to personal development.
(3) There are abundant ways to contribute to growth, but a lot are never tried - it takes effort, belief, and risk to provide 'powerful' help.

One of the most powerful sources of learning, but one which works positively or negatively, is the next theme.

The Power of Imitation

This is yet another concept familiar to readers, but consider its implications for both valued and devalued people and the opportunities with which they so often get faced (Table 2.6).

Although the effects of role modelling are so well known and so powerful, so many of our services to devalued people are provided in segregated settings, with devalued people all herded together, giving little or no opportunity for observing, or even recognising valued behaviour. The implication for normalisation is clear. Allied with imitation is another powerful effect on learning and behaviour, but one which is less often addressed by human services.

The Dynamics and Relevance of Social Imagery

Because, perhaps, we like to think of ourselves as rational, intelligent people, the effect of imagery, of impressions and associations of what we see, tend to be little discussed. We like to think, for instance, that advertising has no effect on us, that we can see through the association of cigars and sex, toothpaste and family life, washing up and success. Well of course we can, if each advertisement is analysed - but we don't for all our cleverness. Images have a great effect - why else would politicians spend thousands on improving their

Table 2.6: Imitation - Opportunities and Results

	Live in/ Observe	Identify with/ Imitate	Learn About	Become
Valued people	Society at large	Persons/role models seen as valued	Valued behaviour	More valued people
Devalued people	Segregated or restricted society	Persons/role models who are devalued	Devalued behaviour	More devalued people

image, and hard-headed businessmen give away thousands on two minutes of trivia.

We are back, of course, to unconsciousness again - this time in the association of images and symbols with positive or negative messages which are then transferred to people, and it is not again just what we do; there are many other media (Table 2.7, adapted from slides used in Thomas, 1984).

As before, many of these things seem obvious, but are very powerful in contributing to the way in which services, and devalued people, are viewed. Unfortunately, perhaps because they are so obvious, there is a tendency to forget about such things, or to regard them as not worth addressing professional attention to. The key aspects from the viewpoint of normalisation are:

(1) Recognise the immense power of imagery.
(2) Be aware of what messages are conveyed by services.
(3) Change them from negative to positive.

Yet again, normalisation is not suggesting evil intent from those who surround their services with images which devalue people; it is simply trying to point out the effects, and thus raise awareness of what is happening in those services.

All such efforts at awareness within human services, which form the basis for analysis using normalisation principles, have underpinning them a fundamental value position, and this in turn leads to a view of what the objective of human services should be. The value position is not peculiar to normalisation, it has been stated in a number of ways in various religious and secular manifestoes. Put at its simplest, it is a belief that all people are of equal value, and it is not the purpose of this chapter to argue the moral and philosophical case for such a belief, but given this belief is held, which is certainly the case for those advocating the principles of normalisation, one particular objective which normalisation then derives for people who are at risk of being devalued forms the final theme.

Personal Social Integration and Valued Social Participation

Most of the previous themes have provided an analysis by which it can readily be seen how societies, and human services that are part of those societies, have

Table 2.7: Image Media and Their Effects - Examples

Media	Aspects of Media	Examples of Image-producing Aspects of Services	Giving Images of
Physical setting	Appearance	Beautiful, ugly	Worthlessness, unimportance
	Physical features	Bars, gates	
	Location	Set apart	Danger, fear
	History	Hospital, workhouse	Difference
Grouping with others	Clients	All the same	Inhumanity, facelessness
	Staff	Warden, medical uniform	
	Others	Adults and children all together	Sickness, prison Eternal children
Personal imagery	Appearance	Socks at 35	Eternal childhood
	Possessions	Children's toys for adults	Eternal childhood
	Autonomy and rights	Overprotection	No personal growth
Language	Personal names and labels	Kids, mentally handicapped	Children, subhumans, sorts of disease
	Service names and labels	'Waifs and strays'	Animals, charity
	Setting and location name	'Sunshine Home', 'Home of Hope'	Burden of charity
Activities	Type of activities	Kids stuff for adults, basket-making	Eternal childhood occupation
	Combination/separation of function	Work and live all in same place	Need for protection, separate existence
	Schedules and routines	Start work at 10, end at 3	Differentness

systematically (though often with the best of original intentions) devalued certain groups of people. Where this book is concerned the group of people are those called mentally handicapped, and one of the primary methods of devaluation used for this group has been to set them apart. As mentioned above, there are many ways in which this segregation has been justified, for example(3):

(1) To protect them from society.
(2) To protect society from them.
(3) They are happier with their own kind.
(4) They can be properly looked after.

All of these place, at best, a devalued image on the people concerned; at worst it kills them - the ultimate form of segregation. What it represents is easing society's conscience and removing a situation of which people, through ignorance, are afraid. Normalisation proposes the reverse, but note the importance of the two parts of the final theme. Physical integration, that is, being there, is a precondition, but it is not enough. The key issue from the point of view of normalisation is the value placed on that integration. Table 2.8 gives a simple example.

Table 2.8: From Segregation to Valued Social Participation

Segregation	Physical Integration	Valued Social Participation
Swimming pool in institution	'Special' swimming lessons at local pool	Going swimming with everyone else

The big mistake has been to assume that physical integration is all you need, hence the vast numbers of hostels, special schools, ATCs, etc. 'in the community'. The ultimate aim of normalisation, and it is a difficult one, is valued social participation.

MYTHS ABOUT NORMALISATION

Given that the segregation of handicapped people, indeed the whole process of devaluation, is meeting certain needs of society, the objective outlined in the final theme will meet with considerable resistance. Changing society's views of people with handicaps is therefore a corollary of carrying out normalisation principles in practice. The problem has been that a number of services have either seen this change of attitude as a precondition for, rather than the possible result of, changes in those services in line with normalisation principles. 'You can't change society' is often used as the end of the argument, whereas, ultimately, normalisation recognises that only through continuous examination of the effects of services on that already difficult society and the provision of 'good models' can society learn about people with handicaps, and overcome the fear that is at the root of devaluation. People can only learn about what they can see, and thus the maximum opportunity for seeing and meeting people with handicaps provides the maximum opportunity for learning how to overcome that ignorance and fear. This suggests a number of ways of going forward from the analysis of what societies and services are doing to people at risk of devaluation which normalisation provides and which tends, initially, to appear very negative. Unfortunately, many of the ways in which this initial examination of what is happening now have been interpreted has led to the growth of a number of myths about normalisation. Still more myths have been created by attempts to answer part of the devaluation process, using the name of normalisation to justify practices which then continue that process. Table 2.9 headlines some of these myths. Readers may again care to think of examples from their own experiences.

CONCLUSIONS

This chapter has, as the author's opening concern noted, only covered the principles of normalisation in a very brief, introductory way. The magnitude of scope of these principles, even when presented in such a way, sometimes leaves people helpless as to where to go next, and this unfortunately is often followed by a rejection of the principles, and thus the devaluing process of human services continues unexamined. PASS and PASSING, as methods of examining services using normalisation principles, are still very little used by services themselves, for essentially the same reasons. Nevertheless there are signs that the practice adopted by CMHERA, of using PASS and PASSING as aids to understanding the principles of normalisation, has produced a growing awareness of the ideas throughout human services. It may be that wider trends in society will prevent this awareness from being realised in changed practices - ideas that involve a lot of thought and hard work are not easily absorbed by the sorts of bureaucratic organisations that run human services - but there are a few examples of work (3) that give grounds for optimism. It is to be hoped that a few people reading this chapter will be stirred to discover more.

Table 2.9: Myths about Normalisation

Normalisation Does Not Mean	Normalisation Does Not Imply
Making devalued/handicapped people 'normal'	Handicapped people are not handicapped
Making everyone conform to the 'norm'	Everyone should be integrated into all aspects of community life
Allowing any sort of behaviour as the 'normal' option of free choice	As long as their image is all right, forget the personal growth
Allowing segregated service settings as long as they are 'homelike'	Never use language which denotes some handicap or impairment

NOTES

1. Information on PASS and PASSING Workshops is obtainable from CMHERA, 12a Maddox Street, London, W1R 9PL.

2. Information on Training Institute Workshops is available from Training Institute for Human Service Planning, Leadership and Change Agency, Syracuse University, 805, South Crouse Avenue, Syracuse, New York 13210, USA.

3. Examples from this author's current organisation can be obtained from him c/o The Church of England Children's Society, Old Town Hall, Kennington Road, London, SE11 4QD.

REFERENCES

Thomas, S. (1984) Two Day Introductory Workshop on Normalisation, Castle Priory College, February

Tyne, A. and O'Brien, J. (1981) The Principle of Normalisation: A Foundation for Effective Services (CMH Publications, London)

Wolfensberger, W. (1972) The Principle of Normalisation in Human Services (Toronto, NIMR)

Wolfensberger, W. and Glenn, L. (1978) Program Analysis of Service Systems (PASS): A Method for the Quantitative Evaluation of Human Services. Handbook and Field Manual, 3rd edn (Toronto, NIMR)

Wolfensberger, W. and Thomas, S. (1983) Program Analysis of Service Systems' Implementation of Normalisation Goals: (PASSING) A method of evaluating the quality of human services according to the principles of normalisation. Normalisation Criteria and Ratings Manual 2nd edn (Toronto, NIMR)

Chapter Three

SHAPING COMMUNITY SERVICES: THE IMPACT OF AN IDEA

Alan Tyne

INTRODUCTION

In the early 1970s, those of us who used public platforms to talk with professionals about the closure of long-stay institutions, and the development of community alternatives for people with substantial handicaps got used to being 'howled down', treated with derision, even abuse. Ten years later we find ourselves in the midst of whirlwind change, with authorities falling over themselves in almost indecent haste to declare their closure plans and their advances in 'community care'. Change in service organisations not only happens, it is endemic. The influences on the pace of change are complex and often exasperating. One significant advocate of change has commented: 'It seemed that for years we were battering away at an obdurate authority over the ordinary housing issue, with very little success; then overnight they turned around to us and said "Okay - but we want it by tomorrow!".' The problem for many of us has been how to influence the path and direction of change so as to safeguard the people who rely most on those organisations for important things happening in their lives - people with handicaps, their families and friends.

Organisations may be limited in responding fully and effectively to people's real situation in a variety of ways. They may lack sufficient or appropriate resources, they may lack adequate processes and techniques of intervention. They may be poorly coordinated, have unclear or inapppropriate goals. Or they may have none of these, yet fail to address themselves to the right problem. Russell Ackoff (1978) observed, 'The failures of modern society and its institutions are more often from failure to ask the right questions than from failure to answer the questions we ask'. We have a panoply of technology and technique, professionally organised. Its failure to shift most of society's more intransigent problems is often attributed to the lack of sufficient professionals with sufficient training; rather like the poor old king calling for 'More horses, more men:' to put Humpty Dumpty together again. Likewise, major problems of service-giving organisations may lie in their failure to address the right questions, or in inadequate understanding of 'the problem', or in failure to secure a match between organisational 'solutions' and the problems addressed.

Definitions of 'the problem' and of appropriate solutions constitute a part of what Charles Perrow described as an organisation's 'premises of action' (Perrow, 1965). He was fascinated by the ways organisations control member's behaviour through control of their 'premises of action'. Later writers describe 'organisational cultures' - the stock of practically available ideas within an organisation which support problem solving and policy-development. Argyris and Schon (1980) refer to organisation's 'theories in action' - that body of current belief, and commitment, which an organisation rewards, and which makes sense for actors of what they are involved in. Organisational learning is a complex and often difficult process of shifting key values and commitments, as well as of established practice and routine. Recent writing (Peters and Waterman, 1983) suggests that organisations coping successfully with turbulent and changing environments pay careful attention to the maintenance and management of key values.

CMHERA AND CMH

What follows is drawn from the story of one small organisation's attempts to influence the cultures of ideas in service-giving organisations over the past seven years, and some of the lessons to be learned from the story. The Community and Mental Handicap Educational and Research Association (CMHERA) has its roots in the Campaign for People with Mental Handicaps (CMH) which originated as a small group of friends meeting regularly in London, with a commitment to high quality community-based services for all people with mental handicaps. CMH's work over the years has disseminated a stream of high quality information through low cost, accessible, well-researched publications. Although never a large organisation it has worked successfully through direct policy 'lobbying' at government level, and through its network of local group connections. The essence of its success has lain in its ability to claim attention for ideas concerning quality in community-based services. A tiny organisation with small resources is likely to have minimal impact on major processes of organisational change, yet it may command attention by generating a debate, by creating the terms for debate, and by influencing agendas for debate. CMHERA's contribution has been to take the debate into direct-service settings through training, evaluation and consultancy with service-giving organisations. Its work over seven years has been a practical exploration of the service world, inviting both service users and providers to join in that exploration.

In evaluating this work we would be hard put to give measures of inputs or outcomes. What experimental designs could lead to the attribution of causes or consequences? A whole school of thought would argue that 'communication' as a concept is a slippery fish, and that 'ideas' are poor predictors of actions. Maybe the most we can claim is that there have been changes in verbal behaviour in key persons developing services for people with mental handicaps, and that we believe there to be some connections at least between verbal behaviour and actions. So that readers may make their own judgements, it is necessary to give some descriptions of the process and structure of the 'explorations'.

PRINCIPLES OF NORMALISATION

The principle of normalisation which formed an intellectual framework for the most part of this work originated with Nils Bank-Mikkelsen in Denmark, and described the goal of 'letting the retarded obtain an existence as close to the normal as possible'. Bengt Nirje's work in Sweden focused on the means of the process, and elaboration of the meaning of patterns of life as much like those of ordinary citizens as possible. (Early statements on the development of the normalisation principle by Nirje, Bank, Mikkelson, Wolfensberger and others can be found in Kugel and Shearer, 1976.) In the late 1960s discussions of normalisation were to be found in the work of English academic psychologists - Gunzburg, the Clarkes and others, yet the ideas seemed to have little impact on the development of social policy. Wolf Wolfensberger's visit here at that time, however, left him impressed with the newly developing adult training centres (ATCs) and the potential they offered for people with substantial handicaps undertaking socially valued employment. Those early influences on English thinking seem hardly to have taken root, however.

Wolfensberger's Contribution

Wolfensberger's has been the major intellectual contribution to thinking about normalisation both in North America and internationally. His work has linked the original egalitarian goals with that broad band of sociological thinking which can be described as 'societal reaction theory', and in particular work on the sociology of deviance. Further, he has developed an analysis which encompasses the social situations of a range of potentially socially devalued people - elders, people with mental illness or physical disabilities, and others. More recently his attention has turned to the quite literal crisis in human service developments and to the major threats existing to elderly and handicapped people in western countries.

The earlier work on normalisation undoubtedly stimulated and fed much thought and action throughout North America. To those observers who were fortunate enough to visit there in the late 1970s, a few examples stood out - ENCOR in Nebraska, the Macomb-Oakland Regional Centre in Michigan, and Canadian services influenced by the COMSERV programme. All seemed to be characterised not only by energy and commitment but by some clearsighted notions of goals and purpose, and some working theories to guide action.

CMHERA was formed in 1978 to apply some of that experience, by developing a UK base for teaching normalisation principles, and normalisation-based service-evaluation and consultancy. It worked at first as a tiny agency, teaching two-day or so 'normalisation workshops' (some 50 or more throughout the country in its first two years). It gradually developed a network of associates who supported this work by teaching on courses, funding and coordinating events, and investing time and effort in adapting and developing teaching materials and methods (O'Brien with Tyne, 1980). From 1980 to 1986 PASS (Wolfensberger and Glenn, 1975) was adopted as the basis for most of its work, together subsequently with PASSING (Wolfensberger and Thomas, 1983).

PASS and PASSING

PASS was developed by Wolfensberger and Glenn as a normalisation-based evaluation instrument. It has a detailed description of 50 distinct aspects of service quality, and also of a process for arriving at judgements of service-quality. It was intended as a quantitative tool for service evaluation, and has been used as such both in the United States and elsewhere, and here in the United Kingdom. Its major use, however, has been in introductory workshops as a framework for 'guided exploration' of service quality, where the major purpose has not been to learn about evaluation methods, but rather about normalisation principles. While major features of the course design have been retained, adaptations have focused on the goal of 'Learning about Normalisation through PASS'.

Subsequently PASSING has been developed by Wolfensberger and Thomas. While PASS combines both ideology-based and system-based or administrative issues, PASSING has only the former. These issues are more extensively analysed in PASSING, and the written texts are designed to be more systematic and more accessible to the ordinary reader. The development of PASSING marked an important shift in Wolfensberger's reconceptualisation of normalisation as 'social role valorisation' - the goal and process of achieving valued social roles, for people who stand at risk of being subject to substantial social devaluation. Again, both in the United States and elsewhere as in the United Kingdom, PASSING's main use has been as a framework for learning through introductory courses.

CMHERA's work with PASS and PASSING has had several distinct strands. The major one has been introductory courses - 35 in all, and a current programme of ten each year. More than 2000 people have passed through these courses during that time. They receive only limited advertising and the main source of referral to the courses is from other people who have experienced them. There is no lessening of demand for places, and the network of people who refer others to them is wide and growing. More than half of participants come from a background in mental handicap services, but a growing proportion come from mental illness services and services to elderly people. Participants range in backgrounds from direct service users, relatives and friends, through service providers at all levels and in all agencies, to elected members and community representatives. The great majority, however, have been middle and senior-level service managers and professionals.

The courses themselves are highly structured and demand skilled leadership. A major endeavour has been to develop a network of more than 50 team leaders with substantial experience, and some good mechanisms for their support. This network sustains the annual programme of introductory courses.

A second-level course - 'Using PASS in Organisational Change' - is conducted annually and provides opportunities for learning about service-evaluation for people who have already attended one or more PASS or PASSING course. Those in 1983, 1984 and 1985 have attempted systemic reviews of sets of interrelated services in three districts. These encourage participants to confront wider systems-issues in negotiating change in service organisations.

A further strand has been evaluation-based consultancy with five organisations. Separate evaluation projects have completed some 20 full PASS evaluations. These projects have given a further opportunity for exploring the part played by external evaluation in the business of changing services.

Finally there has been a small programme of long-term consultancy with local networks of people concerned to explore the implementation of normalisation principles in their own work and in their own agencies and organisations. This has taken a variety of forms including supporting staff in self-conducted service-reviews, managing 'search' conferences for groups seeking to identify new directions in their work, and supporting groups who themselves want to undertake normalisation-based training and service-development within their own organisations.

Our 'explorations' then, of normalisation and its implications for services, have been conducted in several contexts; through direct conversation with several thousands of service workers and others in the context of practice evaluations in workshops; through service evaluations, and through practical consultancy with service-providers.

During this time our sense of the ideas themselves has shifted and changed. It seems less appropriate now to speak of 'the principle' of normalisation as a highly unified body of theory. Indeed there seem to be at least four identifiable strands of useful ideas linked together. They include the following:

(1) Understandings of the life situation of people with handicaps or mental illness, elderly people and those who are homeless or have problems of drug or alcohol abuse - any group, indeed, who are at risk of social processes of devaluation, of being systematically treated as if they were 'of less value' than other citizens.

(2) Images of alternative possibility, which couple basic assumptions about human development, with the ability to imagine attainable ideals in service accomplishment. For a time, some concrete models (such as ENCOR) provided real inspiration for this ability to imagine how things might realistically be in an alternative future. But the ability to think in ideal terms is not limited solely by the availability of real models; it seems some people at least can make 'imaginative leaps'.

(3) A set of theories about the consequences of organising human services in various ways. Both PASS and PASSING are disciplined and structured presentations of sets of hypotheses, arranged within a process designed to test them, and concerned with the consequences of grouping, segregation, imagery and a variety of specific service-practices and administrative arrangements.

(4) Practical agendas for action. As people have taken the normalisation ideas in to their work so there has grown a set of 'worked examples'. These are 'way marks' for others - a store of experience from which to draw strategies and tactics - a 'list of things to do' that are concrete and real. In the mid-1980s there are some things, like the use of ordinary housing, that we know fairly well how to do. Other areas like finding real work for people with substantial handicaps are less well charted. It is in this fourth area that the ideas are least well developed. They offer a challenge to be creative, innovative, to be practical explorers, 'learning by doing'.

These four kinds of ideas inform one another and in turn are informed by broader principles. As a set of values and commitments they draw on egalitarian ideologies and traditions that can also be seen in major religious and humanist moralities as well as specifically today in feminism, racial awareness, ecology, third world consciousness and others. 'Normalisation theory' itself is a low-level set of theorems about service-design. Wolfensberger (Wolfensberger and Thomas, 1983) identifies 'seven key themes' in major treatments of normalisation, including the pervasiveness of unconscious devaluation in human services; the power of the mechanisms of imagery and of role-circularity in sustaining devaluing social processes; the importance of imitation, of positive compensation for disadvantage, and of 'developmental assumptions' in unlocking those processes and reversing them; and the overriding importance of positive, valued relationships in the lives of people who are at risk of being devalued. These themes in turn draw on a very wide range of social science theory and research. Finally, as a set of purposeful service-practices designed to positively counter devaluation, they draw on many elements of past service-practice and on powerful 'stories' and examples from service-giving organisations.

These then have been the ideas that have structured a debate, a series of conversations with service planners and providers through workshops and consultancy over the past seven years.

THE CHALLENGE - SUSTAINING A CREATIVE TENSION

Through these sets of ideas then it seems possible to engage people's attention in a practical exploration of their own work - to discover the 'gaps' between intent and action, to renew and clarify ideologies, to redirect essential commitments and to shift systems of priority, generate a sense of urgency. Practically these may require changes in people's personal behaviours as service-managers, practitioners or planners, and in the ways they organise their days. The analysis on which the principles of normalisation rest is not a comfortable one. There is a wealth of complex information to master, and links and connections with bodies of theory and traditions of thought which may be unfamiliar. It may pose complex moral problems, for instance, of coming to terms with one's own involvement in an organisation which systematically perpetuates the segregation and dehumanisation of potentially devalued people. An analysis as sharp as this exposes dilemmas which (in the nature of dilemmas) are not resolvable, but may have been quietly laid aside for some time. Many people working in service organisations have very little time to master complex arguments, energy to manage moral dilemmas, or personal commitment to the people served. The phenomenon of 'displacement of goals' in organisational life is familiar enough not to need describing here. Maintaining the steady flow, the daily routine may become an end in itself. Ideological change - even reassessment and renewal of direction - can seem profoundly disruptive and disturbing.

Two examples here may give some sense of what is involved in 'sustaining a creative tension'.

PASS Evaluations of Community-based Services

PASS was designed as a scientific evaluation tool. That is not a claim we have pursued for it with any energy. Nevertheless our experience suggests to us that it is a very helpful way that groups of people may learn to make some systematic descriptions of human services, of their accomplishments for the people who use those services, and of the values that underlie them. It helps too, in giving people experience of making some disciplined and principled judgements about 'quality' in services. It has been mainly used as a structure for teaching and learning. There have also, however, been opportunities to use PASS as a basis for consultancy with service-providers - conducting evaluations of service quality, and offering feedback to managers and planners.

In examples during 1984 and 1985, two service-systems were examined, which aimed to bring people from mental handicap hospitals into ordinary houses in ordinary communities. Both had set out to implement the ideas described clearly in the King's Fund Centre's (1984) publication Ordinary Life. (Since 1978 the King's Fund Centre has sustained a working group initiative which has produced a series of publications under the Ordinary Life heading. (2)) In each instance it was possible to use PASS to evaluate a range of services and settings - from hospital wards and villas, through various 'transitional' arrangements (for example, 'rehab' programmes) and into a number of ordinary housing arrangements. All of the people involved had substantial handicaps, and all of the living arrangements were directly supported with staff.

In general, it was found that the move into 'community care' produced a net gain in the lives of people with mental handicaps. In specific areas there were substantial gains, including the following.

(1) People enjoyed physical settings of higher and improving quality.
(2) People had more personal possessions, and many more that were appropriate to their true age.
(3) There was greater personal privacy, accompanied by greater accord of dignity and respect, and more high-quality interactions with those about them.
(4) There was greater access to valued community resources, and greater potential access to valued relationships with non-handicapped citizens who were not 'staff', a potential not always fully realised.

There were also very substantial areas of continuing challenge in these 'leading edge' services including:

(1) They tended to have weak ties with the mainstream of service provision, often being marginal 'projects', with tenuous management structures and insecure finance.
(2) There was a failure to clearly orient staff to the character of the new services, often leaving them uncertain of their roles and unsupported in their work.
(3) There was little provision for review and reflection on the performance of the services.
(4) There was very inadequate attention to the quality of relationships in people's lives.
(5) There were limited and narrow views of what constituted 'development and growth' in people's lives, with often inappropriate attention to limited 'skills programmes', and the use even in these of ineffective and inappropriate 'teaching' methods.

These were some very generalised issues in some 20 separate PASS evaluations. Specific examples varied widely. Institutional environments in general can be shown to actively damage residents. Some of the 'community' settings appeared only marginally less damaging, and one instance was inferior overall to the worst institutional setting we examined. By contrast, one small cluster of housing-based services achieved at or near the very highest levels measured by PASS.

The dilemmas in presenting these results are

clear - as one friend pointed out 'evaluations that bring bad news are Bad News'. Each service was uniquely exposed. Each was among the most advanced of its kind. Both were 'marginal' to the mainstream of provision, and politically 'out on a limb'. Their achievements had been largely against a background of political opposition within authorities and even in communities. Though they had been successful in gaining widespread support, there were still people who would use any 'bad news' to discredit them. For both it was vitally important that they developed clear and accurate accounts of their own performance if they were to manage responsibly their own future development. Yet these same accounts might weigh heavily against them in the competition for scarce resources.

There are several recognisable stages in 'project development'. At an early stage, projects focus attention on developing an effective pattern of service. Later pressure develops to give greater weight to efficiency, and later still to expansion. It was our sense that both projects were still struggling to develop effective service models, and yet already both were threatened with pressure to reduce costs and serve greater numbers, in line with governmental policies and the demands of 'general management' for quick results.

An easy route out of the dilemma posed for service-managers and planners would be to reject the process, deny the validity of the assessment. Another would be to reject the values that underlie the assessment, and to assert a different set of priorities - those of expediency. Either way, the opportunity would be lost of genuinely extending their own notion of what constitutes 'quality' in services, and of engaging their attention with the business of actively revaluing people who are substantially at risk.

Introductory 'Workshops'

Seven years of experience have given us 36 occasions to test out the process of helping people learn about normalisation through an introductory PASS workshop. During this time key features have remained constant. There are opportunities for learning the principles through reading and presentations. A small team provides a context for debate. There is a clear process for making judgements, and an opportunity to apply the learning in the context of a real cooperating service, which offers itself as a 'practice placement'. Unusual attention is given to ensuring that the workshop is coherent throughout, that the elements are well coordinated, and that participants' time is effectively and efficiently used. Supportive materials and presentations have been constantly revised and rewritten to render them more accessible to participants.

Most participants responding to our three month follow-up letter (and most do) comment that the workshop was amongst the most challenging learning-experiences they have known. The challenge lies in the ideas themselves. Whatever is done to make the learning more accessible, the challenge remains. Confronting the true extent of the devaluation of people with handicaps in our society, the individual consequences in people's lives, the ineffectual nature of service-organisations is a painful business. The debate over 'values' is itself an uncomfortable one to some professionals who still cherish notions of their 'objective' role - an idea that dies hard. That people should struggle with the ideas in the workshops is not surprising. If they did not, we should think we had failed. Therein, however, lies the dilemma. To generate a debate over 'values' is to run the risk of appearing to be 'holier than thou'. However clearly you explain in advance to people the objectives of the course, the debate over values will come to many as a surprise, a shock, something they had not bargained for. It is in the very nature of our deepest values that we change them only with difficulty. For many people, the opportunity even to review their own values comes rarely - the busy hurly-burly of workaday life takes care of that.

It was in our first reviews of these workshops that we began to realise people might not always enjoy challenge, yet they might welcome, even celebrate it. Our sense of participants (and ourselves) was that people are often poorly equipped for challenge of any kind, and particularly substained values-led challenge. Most of us have learned only rudimentary responses of fight or flight - reject the challenge aggressively, seek to discredit it, deny it, evade it; accept the 'ideals' but deny any possibility of implementation; cast 'blame' for inability - on service-users, on organisations, on government, on 'society' or whoever. It seemed to us that our role was to maintain a tension, a continuous questioning about the meaning and implication of values in service-organisations. At first it came as a surprise when people welcomed the challenges this presented, and the opportunity to literally 'embrace' the challenge. Latterly it is expected - it should not be surprising that so many people who have chosen a commitment to human services welcome opportunities for exploring their challenges.

How is it then possible for a small organisation to 'sustain a creative tension' with something so huge and amorphous as the social world of human services? Of course it is not. Yet it does seem possible to engage some people's interest, and they, others. The methods are as old as the hills. The first is quite simply using the role of an interested outsider. People who are interested in what they are doing enjoy nothing so much as having someone join them and show an interest too. Within that lie the seeds of a learning process. 'Outsiders' can facilitate the learning in a whole variety of ways. Asking questions is one. Outsiders can ask things that seem obvious, or may seen indecorous - 'how is it that things are done in this way?', 'how is it that person is paid so little?' Setting occasions is another. A workshop or a consultation exercise are occasions for people to mark in diaries spaces to be kept free, which otherwise might get used up in a busy life. Outsiders give permission for agendas which might not otherwise get discussed. Reviewing or reflecting on one's work can be seen as an unwarranted luxury in an organisation under pressure to deliver more, faster, cheaper. They can create agendas by declaring values openly, by modelling an approach that puts values high on a working list. They can set the terms for a debate by ruling some things out of consideration. (For instance, we have only agreed to consulting with those people who showed a commitment to developing high quality community services, we have always refused to discuss 'apartheid' solutions based on a notion that people with handicaps have innate or fundamental cultural differences.) They can create an orderly process for learning by paying attention to learning, by studying where people are in their learning, and by keeping a visible record of that learning so people can see it for themselves.

The second method is to work through networks. Merrelyn Emery has said 'Dispersed but cohesive networks represent the strongest and most powerful infrastructure for both effective implementation of innovation and continued diffusion (1982, personal communication). Networks seem typically good at discerning and introducing new ideas, are decentralised, operate on informal, often face-to-face contacts, and embody high degrees of reciprocity and shared commitment among members. They are in many ways what organisations are not. They are virtually impossible to either create or forestall - they seem to have a life of their own. Within an organisation, individuals committed to values-led change may be isolated, but within a network that stretches across and between many organisations they can derive support and the strength to sustain their commitment. The networks of people working seriously to implement normalisation-based ideas in services stretch across many of the authorities and voluntary organisations in the country. There are 'nodes' around the Campaign for People with Mental Handicaps, the King's Fund Centre An Ordinary Life projects and others. The networks overlap to a degree with those in the various interprofessional organisations (APMH, BIMH) and among professional groups (particularly clinical psychologists). CMHERA's work created another such 'node' - a focusing of attention on particular agendas for action, a concentration of energies, a reinforcement and re-energising of that part of the net.

With whom has the debate been? Not much with academics and our centres of higher learning. There has been a little, but largely they have remained aloof and distant. Occasional articles point out a contradiction between the 'principles' of normalisation, or bemoan the lack of properly conducted research to 'test' the ideas before implementation. Service-designers and planners have entered the debate to a degree. Some are looking mainly for fast solutions and do not stay the course, others seem to have engaged with the dilemmas and are slowly and painfully creating new designs for the services where they work, 'practical agendas for action', and finding out how to 'learn by doing', both for themselves and their organisations.

Mostly though, the debate has been with the 2000 or 3000 direct service workers, managers and consumers with whom our workshops have brought us into conversation. There the learning has been direct and face to face, with little written down. Mostly, if it shows at all, it shows in people doing what they do differently. The group most significantly missing from this debate are the politicians and those who stand for and represent ordinary communities. At the end of the day, when the stories of the changes of the 1980s are written, it may well be the absence of these people from the debate which is seen to be the most significant fact in determining what really happened, unless there is some way that can be addressed.

CONCLUSION

Finally, our grasp of the ideas, and of the ways people may be encouraged to grapple with them, is constantly developing. Our sense of the challenge of the ideas is changing. Of the four different kinds of ideas already described people seem more ready and able to understand the first, to engage their lives directly with those of people with handicaps, and to be informed by them. As time goes by it seems surprising that once this seemed the most difficult step for professionals and practitioners to take. The third kind of ideas - learning the theories which explain how human services work, seems more straightforward too. Much of what once seemed complex and hard now seems more like commonsense.

Two kinds of ideas still remain challenging. The first is the creation of powerful images of alternative possibility. Without people being able to 'see' what futures might be like, they will always be uncertain. Just as in the 1970s the slides that showed people with substantial handicaps living in ENCOR's ordinary houses were an 'eye-opener' - a vision which showed people what to aim for, so today we need clear sharp stories about people and their possibilities.

The 'practical agendas for action' need to change too. In the 1970s we talked a lot about 'standards'. We have since become very good at helping people spot what is going wrong, and teaching people not to do bad things. A major need now seems to be to develop some greater opportunities to positively support creativity and inventiveness, if we are not to get merely repetitive standard solutions 'in the community' which may be as unresponsive to real needs as were the solutions of the past.

We think that the same set of values which has guided the work on normalisation between 1978 and 1986 can guide this next step towards inventing and designing more desirable futures for people with substantial handicaps - futures which actively engage their lives with those of other ordinary citizens. The last seven years have given us a range of stories which show some of the dimensions of what is possible. The next step is to encourage more people to engage with the creative challenges. The processes for achieving it will be the same. It may or may not be possible to change major service-systems, but it does seem possible to invent better futures for some individual people with handicaps. It may or may not be possible to change 'organisations' in an orderly way, but it does seem possible to help individual members to undertake new commitments, adopt new priorities, and for them to support others. Therein lie the seeds of principled change.

ACKNOWLEDGEMENTS

Between 1982 and 1985 the work described here was substantially funded by the Joseph Rowntree Memorial Trust, who also gave very real practical and moral support. Two people who have contributed immeasurably to this work are Paul Williams (Associate Director of CMHERA) and John O'Brien of Responsive Systems Associates, Atlanta, Georgia.

NOTES

1. ENCOR - A Way Ahead, CMH, London. CMH have subsequently published a number of descriptions of American experiences in the late 1970s. Publication lists/order forms are available from CMH, 12a Maddox Street, London W1R 9PL.

2. Further details from the King's Fund Centre, 126 Albert Street, London NW1 7NF.

REFERENCES

Ackoff, R.L. (1978) Problem Solving (John Wiley, New York)

Argyris, C. and Schon, D. (1980) 'What is an Organisation that it May Learn?' In Organisations as Systems (Open University Press, Milton Keynes)

King's Fund Centre (1984) An Ordinary Working Life. Project Paper No. 50

Kugel, R.B. and Shearer, A. (1976) (eds) Changing Patterns in Residential Services for the Mentally Retarded (PIMR, Washington)

O'Brien, J. with Tyne, A. (1980) The Principle of Normalisation: a Foundation for Effective Services (CMH, London)

Perrow, C. (1965) 'Hospitals, technology, structure and goals'. In March, G. (ed.) Handbook of Organisations (Rand-McNally, Chicago)

Peters, T.J. and Waterman, R.H. (1983) In Search of Excellence (Harper and Row, New York)

Wolfensberger, W. and Glenn, L. (1975) PASS 3 - Program Analysis of Service Systems, 3rd edn (NIMR, Toronto)

Wolfensberger, W. and Thomas, S. (1983) PASSING - Program Analysis of Service Systems' Implementation of Normalisation Goals, 2nd edn (NIMR, Toronto)

Chapter Four

PLANNING COMMUNITY-BASED SERVICES FOR MENTALLY HANDICAPPED PEOPLE

John Cubbon

INTRODUCTION

Mental handicap registers are databases holding more extensive information than identifying details on all the mentally handicapped people in an area. They promise to put the planning of mental handicap services on a more rational basis. Though they have been established throughout the country in growing numbers since the early 1970s, no detailed evaluation was carried out until a two-stage survey in 1984; a postal questionnaire was sent in spring to all registers in England and Wales, and then in the summer some of the staff operating them were interviewed (Cubbon and Malin, 1985). The findings of this survey will provide the basis for considering how far it is possible to plan to meet the needs of mentally handicapped people: can their needs be more sensitively assessed with or without a register? can a register measure their needs? how far will the indicators of need provided by a register be taken into consideration in the planning process?

THE NEED FOR A REGISTER IN PLANNING MENTAL HANDICAP SERVICES

Again and again register-operators commented on the haphazardness of planning without a register. 'Guessing' was a word that came up a few times to describe the process. The following remarks were not untypical:

> (The original purpose of the register was to be) a planning tool because of the incredible lack of information that we had ... I think a typical example was when we were looking towards setting

> up two fairly independent living hostels ... We had no idea of the numbers there might be to make use of this facility ... I mean some of the information that we got out in the early days (of the register) was really quite frightening because we had no idea of the likely demands that were going to be made of us. So it was in two senses: we (had been) trying to make plans without knowing how many fitted the target group and we had no idea of the likely future demands.

> A number of projects had gone ahead without really the statistical kind of information that was required to really plan the numbers ... In some ways we were floundering about a little in the dark when it came down to looking at: how many community units do we need? how many hostels do we need? how many ATCs do we need?

Reports produced by two social services departments which at the time had no register revealed that some fundamental questions could not be answered - for example how many adults from the Borough were in mental handicap hospitals, how many children had gone into mental handicap hospitals the previous year, where the mentally handicapped were located, and how handicapped they were (Jones, 1979, p.10; Birmingham Social Services Department, 1983).

The Independent Development Council has recently stated that too little attention had been paid to planning on an individual basis and that planning needs to move away from its emphasis on capital developments and units with so many beds (Independent Development Council for People with Mental Handicap, 1984, pp.14-17). Does this approach significantly reduce the need for a register?

I think not. Even if planning is based as much as it can be on the needs of each individual, and proceeds in a piecemeal fashion, an overall picture of the client population is still essential. The most obvious reason for this is that unless the needs and situation of all the mentally handicapped people to be planned for are known, it is impossible to decide which individuals or groups should be given priority. Setting on one side the question of the strength of need, it may be that the need of some particular group of people should be satisfied first because this would fit in most easily with subsequent developments. But to discover whether this is so, it would be necessary to know everyone's needs. For example, there may be financial, administrative or other grounds for providing one set of four people with a group home before certain other groups, even if all were in roughly equal need. Alternatively, a certain number of people may need a facility of some type. This might be provided in such a way that it cannot easily be adapted to meet the needs of some other group as well. This may not matter - and may indeed be the best option - if there is no other group who could use the facility in question. But to find this out one would need a comprehensive picture of the mentally handicapped population. So, to sum up, individual-based planning is best carried out within a strategy worked out on the basis of register data because priorities should be determined by the urgency of needs of different individuals and the various practical consequences of the provision of the facilities which might meet those needs.

One might suppose that the impressions of an experienced professional or administrator would be sufficient for planning a mental handicap service. However there is no single person who knows the entire mentally handicapped population - so complex and vast are the services. Instead there are a number of people - social workers, community nurses, doctors, staff in institutions, some of which may be distant - each of whom knows only part of what is provided within a district. A doctor explained that she and her colleagues on the Community Mental Handicap team (CMHT) realised that none of them had a satisfactory overview of the needs of the mentally handicapped population:

> I've worked eighteen years in the School Health Service ... so I obviously know an awful lot of people also at the Adult Training Centre (ATC) ... But it was just apparent to all of us that we each worked in different fields. The social worker only worked in one area ... I only know the school and those younger people at the ATC. It was just obvious that we had to get a comprehensive view of it.

No one has an equal level of contact with all parts of the service:

> (The views of experienced professionals) tend to be fragmented and people's own individual personal views override. Their knowledge of a ward sometimes make them look very insularly at the needs of their ward.

Without a register individual professionals or administrators may be the only people with access to some of the facts relevant to planning. They are thus able to present the facts in any way they choose. However, as a Health Service administrator pointed out, the beauty of a register was that it made the facts available to everyone, however one might choose to interpret them.

Professional interest may lead to bias. The opinions of some professional group might be coloured by the desire to preserve its sphere of activity. This was given as a reason for using a register to take planning decisions centrally rather than relying wholly on the opinions of staff of the establishments which would be affected. A social services planning and research officer considered that professionals in the field were less able to take a balanced overview because they were concerned with individual clients.

MENTAL HANDICAP REGISTERS AS AN INDICATIVE SOURCE OF THE NEEDS OF A MENTALLY HANDICAPPED POPULATION

In its most basic form a register holds each subject's name, address, date of birth and details of services used. These items of information are easy to collect and can make an important contribution to the planning process.

If a local authority knows the number of people at mental handicap hospitals who are its responsibility it is able to make a start on planning their return. Knowledge of numbers of people not using some service can provide a basic indicator of need - for example, the numbers of people in the community who are not attending an ATC. Addresses of mentally handicapped people in the community and the addresses from which the rest were admitted to residential establishments can provide an invaluable guide to the siting of services. Ages can give an indication of future demands. For instance the number of those approaching school-leaving age will give a forecast of the number of places needed at ATCs. The numbers of subjects over 60 will give an indication of the type of need for special day or residential facilities for elderly mentally handicapped people. Statistics of age, geographical location or origin and service use can combine in a mass of ways with the impressions of professionals and administrators in the formulation of plans. But useful though these data are, alone they provide little guide to services needed. For this some type of assessment of ability or need is required. Several of the staff involved with registers holding only basic and service information said that they wished that their registers held also an assessment of this type.

The method of assessing need which is used most frequently by mental handicap registers is Kushlick's Wessex Behaviour Rating System. It is made up of two scales - the Social and Physical Incapacity (SPI) scale, and the Speech, Self-Help and Literary (SSL) scale. The SPI scale collects information on incontinence, mobility and behaviour problems; and the SSL scale records the level of speech, self-help (feeding, washing and dressing) and literacy (reading, writing and counting). A three-point scale is used to answer each question except for those of speech where a four-point scale is used. Overall SPI and SSL scales can then be calculated. The SPI scale allows subjects to be divided into CAN ('continent, ambulant and having no severe behavioural disorder') or CANT (the remainder) (Kushlick, Blunden, and Cox, 1973). The Development Team divided scores on the Wessex scale into four groups and suggested that the numbers falling into each group should be a guide to the numbers needing a specific type of residential accommodation and a specific level of staffing (1979, para. 10).

Perhaps the most significant finding of the interviews was that a very large number of register operators were dissatisfied with the Wessex scale as a guide in the planning of services and felt that a more direct assessment of need was required.

A general criticism of the scale was that it was not an indicator of services needed:

> The problem is ... the Kushlick bit describes the person but you've got to guess what the need is.

> (Wessex scores) invariably grossly underestimate people's potential ... They function as photographs of a moment in time.

> It doesn't really seem to address the problem of how self-sufficient people are.

Several interviewees pointed out that people with similar Wessex scores could have very different service needs. In some cases the score may be a reflection of particular features of the environment; in others it might remain constant in all circumstances. Someone, for example, might be rated as having severe behaviour problems because of his environment; the problems of someone else might be independent of the environment. Equally the same behaviour might be regarded as difficult and disruptive in one situation and unremarkable in another. There may be someone who is permanently incontinent and will always need incontinence aids. However, another client may have the same scores on the incontinence subscale not because of any physiological condition making his incontinence permanent rather because he has not been toilet-trained. Such a person would require training more than aids and so would make very different demands on the service. The training might lead to a greatly improved score - which the permanently incontinent person could never attain. Moreover scores on the Wessex system do not necessarily give even a rough indication of how a client's family is likely to be coping with him.

More than one interviewee gave examples of clients with high scores on the Wessex scale who were nevertheless unsuited to the community-based accommodation on offer:

> As an example we've got a girl here who's a resident of our one heavily handicapped house .. She's an obsessive rocker ... People leave her pretty much to her own devices ... she's not someone who really participates in the Activity Centre programme. She wanders about on the site ... People would be able to say that she's able to dress herself with some help. She's not a major behavioural problem. She's continent; she's ambulant. And, as a consequence, she gets quite a high score on the Kushlick behaviour rating scale and comes out as one of the people who really ought to be discharged. But ... she wouldn't be able to function in a Social Services hostel at all, if for no other reason, of course, than that they don't really have working night staff.

Similar levels of dependence or types of problem do not necessarily imply the need for similar treatment. In fact the greater a client's problems, the less likely he is to benefit from being mainly with others with similar problems (Guy's Health District, 1981, p.24).

There are grounds for dissatisfaction with regarding the numbers of people falling into a

Development Team category as a basis for planning corresponding numbers of places in certain types of residential establishments. A detailed study of group homes has shown the importance of group behaviour for their success. 'Leader/follower' and 'mothering' relationships enable the more able to assist the less able, thereby lessening the need for outside support. The study concludes that a wide range of mentally handicapped people are suited to group homes. No clearcut criteria for admission can be given since the right combination of individuals is essential (Malin, 1980 pp.104-5, 108). A register operator said:

> My own personal view is that the (Wessex scale) makes less and less of a contribution ... The whole concept of mental handicap is changing. A person's potential in relationship to some form of alternative living accommodation is not so much now dictated by the Wessex grouping as it was. I mean once upon a time it was absolutely rigid: if it was Category I or II (the development team categories derived from the Wessex scale) they should be out. But since that time we've learnt that that isn't always the case and that now category III and IV (can) live perfectly reasonable lives in the community depending on staff input to them. So I don't think (the Wessex scale) is as important as it was.

The Wessex scale had been felt too institution-orientated:

> There's been quite a lot of resistance (to the Wessex scale) particularly among Clinical Psychologists ... because they say it's too crude and in any case was designed for use in a more institutional setting.

> Broadly (Wessex scores) were very helpful in planning hospital discharges. I don't think they would be so helpful on people living in the community because in a way we need more sophisticated assessments ... I suppose it reflects the sort of service we provide.

Another bias of the Wessex scale which was pointed out was that it overpenalised disruptive behaviour. Even considered as a measure of behaviour, the Wessex scale was criticised for being insensitive:

> The questions are so black-or-white ... For instance ... there's a question on there about speech - 'Does the client (a) have no speech at all, (b) ask for basic needs, or (c) can he hold a conversation?' Well, OK, if you put: 'He doesn't ask for basic needs - i.e. can I go to the toilet?' or 'can I have a drink?' ... But he does ... say 'dog' or 'cat' ... But there's nothing in between. You've either got to say: he asks for basic needs or he's got no speech at all. And there's a big difference. And that is in a lot of cases - there are a lot of questions there which you can only answer (a) or (b) to (with) nothing in between.

A number of register operators were unhappy about the level of interobserver agreement in the classification of people on the scale. It was pointed out that the same person was often given a higher rating at school than at home where he would be overprotected; more experienced staff would make different ratings from less experienced ones; and staff at hospitals are inclined to make different assessments from staff at local authority hostels. However nobobdy contradicted the conclusion of Palmer and Jenkins (1982) that the inter-rater reliability of the Wessex scale was such that it could be used in large-scale surveys but in the assessment of individual clients it should be treated with great caution.

There were some who were happy with the Wessex scale. One operator reported that low-scorers on a 0-6 scale derived from Wessex had tended to attain near-independence while those with higher scores, in particular those with behaviour problems, had been less successfully rehabilitated. He still felt that his register should be used to conduct sample-surveys in which professional assessments of need for service could be recorded. Another operator said that the Wessex scale indicated the level of staffing needed - this was a guide to the crucial question of the level of resources required. The Wessex scale may be a better guide to levels of staffing than to types of service needed - that is, to numbers of group homes or sheltered lodgings or ATC places - though even this is questionable.

How beneficial, then, is the contribution to planning made by statistics derived from scores on the Wessex scale? The evidence assembled here makes an answer to this question difficult. Nevertheless, it seems likely that Wessex scale statistics have led to the implementation of policies which have been in line with a philosophy of mental handicap which has ceased to be the conventional wisdom. This is not perhaps a fault so much of registers as of the attitudes towards mental handicap services of many of those who have set them up.

Many register operators said that they wished that their registers held information specifically on the services which clients needed. A register organiser whose register held a version of the Wessex scale said:

> I feel personally that it could be improved to incorporate more detailed assessment of needs which are being met and which aren't being met and in that way could be a far more useful tool for planning ... You would then be able to say: 'we have four people in a particular area ... who have shown a need for a particular type of service'. Therefore we can set up a very local service from that information.

Assessments of the service needs of a subject are likely to depend even more on the individual making them than those on the Wessex scale. Professional training and roles would determine the assessments made. As a social services administrator put it, a charge nurse in a hospital would not assess for hospitalisation like an ATC manager. Some professionals would not have sufficient knowledge of all the services available. Also some members of staff would be more progressive in their thinking about mental handicap than others. It would therefore seem better for assessments of need to be made by a group of staff rather than an individual. Such assessments can be made at multidisciplinary reviews; and, as I have explained, a register can feed off them.

Though no register has yet been based on individual programme plans, registers based on annual multidisciplinary reviews have recorded needs in general terms - for example, current need for residential accommodation broken down into 'own home with relatives', 'hospital', 'residential home for the mentally handicapped', 'minimum support hostel', 'fostering', 'sheltered lodgings', 'warden service accommodation', 'group home', 'own independent home' and 'other'. Another register specified need in terms of five alternative settings with different levels of support. Both held assessments of both present and likely future needs. However, there were few others holding judgments of service needs as formulated in general terms at annual multidisciplinary reviews. It is too early to assess the benefits or otherwise of information of this type. Despite its difficulties it can assess overall service-needs in accordance with the latest thinking on mental handicap which the Wessex Behaviour Rating System cannot.

Any assessment of services needed derived from a register is open to criticism based on Smith's (1980) study - that professionals impose their highly routinised categories of need on clients. 'Need' is not a single concept but a set of interrelated notions and assumptions with ideological variations on several dimensions. On the basis of detailed qualitative research into client intake and allocation procedures, Smith concludes that 'need' is largely an administrative construct for the accomplishment of the organisational task of client management. According to this view by making need-assessments the basis of planning decisions one is allowing priorities to be determined by professional and bureaucratic interests. If this attack is valid, social workers and others need to adopt a radically different outlook. It is impossible to do justice to Smith's thesis in a short space. Suffice it to say that the interests, beliefs and motives underlying professionals' assessments of the needs of individuals should be taken into account in interpreting statistics from registers which are made up in part of those assessments.

OBSTACLES TO THE FULLEST USE OF MENTAL HANDICAP REGISTERS

There was overwhelming enthusiasm for the contribution that registers could make to the planning and management of services. However this potential was not, it seems, always realised.

The underuse of registers is perhaps not surprising in view of other more general tendencies. Since they provide fairly objective statistical data as a result ultimately of direct contact with the mentally handicapped population, registers may be regarded as research tools. It is widely recognised that research has not made as much of an impact on policy-making as it might have. The main reason for this has frequently been the lack of any suitable link between researchers and administrators (Leigh,

1977). A research manager who can move easily between the two sides can, however, in Leigh's view provide such a link. He also makes the point that the determination of researchers to make a contribution to decision-making has been a significant reason for such success as they have had. The need for close liaison between research and administration springs in part from the format in which research is presented. Many of the findings of surveys carried out by researchers in social services departments have been written up in booklets of well over 20 pages which a busy councillor or high-ranking officer will be unable to digest fully. There are widely held attitudes to planning which detract from the fullest consideration and appreciation of locally conducted research. There is still a tendency to see planning in bricks-and-mortar terms: since the 1962 Hospital Plan the emphasis of health service planning has been on capital developments. There remains an inclination to rely on norms laid down by the DHSS which, of course, make no allowance for local variations. As well as a disinclination to make use of research-findings in planning, there is a tendency to ignore the possibilities of evaluation: policies arising from the planning system are seldom evaluated to ascertain their impact on the public nor indeed to see if the original aims of the policies have been achieved (Barnard et al., 1980).

Many of these points were echoed in the findings of the survey and the interviews.

There were 24 respondents to the postal questionnaire who considered that service providers and planners made generally as much use of the register as they reasonably could, while 18 felt that they did not make as much use of the data as they might. There were indications that the relevant question may have been misunderstood by some respondents and that more than 18 considered that their registers could be put to significantly greater use. Some of those who had written that sufficient use was made of their registers revealed serious reservations in the interviews.

Table 4.1 shows that organisational failure and ignorance are important reasons for lack of use. Reasons A, C, D and G may often be closely related: they all point to a lack of coordination. The two most frequently cited specific reasons both mention ignorance on the part of service providers and planners. Of the eleven respondents who gave some reason other than those specified on the questionnaire, four mentioned the incompleteness of the database, three organisational factors, two the low level of planning in the area and two ignorance of some type on the part of service providers and planners.

Table 4.1: Frequency of Reasons for Lack of Use Cited in the Postal Questionnaire Responses

Reason	Frequency
A: Because the planners and providers of the service do not know enough about the register	7
B: Because staff working on the register do not themselves know what their information needs are	7
C: Because staff working on the register do not have enough liaison with the planners and providers of the service	3
D: Because the register is not located close enough to the planners and providers of the service	2
E: Because the provision and planning of services for mentally handicapped people is a low priority in the area	2
F: Because the planners and providers of the service are sceptical about the value of the information on the register	1
G: Because the agency which funds the register has insufficient liaison with the other agencies concerned with mentally handicapped people	0
H: For some other reason	11

Only one respondent indicated that scepticism of potential users about the register was a reason for lack of use. He in fact substituted 'accuracy' for 'value' in F. One might argue that register operators would be reluctant to admit to scepticism about the value of the register, because this would cast doubt on the value of the work that they were doing. But scepticism about the value of the register hardly ever came up in the interviews in which operators were usually very frank about the deficiences of their systems. So service providers and planners are probably not hostile to registers even if they do not always exploit them to the full.

The lack of an adequate link between registers and the planning process is typical of the organisational separation between researchers and the decision-making process. It is widely recognised that this separation is a major reason for the frequent neglect of research-findings (Leigh, 1977).

The organisational gulf between the register and decision-makers was discussed on several occasions in the interviews. On a few occasions the barrier was practical: data were inaccessible or inconvenient to extract. In at least two cases the location of the register in one agency was said to be a reason for lack of use by the other agencies - in one case, the agency concerned was a health authority and in the other it was a social services department. Twice the direct accessibility of data to a single person was said to be a handicap. Physical remoteness of the register and delays in responding to enquiries, such as might be caused by a mainframe computer, also reduce willingness to make requests. Registers have often also been underused because inferences from them have not been made known to the planners:

> You can't keep a register going without somebody who is going to go out and literally twist people's arms and say: 'Look here. We have got the register here and you are not using it.' And we just haven't got the manpower to do that - that is what a director is for ... I think you can't expect people to come and ask for things. People are making decisions all the time and they should be asking you for information: but they just won't. You have to go and say: 'come and ask for me'. You have to take the first steps and then hope that the next time they have a problem they will immediately think about you. But you have to do the initial thing.

> The senior managers - the ones who really ought to be capable of handling the detail and looking at it closely and interpreting what it means and turning it into a plan or policy - they're the ones either with the least time to do it or the ones who don't want to do it - it's too nitty-gritty for them. And it leaves a bit of a gap which only somebody like (the newly appointed Senior Officer spending half his time on the register) can fill really or somebody like my section if we have the time to do it ...

The form that the relationship between the register and its potential users should take will depend on a mass of characteristics of the district in question. However, the involvement of a member of the register-staff in the decision-making process was often a crucial determinant of the extent to which register-data made their due impact. A unit administrator for mental handicap services who was in overall charge of an underused register said:

> On the new Joint Development Team ... there are only two representatives (of the Unit) - a Director of Nursing Services and a consultant ... there wasn't direct input from (the register operator). And ... they didn't actually invite her along to talk about it.

Equally a number of register operators regarded their involvement in the planning process as the principal mechanism by which data from the register came to the attention of the decision-makers:

> Q. How do service providers and planners in the various agencies know about the register and its potential?
> A. ... Partly they know about it because I'm a Social Services planner ... On the Health Service side my boss and I are on the various teams for joint planning and therefore we can say: 'Ah well, the register can give you the information on that' ... or we can present the register's findings.

> Q. So data from the register come to the attention of people involved in planning through you?
> A. I'm responsible ... for managing and planning services within this Authority. And I'm also a member of the Joint Planning Team between ourselves and the Health Authority ... It's my personal knowledge of the information (on the register) that helps us as a Division and as an interface with the Health Authority.

> Now I'm a member of the (extended) Community Mental Handicap Team ... I am in much easier contact with the (Health Service staff) ... I'm in more direct contact with them and they appreciate the amount of information I shall be able to give them ... I don't think it was so much that they probably didn't know, because they've been told umpteen times; but ... you see it on a piece of paper, but when you see a person and you happen to mention something and they come back with all the information, you

> think: 'my word, they really do know something ... it's all getting about.'

Until recently the person in charge of a sophisticated register covering a metropolitan district worked on it full-time but was not a member of the joint officer body responsible for planning mental handicap services and was only involved in planning in an advisory capacity. Recently the post has been changed into that of Principal Adminstrative Assistant in the Mental Handicap Unit of the Health Authority with responsibility for planning and information as well as the register. The post-holder is also now a member of the joint officer body responsible for planning. The present incumbent regards his membership of this body as the ideal mechanism for ensuring that information from the register is available to all the agencies. A colleague in social services felt that the new arrangement was better:

> It certainly makes a difference in that the (person in charge of the register) is part of the planning process and that he isn't shut away in his little computer box ... In a meeting he might say: 'Oh yes; but that might be on the register', where people hadn't even thought that we could get that information out of the register.

Unsuitable approaches to planning were held by several operators to prevent the fullest use of their registers. There was apparently a tendency to view planning as expansion of services without a detailed appraisal of what was needed:

> You should be able to develop ... a profile of who our customers are ... We ought to do that first ... and tailor our services to meet the needs of our customers ... Of course it tends to work backwards way on ... They decide they'd like to build an ATC ... and then they say: 'now if we do that, who's going to use it?' - which is really putting the cart before the horse ... People still look upon planning in terms of bricks and mortar. Planning is ... things like saying ... where we want Day Centres or where we want Community Houses or where we want ATCs. Planning isn't about saying: '... within five years ... we're going to have <u>x</u> number of elderly mentally handicapped people - what are

we going to do for them?'

Another interviewee said that a great shortfall in ATC places had led to the decision to build a new ATC but no close examination of the need was carried out. Similarly, more community nurses had been appointed without any investigation of the work undertaken by those already in post. He felt that planning in mental handicap was conceived too much as a matter of pouring resources into the service:

> We are not that sophisticated in our planning ... We either throw in more resources to what seems an almost bottomless pit - so we needn't think too much about how we plan - or alternatively there are things given to the mentally handicapped by the Health Service and are assumed to be a good thing and no one wants to question.

Many of those involved in planning are used to thinking in terms of individuals and so may find it uncongenial to think in aggregate terms:

> The service providers are not used to using statistical information in this way ... Their training and the bulk of their work is dealing with individuals ... and many of them would not particularly be numerate in the sense that they would need to be to use planning information of the (sort produced by registers).

One register operator felt that the unfamiliarity of practitioners with statistical data made them uncertain about what types of data they wanted on the register:

> I think it's because the people who're doing the planning are the social workers, medical workers - they're not administrators, they're not people who normally work with paper. They work with people - they don't see people in the aggregate as administrators and researchers do.

The tendency of people involved in planning to underuse the register because of a lack of sophistication - in particular, an inclination not to think in statistical terms - is probably greatest among those who are specialists in mental handicap, since their main function is client care. One would suppose that the senior administrators and others with more general responsibilities would be more likely to think in the numerical terms necessary to make use of the register. However, they would know less about mental handicap than the specialists and so they might not fully exploit the register. In fact two operators said that the ignorance of the planners about mental handicap had been a reason for lack of use. A related point was made by another:

> The ... problem ... is ... the special nature of mental handicap, that all the other services ... you plan on a provision norm per 1000 population - homes for the elderly, hospitals for the elderly - you try and plan on so many beds per 1000 population ... For mental handicap it's different ... you can actually identify your population which stays comparatively static and you're going to have to provide services for those people for the rest of their lives ... that's a difficult concept ... for people to get to grips with. They have to make ... a bit of a mental adjustment.

As expected several registers were wasted because there was no effective joint planning body - and even on occasions no planning. One interviewee said that the creation of a mental handicap service with specialist posts would give a boost to interest in the register. An operator of a health authority-run register felt that it might not be adequately used by the social services department because of the lack of a structure linking health service and social services administration. On the other hand, where agencies were cooperating satisfactorily in service-planning, it was a different story:

> I suppose the fact that we do work very, very closely together - the main agencies ... does help. Because we have Social Services and Education representatives on the Community Mental Handicap Team and because particularly the Social Services representatives and myself do most of the planning we work very, very closely together and therefore can use the register creatively.

REGISTERS AND PLANNING

Most authorities have had, and continue to have, as a medium or long-term aim the creation of a new mental handicap service. This will require a shift of resources affecting the lives of hundreds of people. Great opportunities could be missed and funds could be wasted with effects which would last for years. Against this background the cost of registers is small. However the degree to which registers have realised their potential has been mixed. To some extent this has been the result of their novelty; but the essential reason is that the changes in organisation and attitude which have made their emergence possible have not been either sufficiently widespread or deep enough. There has been greater emphasis on rationality in planning with more attention paid to objective factual data on service delivery and to social research. There has been a movement towards joint planning with much of the pressure coming from central government. These developments have made those involved in planning and management more receptive to the type of quantitative information supplied by mental handicap registers. However conflicting attitudes and organisational arrangements remain. There is still a reliance on the impressions of professionals and DHSS norms; planning is still conceived in non-numerate terms; and information-collection is often too remote from planning. Attempts by the DHSS to induce authorities to plan jointly through joint finance and the requirement to establish joint bodies may sometimes have led to the formation of registers; however such external pressure has not been sufficient to produce genuinely collaborative bodies which have systematically and comprehensively planned mental handicap services. Joint planning tools require effective joint planning bodies. Their absence has often led to neglect of registers.

REFERENCES

Barnard, K., Lee, K., Mills, A. and Reynolds, J. (1980) NHS Planning: an assessment. Hospital and Health Services Review, 76, 262-265

Birmingham Social Services Department (1983) Birmingham Mental Handicap Register - The Need and Current Developments (Social Services Department, Birmingham)

Cubbon, J. and Malin, N. (1985) A National Survey of Registers of Mentally Handicapped People: A Summary of the Report to The ESRC (Department of Health Studies, Sheffield City Polytechnic)

Guy's Health District (1981) Development Group for Services for Mentally Handicapped People: Report to the District Management Team (Guy's Hospital Health District, London)

Independent Development Council for People with Mental Handicap (1984) Next Steps: An Independent Review of Progress, Problems and Priorities in the Development of Services for People with Mental Handicap (King's Fund Centre, London)

Jones, P. (1979) Mental Handicap Register: Does Wandsworth Need One? (London Borough of Wandsworth Social Services Department and Merton, Sutton and Wandsworth Area Health Authority)

Kushlick, A., Blunden, R. and Cox, G. (1973) A Method of Rating Behaviour Characteristic for use in Large Scale Surveys of Mental Handicap, Psychological Medicine, 3, 466-478

Leigh, A. (1977) The work of Social Services Researchers and its Impact on Social Policy, Social and Economic Administration, Summer

Malin, N.A. (1980) Group Homes for Mentally Handicapped Adults, ERG Report No. 9 (Department of Psychology, University of Sheffield)

Palmer, J. and Jenkins, J. (1982) The Wessex Behaviour Rating System for Mentally Handicapped People: Reliability Study, British Journal of Mental Subnormality, 28, 88-96

Smith, G. (1980) Social Need (Routledge and Kegan Paul, London)

Chapter Five

COMMUNITY CARE FOR PROFOUNDLY MENTALLY HANDICAPPED CHILDREN

Andy Alaszewski and Bie Nio Ong

For the past 150 years institutions have been the main means by which the state has cared for and controlled dependent individuals. Since the 1960s most western governments have adopted some form of community programme. At first these programmmes involved the creation of community facilities for less dependent individuals and these facilities duplicated existing institutions, but increasingly there has been pressure for total deinstitutionalisation and the closure of large institutions, such as mental handicap hospitals. Total deinstitutionalisation means that community facilities have to cope with all dependent people. Not only will special services have to be developed to support highly dependent people in the community but existing generic services will have to adapt to and meet the needs of these new clients. In England the policy of moving clients out of hospital has progressed furthest with mentally handicapped children. The Secretary of State for Social Services has accepted that large hospitals 'are not the right place for any child to grow up in' (DHSS, 1985a).

A major challenge in providing community services is providing services for people who are currently in hospital and who are highly dependent, for example, mentally handicapped children who are medically fragile or who have behaviour problems (Stark, McGee and Menolascino, 1984). In this chapter we discuss the experiences of one unit established to take medically fragile children out of long-stay hospitals and place them in the community - Dr Barnardo's Intensive Support Unit for Profoundly Mentally Handicapped Children in Liverpool. Our account of this service development is organised in three sections. In the first section we consider the background to the establishment of the Unit, in the second section activities associated with the establishment of the Unit, and in the third section activities associated with the routine management of the Unit.

THE BACKGROUND TO THE ESTABLISHMENT OF THE INTENSIVE SUPPORT UNIT

The development of services for mentally handicapped people was closely associated with the development of institutions, which were initially referred to as colonies and subsequently renamed hospitals (Ayer and Alaszewski, 1984). We have discussed the development and structure of these institutions in detail (Alaszewski, 1986) and we have defined institutions as:

> organisations in which inmates are dependent on staff for some or all of the basic necessities of life (and which) are large ... with distinctive buildings that separate inmates from the rest of society, that classify inmates into groups and that structure their everyday activities through an institutional regime (Alaszewski, 1986, p.33)

In the late 1960s large-scale institutions for the mentally handicapped and the mentally ill were criticised by researchers. Goffman (see discussion in Jones and Fowles, 1984) developed a model of the 'total institution' in which mechanisms of subordination enhanced and maintained the incapacity and dependency of inmates. A number of empirical studies were based on his theoretical insights (see, for example, Tizard, 1964).

In the late 1960s there was a spate of scandal in mental handicap hospitals (Martin, 1984) and a Working Party was established by the DHSS to review policies for the mentally handicapped. Its report was published as a White Paper (DHSS, 1971). The White Paper emphasised the problems of mental handicap hospitals. In England and Wales, it was estimated that there were 120000 severely mentally handicapped people, of whom 50000 were children. The residential care of these people had been centred in 59000 hospital beds, mainly situated in old Victorian buildings. In the White Paper it was proposed that these hospitals were to provide specific medical and nursing treatments not just social care. Local authorities were to take on the responsibility of providing residential care in small units. These proposals meant a major change in the balance of services for mentally handicapped people. Hospital beds for adults were to be cut by 50 per cent although it was not envisaged that hospital provision for mentally handicapped children would be reduced so drastically. There was to be a commensurate increase in local authority facilities.

This represented a radical change in policy which has been described by the Chief Nursing Officer of the DHSS as:

> the replacement of services concentrated in large mental handicap hospitals with an integrated network of local domiciliary, residential and day services catering for mentally handicapped people according to their individual needs (DHSS, 1985b).

This change has considerable implications for the pattern of services as well as the role of service providers. For example nurse training had to adjust to the changing pattern:

> away from custodial treatment within institutions, and (aim) to prepare nurses to meet the training and educational needs of people with a mental handicap within the context of an increasing emphasis on community care (DHSS, 1985b, p.1).

A major challenge in developing this new pattern of services was developing a form of residential care that did not isolate mentally handicapped people from the community and that enhanced their development and independence. In 1979 the Jay Committee addressed this problem. The Committee felt it was important to start afresh, with a new model of care, and it argued that any system of care should be based on respect for both mentally handicapped persons and for the care givers. The Jay Committee stressed that residential facilities should not separate mentally handicapped children from their neighbourhood and from their families. They argued that all residential care should be in small ordinary family houses with residents sharing experiences with staff.

A particular concern of the DHSS in the early 1980s was the plight of mentally handicapped children in long-stay hospitals. In 1982 the Secretary of State for Social Services stated that it was of the utmost urgency to get the remaining 2000 mentally handicapped children out of mental handicap hospitals (DHSS, 1982). He asked responsible health and local authorities to review the needs of every child in hospital and to set a date by which they expected to get each child out of hospital. He asked for an annual report from each authority describing the progress they had made in moving mentally handicapped children out of hospital. He also offered additional funds to authorities who had special problems in finding extra money to provide small homely units.

Dr Barnardo's Intensive Support Unit

One project funded by the DHSS was Dr Barnardo's Intensive Support Unit in Liverpool. On 9 December 1983, Norman Fowler officially opened the Unit and he said:

> This is a unique and exciting new project. The houses here are not specially designed and built for mentally handicapped people. Apart from a few adaptations they are just the same as the houses in which their neighbours will be living. The homes are so normal and ordinary that anyone could be forgiven for not realising what an achievement they represent in providing for such severely mentally handicapped children.
>
> All this shows a recognition of the fact that it is not enough merely to bring children out of hospital - important though it is. We have to make sure that they are brought out with a purpose - to acquire new skills, to live more normal lives and to develop their full potential. (DHSS, 1983)

Dr Barnardo's is a large and well-established voluntary agency with extensive experience of caring for and fostering children. It has established a reputation for providing high quality services and of pioneering new forms of care. The initiative for the establishment of the Unit came from the North-West Division of Dr Barnardo's but it fitted in well with DHSS policy. The Secretary of State agreed to provide half the capital costs and the revenue expenditure for 3 years.

The ISU is an experimental unit pioneering a new model of care for a highly selected group of mentally handicapped children. Therefore the establishment of the ISU represents the creation of a new social organisation with its own goals and objectives. As Dr

Barnardo's is a social work agency, the ideology on which the ISU is run is drawn from social work practice and makes use of the principles of normalisation as discussed in Chapter 2.

The ISU makes use of some aspects of everyday family life. For example the Unit is located in four recently constructed bungalows on a middle-class housing estate rather than in purpose-built premises. Minimal alterations have been made to these bungalows so that from the outside they look like any other house in the street. The daily life of the children in the ISU is modelled on the life of children living at home. The staff try to follow the same rhythms, provide the same range of experiences and social contacts as enjoyed by children living at home.

The ISU is not seen as only a long-term care facility. The staff would like to place every child in a family, either by returning them to their natal family or by placing them in professional fostering schemes. The staff of the Unit aim to act as good neighbours on the estate and recruit volunteers, thereby encouraging the understanding and acceptance of the mentally handicapped children in the Unit.

The staff working in the ISU can be divided into two categories - those providing support and those providing care. The support staff comprise one Project Leader and two Assistant Project Leaders (both also involved in child care), who between them are responsible for the management of the ISU. There is also support from an educational psychologist who provides advice on goal planning for the children and a part-time project secretary. There are four domestics.

The care staff consist of ten residential social workers (RSWs), five night staff plus a relief and eight Youth Training Scheme (YTS) trainees. All the care staff provide residential care for the children. The RSWs have special responsibilities for the daily running of the ISU and the care of the children. Eight of the ten RSWs are designated link workers. A link worker not only cares for a child but also monitors the overall care of this child, coordinates the activities of other individuals in relation to the child and develops and implements goal-plans for the child.

If the ISU is to successfully demonstrate that the profoundly mentally handicapped can be cared for in the community, it is crucial that the children selected are indeed profoundly mentally handicapped. The term profound mental handicap is applied to a wide and heterogeneous group of people. The clinical psychologist (Lovett, 1984) providing independent psychological assessment of the children for the ISU used a number of characteristics identified by Landesman-Dwyer (1974) as being associated with profound mental handicap. These characteristics were:

(1) an extremely limited response to external stimulation;
(2) obvious severe neuromuscular dysfunction;
(3) an inability to move by means other than simple turning;
(4) an inability to achieve or maintain a seated position;
(5) poor head control;
(6) an abnormally small body size for chronological age;
(7) the existence of records indicating a hopeless prognosis for behavioural and psychological development even with treatment.

Generally the children selected for the Unit should not be functioning above six months in developmental terms.

The policy of community care is now well established. However, progress towards shutting institutions has been relatively slow. The policy of moving all children out of mental handicap hospitals is important. The remaining mentally handicapped children in hospital are severely handicapped and present considerable care problems. If these individuals can be placed within community facilities then there may be important lessons for the placement of other severely dependent groups. The ISU represents an alternative model of care. It is staffed by social workers and has been established in four bungalows on a newly built housing estate. If this unit is successful then the model could be adopted for other similar units.

THE ESTABLISHMENT OF THE INTENSIVE SUPPORT UNIT

The establishment of a residential unit involves three discrete but interrelated activities: the selection and training of staff, the selection and transfer of the children and the acquisition of suitable premises.

The Selection and Training of Staff

When the Unit was set up the same individuals were involved in the staff selection, training and management. A major objective of the selectors was to select individuals with the right attitude to the children and to child care. The right attitude was defined in a relatively all-encompassing manner. It was not restricted to a specific or detailed knowledge of the principles of normalisation or to care of the mentally handicapped children, but included a willingness to work with and care for children. As senior personnel were setting up a new unit they were concerned to create a balanced team. They wanted to select individuals of varying ages, experience and skills who could work together. The concern to select a balanced team explained the attitudes to qualifications such as nurse training. The selectors did not attach overwhelming importance to qualifications, either positively or negatively, but rather viewed them as one factor to be considered among many others. The selectors were conscious of the need to take into account personality factors. These were difficult to assess in interview. They wanted to select staff who could cooperate and work together and were concerned about having people with forceful personalities as these might disrupt teamwork.

The senior personnel did not see training as merely a way of transferring information to care staff; they were more ambitious. They saw the preliminary staff training programme as an essential method of developing the right work practices, especially through the development of attitudes and development of group working as well as the development of child care skills.

The selection of care staff for the Unit followed the normal practice of recruitment for residential projects in the Agency. The Agency placed advertisements in the local papers and specialist journals inviting applications. Applicants were sent a job description and a standard application form. For each phase of the project some 13 applicants were shortlisted for five RSW posts and invited to a selection day. The selection day started with a general session for all applicants in which senior personnel describe the background of the project and explain to the applicants the objectives and nature of the Unit. Each applicant was then interviewed by a member of an interviewing panel. This was a fairly short informal interview. Following this preliminary interview the panel met to discuss the applicants.

There were no clear criteria for exclusion but generally inexperienced and/or inarticulate applicants were excluded. The interviewers formed an interviewing panel for formal interviews. These did not follow a fixed pattern but each member of the panel questioned the applicant about one area of work in the Unit. Following each formal interview the panel discussed the applicants' suitability for work in the Unit in terms of their ability to care for the children, their ability to work with other care staff and their sympathy with the overall philosophy of the Unit. The formal interview was a difficult experience for both the interviewers and the applicants. The panel had to decide whether applicants were suitable on the basis of their application form, references and two interviews.

Successful applicants were provided with an induction training programme. The induction training for one group of RSWs consisted of five weeks class-based training followed by eight weeks of practical experience in the hospital setting. There were approximately 50 sessions in the five-week programme; 17 of these sessions were primarily concerned with the development of child care skills, 13 with team building, ten with attitude development, seven with background information, and six with preparation for work in the hospital.

Since an important aspect was for the RSWs to develop the right attitudes and to work as a team, the course tutors wanted them to take on responsibility and to be involved in decision-making processes as part of a team. Most of the sessions were designed to encourage the active participation of care staff either through discussion, through role play or through the allocation of specific tasks to individuals. This process of group decision-making was both time-consuming and could at times be emotionally demanding.

The selection and training were two aspects of the same process. The selection was a screening or filtering process. The selectors did not want to recruit people who had traditional attitudes to the care of mentally handicapped children. As a result the majority of the RSWs did not have professional qualifications or extensive experience of caring for mentally handicapped children. The training programme was therefore extremely important. In it the tutors had to explain the principles of normalisation, to develop a team that could implement these principles in 'child-centred' care. Both the tutors and the RSWs were generally satisfied with the programme. The tutors had some reservations about specific RSWs and the extent to which they understood and were willing to care in the consequences of the different personalities rather than a shortcoming of the programme. The RSWs found the participatory learning style difficult to adapt to, and some felt that some major areas had been neglected such as medical information and nursing skills. They felt that these sorts of skills and information would enhance their ability to care for the children and were also important in establishing their status and credibility as competent carers. It is possible that these views could bring into question the extent to which care staff accepted the principles of normalisation. It could indicate that some care staff felt that the children had 'special needs' that could only be managed with discrete skills. The care staff recognised this particular conflict but argued that the parents of the children would want this kind of information and these sorts of skills, and therefore it was normal for them as carers to seek these.

The Selection and Transfer of the Children

The selection and transfer of the children from local hospitals to the Unit was a complex process. Many different professionals were involved in the decision-making. Many of these professionals had different views of the role and function of the Unit and different perceptions of the type of child that would be suitable for admission to the Unit. Here we concentrate on the perceptions of senior personnel in the North-West Division of Dr Barnardo's and contrast them with perceptions of the hospital ward staff.

Senior personnel in the Agency established a clear set of criteria for selecting the children for the Unit. The main objective of the Unit was to care for children 'whose mental handicap is so profound or so exacerbated by multiple physical handicaps that they would not normally be considered for admission to any residential unit other than mental handicap hospital'. Senior personnel were conscious that they required the goodwill of the health service. Not only was this essential for the smooth transfer of the first eight children, and subsequent specialist advice for these children, but if the Unit succeeded in placing these children in foster care then the Unit would need replacement children.

There was indeed some disagreement in criteria for selection. All the hospital staff we interviewed supported the general principle of moving mentally handicapped children out of hospital care into residential care within the community. However, they disagreed with the Agency about which children should be moved first. They wanted to discharge the most able children, who they felt could benefit most from living in small residential Units in the community. This underlying tension created difficulties and problems in various aspects of the negotiations.

The process of selecting and transferring the children involved the collection of information about children resident in local hospitals; the identification and shortlisting of suitable children; discussions with the parents of short listed children and discussions with nursing and medical staff in the hospitals. These activities were initially carried out by a planning team and became the responsibility of the project leader when he was appointed. Most of the information was collected by psychologists employed by Barnardo's and the initial discussions with parents were conducted by the hospital social workers. As a result of these various activities a final shortlist of ten children was produced.

Two late changes were made to this list. The parents of one of the children withdrew their agreement for their child to be transferred to the Unit, and a late replacement was made for this child. Although the child fitted all the criteria proposed by the Agency, the senior personnel were unhappy about the way she was selected. They felt that they had not been fully consulted, and that the transfer had been agreed by the social workers in the hospital and the ward staff at the hospital.

Another child was also withdrawn from the shortlist, as the nurses on the ward felt that she would not benefit from transfer to the Unit. Following discussions between the ward nurses and the consultant responsible for her care, the consultant informed the Agency that he could not agree to her transfer to the Unit, suggesting instead that another child should be transferred. Again senior personnel were unhappy about this process of making decisions. The replacement child had not been on the shortlist and had therefore not been fully assessed. The RSW, who had been designated as link worker for the original child, had already started working with her in hospital and the withdrawal of this child from the shortlist was implicit criticism. Divisional staff felt that the hospital staff were not sufficiently understanding and sympathetic to this RSW. However, despite these reservations the senior personnel felt it was important to maintain the cooperation of the consultant and the ward staff and therefore they accepted the replacement child.

The last stage of the negotiations involved the actual move of the eight children. The senior personnel wanted the care staff to work in hospital alongside the nursing staff and to gradually take over responsibility of the children. Initially this was seen as a fairly short transitional period. However, there were misunderstandings about the precise length of the transfer. Ward nurses were initially informed by senior hospital staff that this transfer would take three days. They argued that there should be a longer transitional period. The senior divisional personnel felt that ward staff had been misinformed. They felt that they had not specified any particular length of time.

Following discussions with staff in the hospital it was agreed that the care staff should spend a minimum of two weeks on the hospital wards. The transfer of the children to the first phase of the Unit took between two and four weeks. The process of transferring the children to the second phase was more formally organised. Before the transfer a four-week timetable was drawn up in consultation with ward staff and the RSWs were rotated between hospitals so that all the RSWs and all the children would be familiar with each other. Generally there appeared to be less tension between the ward staff and the RSWs with the transfer of the second four children.

The actual move of the children from the hospital to the Unit went relatively smoothly. Although the eight children are severely handicapped and require constant care and attention, the RSWs felt confident in their ability to provide the necessary care. The RSWs who stayed longest in hospital were most confident. They felt more capable to deal with crises such as ill-health.

The process of selecting and transferring the children from the hospital to the Intensive Support Unit was both complex and at times difficult. The senior personnel saw the Unit as first and foremost an experimental unit which would demonstrate that profoundly handicapped children could be cared for in small residential units in the community, staffed by residential social workers. The hospital staff saw the Unit as another community Unit into which they could place their children. They wanted to place the children who they felt would be most suitable for the Unit, that is, the children who they felt had the most developmental potential and most awareness of their environment. Although there were different opinions amongst hospital staff about specific criteria there was a general feeling amongst ward staff that only three of the eight children were suitable for admission to the Unit. These were the three most able children. Despite these disagreements, with one possible exception, the senior personnel at Dr Barnardo's felt that they had been able to get the children who were suitable for placement within the Unit.

Selecting the Houses

Advocates of normalisation criticise traditional facilities because they do not provide individuals with privacy, living space and the necessary facilities for personal growth and development. They argue that the physical environment is extremely important in allowing mentally handicapped people to develop their own personalities. They believe that the use of ordinary, high quality housing is important because it shows that service planners see mentally handicapped people as valued people whose lives can be enriched by this sort of facility.

The importance of selecting the right sort of housing was stressed from the very early stages of the planning of the Unit. An important member of the planning team was the Barnardo's architect. Although it was accepted that the Unit should be set up in ordinary housing, there were a number of options. The Agency could rent accommodation from a housing association or the local authority or could buy accommodation. At an early stage it was decided to buy rather than rent as this would provide a wider choice and would allow the Agency greater control. The next major decision was about the type of accommodation to be purchased. Traditionally community units have been set up in established housing areas. Usually there are large relatively cheap houses available in these areas and established facilities. However, setting up a unit in an established area requires negotiations with existing residents and often means that cheap houses are selected. The Working Party decided to buy accommodation on a new middle-class housing estate and single-storey buildings were selected.

The architect and building inspector in the Division spent nine months in Liverpool looking for suitable bungalows. In the north-east section of the city they found a new housing development. The developer had purchased two large areas and planned to build, over a period of seven or eight years, a large community with a range of housing, schools, shops and a community centre. At the time Barnardo's were looking for houses for the Unit, the builders had only just started work. Barnardo's approached the builders and they identified two pairs of bungalows that would be suitable for the Unit. These bungalows had not yet been built so that the agency could influence the construction. A major reason for selecting these houses was that other people were buying them and considered them attractive. They also were a good property investment so that they could be resold if necessary.

Once a preliminary agreement had been made to purchase these bungalows the Barnardo's Working Party discussed adaptions. The main criteria for these adaptions was that they should not influence the external appearance of the house and so differentiate it as a 'children's home', and that they should not affect the resale value of the house. Initially the architect discussed building a covered link between each pair of bungalows to facilitate movement between bungalows. However, this was rejected as it might create a 'mini-institution'.

It is general policy of the builders not to make structural alterations but they agreed to make minor alterations for Barnardo's. In the bathroom the position and shape of the baths were altered. The corridors in the bungalows and the doors were altered so that wheelchairs could pass through them easily. Externally there have been few alterations. All the houses on the estate have a step down to the drive but these were omitted and the drives raised so that there was direct access for wheelchairs.

The selection of the interior decor and furniture was done by Barnardo's. In the first pair of bungalows, the decisions had to be made before the appointment of the care staff. The domestic adviser from Barnardo's head office, selected the decorations and the furniture. The process was rather time-consuming as all decisions had to be approved by headquarters. The RSWs in this phase only chose minor items such as lamps, bedding and bathroom fitments. In the second pair of bungalows the RSWs were involved in all the decisions.

The bungalows look like other houses on the estate. Internally each house has its own individual atmosphere and different furniture, decorations, pictures on the wall and photographs of the children. For example, one house has a bird cage whereas another house has a basket for a cat. At birthdays and Christmas the houses are decorated in the same way as other houses on the estate.

Generally space is used in the house in the same way as in other households. There is a living room that is used for leisure activities such as listening to music and entertaining guests. A dining room is connected to the living room, and the children sit at a table for their meals. They also use the dining area for some leisure activities such as painting. The kitchen is separated from the dining area by a door and is used for the preparation of food. All meals are prepared in the kitchen. The bedrooms are relatively small and cannot be used as play areas. The children are always cleaned and changed in the privacy of their bedroom with the door closed. At night they have a quiet period with one of the care staff, reading a story in their room or having a chat and a cuddle. The bathrooms have toilet facilities which are used by everyone. All the children's bathing equipment is kept in the bathroom and it also has other features that one would find in a normal bathroom such as a linen basket.

However, these areas are also used for other activities that do not normally take place in a household. The living room is used for physiotherapy sessions as it has more space than any other room. When the children are at school it is also used for staff meetings and general administrative activities. The kitchen tends to double as an informal staff area where staff can talk over a cup of coffee. One of the spare bedrooms in each pair of bungalows is used as a sleeping-in room and also provides a storage area where old notes, supplies and staff coats and personal belongings can be kept. It also contains a notice board where staff notices are pinned up. The other spare bedroom in each pair of bungalows is used as an office and has a telephone.

The bungalows are relatively small and space has to be used efficiently. Living space has to be provided but space must be made for the other activities associated with running the Unit. Living space is always given priority and determines the characteristics of the bungalows. For example, meetings and administration take place when the children are not at home. There is a continual problem of storage. Like many modern houses storage space is minimal and a lot of play equipment has to be put behind sofas in the living room or put in cupboards. The only problem in moving around the house is carrying children between their bedrooms and the bathroom. Children are undressed in their own room and carried to the bathroom. With older heavier children this can be quite a strain for the staff, and following discussions dressing tables have been placed in the bathrooms.

The bungalows do not have car parks. The first pair of bungalows are in a cul-de-sac and there is only space for three cars in front of the house. Staff park their cars in the drive leading to the garage. However, there are still occasions in which these parking facilities are full and there are quite a lot of cars parked along the street. The second pair of bungalows are situated nearer a junction, and therefore there is far more on-street parking and less of a problem. However, even in this house when a large number of people have come to the Unit, for example for a childrens' review, parking can become a problem. However, this does not seem to have created any difficulties with the neighbours.

The estate is new and as yet few community facilities have developed. There is no public transport on the estate and the second pair of bungalows, in particular, is quite a distance from the bus stop. At night the walk from the houses along deserted roads can be quite intimidating and the staff use cars for transport.

Advocates of normalisation stress the importance of enhancing the social status of mentally handicapped people. One way of doing this is buying and equipping houses to the highest possible standard. Dr Barnardo's has pursued this policy and the houses they have purchased are undoubtedly very desirable. However, buying houses on new estates does create some problems. The houses are small and have limited space and therefore the internal environment of the Unit has to be carefully managed. There are limited community facilities on the estate and no public transport. This can be a barrier to people who do not have their own transport and can involve the Unit in quite high transport costs.

RUNNING THE UNIT

Although it is important to set up a community unit properly, the real test of such a unit is the ways in which routine methods of caring for the children are established and additional support that these children require is obtained. In this section we shall discuss the internal operation of the unit and the ways in which it has established contact with the informal sector and with formal agencies as the NHS.

Child Care

Caring for dependent people, especially for profoundly mentally handicapped children, who have extremely limited abilities to help themselves and to communicate their needs, is a difficult and stressful job. These children are likely to have health problems that require careful nursing. As the ISU is an experimental Unit subject to external evaluation, this creates its own strain. One aspect of the success of the Unit, therefore, depends on the extent to which the staff in the Unit can cope with the various stresses and strains and the ability of the internal management arrangement to resolve the inevitable difficulties. In this section we shall discuss some of the problems that arise in staffing a small community Unit and we shall discuss some of the mechanisms, including goal planning and supervision, that are used in the Unit to ensure its smooth operation.

When the Unit was established an educational psychologist took on responsibility for advising the RSWs on the developmental needs of the children and on the methods of establishing and maintaining goal plans for the children. The RSWs were expected to monitor the progress of the children in relationship to the plan. The psychologist discussed the goal plans with the RSWs during the induction training and the RSWs developed plans for each of the children. Initially these plans were maintained and regularly reviewed. However when this psychologist went on maternity leave there was only limited external support for goal planning.

The project leader consulted another psychologist about alternative methods of goal planning, and as a result of his discussions decided to purchase the Bereweeke package and all the RSWs and the project leader were trained in the system. The programme is tightly organised with clearcut goals and timetables, and once it has been established it gives the RSWs a clear idea of how and in what way they should develop the skills of their children. The RSWs are enthusiastic about the scheme and it has clearly resulted in the progress of some of the children. The feedback from the goal plans is clear and gives them faith in the childrens' ability and ideas on how to stimulate the children. The step-by-step, week-by-week organisation of the programme makes the identification and achievement of long-term goals realistic. As the staff have been trained in the system and can monitor and develop it, this has been important in maintaining their self-confidence and self-reliance and reducing their reliance on outside experts.

The ISU is classified as a residential project, and has generous staffing levels compared to both mental handicap hospitals and other residential units. However child management practices do not depend on number of staff alone, but are related to the ways in which these staff are used and the philosophy of work adopted. Within the normalisation philosophy there is great stress on individual child care and therefore to maintain this system, staff must be willing to work the hours that suit the children. This means that the rota of staff duties is both important to the achievement of child-centred care and is also difficult to organise. The eight children in the Unit are divided between four houses. During the day each house should have at least one member of staff on duty whenever a child is at home.

When pressure on staff increases because of staff vacancies and staff sicknesses the project staff have several ways of coping with the situation. The major one is an adjustment of the staff rota. During periods of staffing shortages, the staff in the Unit maintained their commitment to the children and ensured that the children did not suffer. They maintained a high quality of care. However, it was inevitable that there was less time to maintain activities that were important but not necessarily considered essential, for example, activities associated with the childrens' goal plans, social interactions and outings. In all residential settings, as staff become tired they inevitably lose enthusiasm and tend to operate at lower levels of efficiency and the ISU is no exception.

Because of the difficulty of residential care in general and caring for profoundly mentally handicapped children in particular, it is important that front-line staff receive adequate support. A major mechanism of support in the Unit is the chain of staff supervision, each member of staff receiving supervision from his or her immediate superior. We concentrate here on the supervision between the Project Leader and his deputies as this supervision is important in the management of the Unit and also sets the tone for the supervision given by the APLs to the RSWs. Supervision sessions were both lengthy and covered a wide range of topics. The majority of the issues discussed between the Project Leader and his assistants concern the running of the Unit. In both supervision relationships discussion of specific and general personnel issues dominate; 144

of the 239 separate topics identified in 13 sessions were concerned with administrative or management issues. Neither the relationship between the Unit and parents, neighbours and volunteers nor relationships with other agencies figured prominently in either supervision relationship.

Supervision is an important mechanism of professional development and management accountability in social work, and best developed among professionally qualified field social workers. The ISU is a residential unit and, apart from the project leader, none of the staff are qualified social workers. It is unusual to find such systematic use of supervision in a residential unit. The data we have indicates that supervision is a well-developed mechanism of management accountability.

An important part of the internal management of the Unit are the various staff meetings held in the Unit. There were two main types of meetings, staff meetings and group meetings. Formal staff meetings formed the main link between the staff in the Unit and the rest of the division, they were held once a month and chaired by the project leader. The current practice is to have separate staff meetings for each phase because of the problems of the rota and staff availability. The project leader set the agenda, incorporating items from the staff. The meetings focused on information about the agency. However the project leader has been concerned to discuss policy issues in the Unit and has created more time to discuss Unit issues. When the meeting concentrated on agency issues, the staff found it difficult to contribute but with a changed emphasis their participation increased.

Each phase held a weekly group meeting of about an hour. In comparison to the staff meetings, these were informal. Although general management issues and general policy issues were discussed at group meetings, the bulk of the discussion concentrated on specific operational issues such as staff rotas and the care of the children. Generally the Unit staff seemed to enjoy and contribute to the group meetings far more than they contributed to the staff meetings.

The ISU shares many of the characteristics of other residential units. For example, during the period under review there were interpersonal tensions, and tensions between the different groups of staff about the precise responsibilities of each group of staff. These tensions seem inevitable and the difference between successful units and other units are not so much in the existence of these tensions but in the mechanisms that exist to cope with them and to prevent them disrupting the care of the residents. The Intensive Support Unit has two major mechanisms for resolving and managing these tensions: the staff supervision and the various Unit meetings.

Relating to the Community

One objective of normalisation is to integrate handicapped people into society. This means moving them out of institutions as quickly as possible and also altering social attitudes so that society is more willing to accept them. The development of positive community relations is one way of altering social attitudes and of enhancing the social value of the mentally handicapped children in the Unit.

As the Unit is located in four bungalows in a newly developed middle-class housing estate there are few ready made social networks on this estate and no ready made 'community'. The Unit and its staff have, therefore, adopted a pragmatic definition of the community, as the parents and foster parents of the children, the residents, who live in the neighbouring houses on the estate, and volunteers who have been recruited to help in the Unit.

Volunteers. Volunteers are recruited to benefit the children. In the initial planning stages, volunteers were clearly seen as relating to individual children. As the project has developed so the emphasis on the role of the volunteers has altered. There is no longer a clear distinction between the activities that the staff and volunteers can perform but rather there is a difference in the objectives of their actions and in responsibility and accountability. The RSWs are responsible for the children and the volunteers should act under the advice and guidance of the RSWs.

In the North-West Division residential projects normally recruit their own volunteers. In the ISU, senior divisional officers felt that it was important that volunteers began working at the same time as paid staff. Therefore, the volunteers for phase 1 were recruited in advance and the project leader in the Division responsible for volunteers used her expertise to recruit and train the volunteers for the first phase. The planning team aimed to recruit 12 volunteers for each phase of the project, and the voluntary work project leader advertised in the local press for volunteers. All applicants were invited for an interview, as the interviewers wanted to be sure that the applicants were 'sound people'. The Unit selected volunteers on the basis of the interviews, references and police checks. The volunteers recruited to the first phase had a training session modelled on the RSWs training session, which had to be adjusted to the more limited availability of the volunteers.

It was generally agreed that the initial recruitment of volunteers was not very successful. Of the 24 volunteers initially recruited to the Unit only one continued visiting. She was fairly exceptional in that she came to the Unit three evenings a week, and developed an exceptionally high degree of commitment to the Unit. This volunteer built up a very close relationship with one of the most handicapped children and applied to be and was accepted as his respite foster parent. One major difficulty with the initial recruits was the problem of transport. Although the volunteers could claim expenses from Barnardo's for travelling, unless they had their own transport reaching the Unit could be very inconvenient and time-consuming. The greatest dropout of volunteers occurred in the first few weeks. The volunteers were probably unrealistic about the Unit and its children, as they had no experience of this Unit and had not visited it.

Subsequently the Unit has recruited volunteers through personal contact. The staff in the Unit generally agreed that volunteers recruited in this way were more successful; they appeared to be realistic since they already had some knowledge of and a genuine interest in the Unit and the children. They had generally been able to develop from one pattern of relationship with the Unit, for instance as a neighbour or a domestic worker, into another style of relating to the Unit.

Neighbours. Barnardo's wanted the Unit and its children to be part of the neighbourhood, but they did not want sympathy or pity for the children. In some ways the neighbours were similar to the volunteers and the Unit policy was that relationships between the children and informal contacts such as volunteers and neighbours should be allowed to develop at their own pace and in their own way. However, in the case of mentally handicapped children this does require some facilitation from the Unit staff. In both phases positive attempts were made to involve the neighbours. Each phase was opened with a housewarming party, to which neighbours were invited. Link workers also visited neighbouring houses to talk about the Unit and its children. Children in the neighbourhood were invited to the Unit both for more formal occasions such as birthday parties and, less formally, to play after school.

The first phase is located in a cul-de-sac, and here the relationship with the neighbours is fairly limited. Some of the neighbourhood children visit the Unit but most of the parents have kept their distance from the Unit. In contrast, the second phase is on one of the major estate roads. The number of houses in close proximity to the Unit is far larger, and the neighbours in this part of the estate have responded far more positively to the Unit. The major points of contact are again the neighbourhood children, who visit the Unit regularly. However, in the second phase the parents have tended to follow their children.

Parents and Fostering. Barnardo's has a commitment to family life and accepts that families are the best place for children. This commitment is evident not only in the way in which the Unit is modelled on domestic households, but in the commitment of the Unit to enhance the relationship of the children with their natural parents and if possible to place the children in foster families. The Unit aims to involve parents in the progress and development of their children, in all significant changes in the child's progress, and in all aspects of the decision-making process. The Unit operates an open-house policy for parents, to encouarge them to visit the Unit whenever they want.

The commitment to family placement has developed, and staff have gained experience and increased in their confidence in the project and the children. The Division has operated a professional fostering scheme since 1979, which places children with severe mental and/or physical handicaps in local foster homes. Shortly before the Unit was opened the planning group had discussions with the fostering team about the possibility of family placements. As a result of these discussions the fostering team attached one part-time social worker to the Unit to be responsible for fostering children. This social worker liaises with the residential staff, with the children's parents and with appropriate authorities. The fostering process is organised as an annual cycle. The Agency advertises for foster parents and individuals who respond to the advert are interviewed and approved. These parents then undergo a training programme, and at the end of this programme they receive the information on all the children who have been accepted for fostering. Potential foster parents can then express their preference for specific children, and these are then discussed with the social workers who make recommendations to a fostering advisory group. Decisions about the fostering of each child are made by this group. After this a programme is drawn up for establishing a relationship between the child and his or her foster parents and transferring care.

Four children in the Unit have been placed under the normal procedure, and there have been few problems with locating foster parents and transferring care, except in one case. One foster mother was accepted but did not live in suitable housing and the transfer of care was delayed until the local authority housing department provided suitable alternative housing. One child was accepted for fostering outside the normal cycle. In this case there had been considerable tension between the needs of the parents and the desire of the Unit staff to foster the child. Initially the parents had been very hostile to their child and had refused to acknowledge that their child had a future. For example they would not give their consent for the use of antibiotics. However, following considerable effort by the Unit staff and the field social worker, the parents developed a more positive attitude and they agreed that their child could be put forward for foster care. As this represented a major change in parental attitudes, senior personnel in the Agency felt that it was important that they should react quickly and positively to the parents' difficult decision. A special case conference was held outside the normal cycle of reviews, and here the chlid was accepted for fostering and special arrangements were made to find a foster family. A family was identified and a programme was established for building up a relationship between the child and his new foster parents. This child has now been transferred to the care of his foster parents.

In some ways the process of relating to the informal sector is best described as an attitude of mind rather than as a set of activities undertaken by the Unit staff, who have been friendly and welcoming and attempted to identify the skills and potential contributions of volunteers, neighbours and parents to child care. Where the Unit has adopted a more formal method of relating to the informal sector as in the recruitment, training and rota system of the first group of volunteers, it has been less successful.

It is difficult to categorise the relationship between the Unit and the informal sector. Interpersonal relationships have developed and been used in different ways. For example, some parents and neighbours have chosen to visit the Unit and to become involved in its operation. These individuals have made positive contributions to the general running of the Unit and to the development of the children in the Unit. On the other hand, many of the volunteers, some of the neighbours and some of the parents, have chosen <u>not</u> to become closely involved in the operation of the Unit. In the case of volunteers this has meant that they have stopped coming. Parents and neighbours do not have the same choice. They often maintain formal but fairly distant relationships with the Unit.

Rather than seeing the informal sector as falling into distinctive categories of people such as neighbours, volunteers and parents, it is probably more useful to see the informal sector as individuals with varying degrees of involvement in the operation of the Unit. There is a core of people who are closely involved in the operation and activities of the Unit. These people visit regularly and they know the staff and the children. They feel involved and for them the Unit is an important place. There are then a group of people who know about the Unit, who may occasionally visit the Unit but who make a limited contribution to the operation of the Unit. The third and final group of people are those who have had some contact with the Unit but for various reasons have withdrawn or seek to maintain a distance from the Unit.

Relationship with the Statutory Services

The Intensive Support Unit provides residential care. It must draw on the various statutory services available to the general population to provide the necessary comprehensive care for the children. As the residents in the Unit are profoundly handicapped children, the Unit makes fairly extensive use of the statutory services and its success in caring for these children depends on its ability to establish close working relationships, especially with the health service and the education service.

Most profoundly handicapped children have a range of health problems, indeed many have short life expectancies, and therefore require frequent medical treatment. The children in the Unit are no exception and therefore methods have been developed of rapidly obtaining medical advice and treatment. To ensure that proper medical services are available to the Unit, its staff have had to develop relationships with a range of health workers. The Unit does not have a special arrangement for access to in-patient facilities but uses the normal channels of admission. There have been no problems in obtaining services and the Unit staff have been able to obtain rapid access to facilities when needed.

Since their admission to the Intensive Support Unit, the children have received intensive medical investigation and treatment. The Unit staff have not been prepared to accept certain physical handicaps as irremedial. The Unit staff have found the hospital and the medical staff cooperative and helpful. When they felt that they required help and advice and investigation of the children, the health service has always responded. The Unit staff have never been willing to transfer the full care of the children to the hospital service but has insisted on providing care in the hospital. This has been a strain on the resources of the Unit as, during most of the winter, at least one of the children was having some form of hospital care or treatment.

All the children have been accepted as patients by the same local group practice. The general practitioners in this practice have no special interest in mental handicap and no special experience apart from their contacts with handicapped patients on their own lists. They do not provide the Unit with any extra or additional assistance but respond to requests from the Unit staff.

Initially physiotherapy was a great problem, in spite of efforts by the project leader to negotiate an improved service. The children only received limited physiotherapy at school. The community physiotherapy service was seriously overstretched. Barnardo's have now funded extra services from the health authority. All the children have been assessed by the occupational therapist for aids and equipment. Some of the children have been assessed in the orthopaedic clinic for special aids to help their mobility.

All the children attend special schools run by Liverpool Education Authority. Most of the children attend a special school for ESN(S) children, this is located in the grounds of a mental handicap hospital and until 1971 was administered by the hospital management committee. In the first phase there was some difficulty in developing a good working relationship with the school. The Unit staff felt that some of the work methods of specific teachers were unhelpful in the development of the children. It proved difficult to improve the relationship although a lot of work has been done through the deputy head teacher and through having coffee mornings at which the teachers and RSWs can meet. The relationship between the second phase and the school developed well. There were some hiccups but these have been ironed out, and there is now regular liaison with the school through visits and talks, and a home/school diary.

As the Unit is primarily residential, it must establish relationships with a variety of statutory services to obtain the necessary health and educational services for the children. Although these other agencies have a statutory responsibility to provide services, this does not guarantee they will provide help with the necessary speed and enthusiasm. Generally the Unit has asked for and received the support it requires.

CONCLUSION

The ISU is an experimental Unit which aims to demonstrate that profoundly handicapped children can be cared for in normal housing staffed by residential social workers using concepts of normalisation. The Unit has undoubtedly been successful in demonstrating this. In the Unit the emphasis is on child-centred care, and the interests of the children have been given a dominant position in the operation of the Unit, and the children have received a high quality of care. The psychological assessments indicate a considerable initial increment of development, most of the children experiencing an initial 30% gain. This was followed by a period of stabilisation, and in the second year there were small but significant increments in the children's development.

The Unit has successfully placed four children in foster care and another child will move when suitable housing has been found. In view of the extent of these children's handicaps and the ill-health that is associated with these, this represents a remarkable achievement. Not only has Barnardo's shown that these children can be cared for in a community unit, it has also provided that they thrive and can be successfully placed in families.

REFERENCES

Alaszewski, A. (1986) Institutional Care and the Mentally Handicapped: The Mental Handicap Hospital (Croom Helm, London)

Ayer, S. and Alaszewski, A. (1984) Community Care and the Mentally Handicapped: Services for Mothers and their Mentally Handicapped Children (Croom Helm, London)

DHSS (1971) Better Services for the Mentally Handicapped, Cmnd 4683 (HMSO, London)

DHSS (1980) Mental Handicap: Progress, Problems and Priorities (DHSS, London)

DHSS (1981) Care in Action: A Handbook of Policies and Priorities for the Health and Personal Social Services in England (HMSO, London)

DHSS (1982) Mental Handicap Services 'A Majority Priority' - Norman Fowler, press release (DHSS, London)

DHSS (1983) Norman Fowler opens Homes for Severely Mentally Handicapped - Government Cash for Dr Barnardo's, press release, (DHSS, London)

DHSS (1985a) Baroness Trumpington Opens new Mental Handicap Home, press release, 85/298 (DHSS, London)

DHSS (1985b) The Role of the Nurse in Caring for People with Mental Handicap, CNO(85)5 (DHSS, London)

Jay, P. (1979) Report of the Committee of Enquiry into Mental Handicap Nursing and Care (Chairman: P. Jay) Cmnd 7468 I and II (HMSO, London)

Jones, K. and Fowles, A.J. (1984) Ideas on Institutions: Analysing the Literature on Long-Term Care and Custody (Routledge and Kegan Paul, London)

Landesman-Dwyer, A. (1974) A Description and Modification of the Behaviour of Non-Ambulatory, Profoundly Mentally Retarded Children, unpublished PhD thesis (University of Washington, USA)

Lovett, S. (1984) A Psychological Assessment of the Children Admitted to the ISU, unpublished working paper (University of Hull, UK)

Martin, J.P. (1984) Hospitals in Trouble (Blackwell, Oxford)

Stark, J.A., McGee, J.J. and Menolascino, F.J. (1984) International Handbook of Community Services for the Mentally Retarded (Lawrence Erlbaum Associates, Hillsdale, New Jersey)

Tizard, J. (1964) Community Services for the Mentally Handicapped (Oxford University Press, Oxford)

Chapter Six

COMMUNITY NURSING IN MENTAL DISORDER

Val Reed

THE BACKGROUND

Methods of thinking about and delivering health care tend to reflect both the 'state of the art' in professional terms, and the contemporary social ethos. Until the late 1950s both psychiatric and mental handicap nursing were deeply influenced by their shared inheritance of a predominantly custodial tradition of care, based in residential hospitals and implying relatively limited individual interventions (Barton, 1958; Jones, 1980). Both nursing specialties occupied a 'medical handmaid' role within an exclusively nosological view of causality. Mental handicap studies were seen as a (not very prestigious) subset of general psychiatry. Contributions from clinical and social psychology were scanty and based on laboratory or statistical studies divorced from the living contexts of psychiatric and mental handicap nursing care (see, for example, Davis, 1946; Penrose, 1949).

Within two decades the intellectual, professional and social climates of nursing care were to change dramatically. This occurred partly as a result of a complex of factors, including the steady increase in contextual studies of mental illness and mental handicap and related social care research (see for example, Carstairs and Kennedy, 1978; Jones *et al*., 1975); altered models of the nature and causes of mental illness and mental handicap resulting from such studies (Bateson, 1972; Szasz, 1962; Laing, 1960, 1961; Clarke and Clarke, 1974); spectacular progress in controlling emotional and behavioural aspects of mental disorder by means of long-acting psychotropic drugs (Eccleston, 1978); and analogous progress in assessing mental, educational, psychotherapeutic and behavioural techniques (Mittler *et* al., 1970; Blackham and Silberman, 1975; Karoly and Steffen, 1980). Change was further supported by public attitudes towards reports of prolonged incarceration and substandard conditions emerging from some residential hospitals; and by resultant legislation and policy statements advocating community care for the mentally ill and mentally handicapped (Jones et al., 1975, pp.3-15).

Equally compelling as determinants of change were two parallel debates which radically altered the professional self-image of nurses. The first of these concerned the implementation of the 'nursing process' in psychiatric and other contexts of nursing care (Chapman, 1974; Altschul, 1978; Jasmin and Trygstad, 1979; Kratz, 1979; DHSS, 1981). In essence, the 'nursing process' is concerned with the adoption of a problem-oriented approach to the traditional concerns of nursing: that is, with making nursing care and treatment more systematic by the application of a simple, four-stage algorithm to the descriptive, analytical, interventive and evaluative aspects of nursing care. Classically the process may be presented in Figure 6.1.

Figure 6.1: Characteristics of the Nursing Process

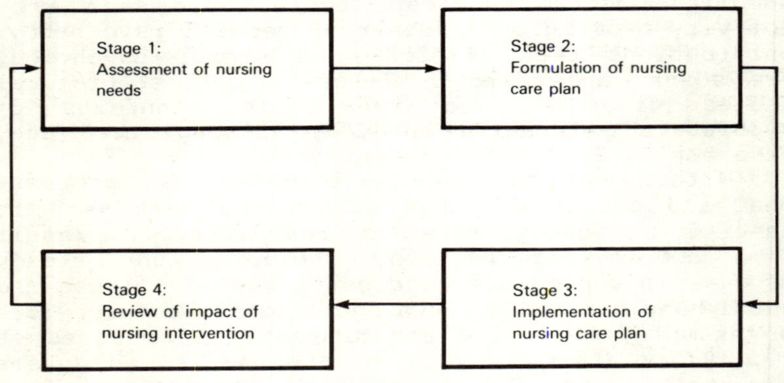

Clearly this approach has much in common with traditional problem-solving strategies in the natural and social sciences; it is similarly reliant for its success upon the collection, analysis and interpretation of a variety of evidence, for example in the form of instrumental readings, more global observations, and reports upon the patient's condition made by himself and others (Hayward, 1975). Here the underlying intention is to transform the professional activities of nurses, traditionally intuitive, reactive and based upon 'received' wisdom, into a systematic, research-based process reliant upon a relatively rigorous system of empirical evaluation of outcomes.

Parallel to the emergence of nursing as a research-based profession comes a development in the professional autonomy of its practitioners. Of special relevance here is the increasing autonomy of the community psychiatric nurse and the community mental handicap nurse as independent therapists, operating in the case of the former partly within a nosological and partly within a social-psychological framework for 'mental illness' (for a useful review see Sladden, 1979, pp.6-51) - and in the case of the latter, now almost exclusively within a social-psychological framework for 'mental handicap'. As early as 1973, Marks, Conolly and Hallam reported an experimental scheme in which nurse therapists, after receiving special training, carried out psychological treatment programmes with patients at home; in a residential hospital; and during their attendance at outpatient clinics. The aim was to produce '... a more independent therapist', who could perform an active psychotherapeutic role in parallel with existing nosological roles such as the monitoring of medically prescribed treatments; administration of psychotropic drugs; and the giving of advice, support and (where necessary) physical care. This same ideal of intervention to anticipate crisis and to promote social adaptation in the normal environment is being reflected in numerous local service contexts at the present time (Haque, 1973; Zeal, 1973; Marais et al., 1976; Leopoldt, 1973, 1974, 1975; Lonsdale, Flowers and Saunders, 1980; Tough, Tingerlee and Elliott, 1980; Hall and Russell, 1982). The growth and development of the role of the community psychiatric nurse (CPN), and of the community mental handicap nurse (CMHN) is thus beginning to see their emergence, not only as specialist therapists (Conolly, 1973; Marks, Conolly and Hallam, 1973), but also as colleagues and resource persons for other members of the primary health care team (DHSS, 1975; Parnell, 1978; Sladden, 1979).

In a recent policy document, the Community Psychiatric Nurses' Association (CPNA) emphasises the issues both of professional autonomy and of systematic care as focal issues in the clinical responsibilities of the CPN` basing the discussion on a recommendation of the Royal College of Nursing Committee of Standards of Nursing Care, that the clinical nurse should assume individual responsibility for systematically assessing each patient's needs (RCN, 1981; CPNA, 1985a). In the Association's view, accountability (that is, being answerable for work and/or decisions about work) forms the basis of professional standards. Nursing accountability in this sense is a relatively new concept; and nurses are now answerable for their output in a much more individual and explicit way than was previously the case in their 'medical handmaid' days. The Clinical Practice Group of the CPNA expresses its conviction that the essence of effective psychiatric nursing care lies in the development of '... community-oriented systematic care plans', employing the canons of the 'nursing process' to produce such care plans as a basis for sound clinical practice. The Group's interpretation of the process may be equated to the various 'stages' as shown in Figure 6.1 as follows.

Stage 1 (assessment)

This is a continuous process enabling the CPN to gather information; to understand and individualise the problems and settings; to empathise with the feelings and behaviour of patients and their families, so that relevant factors can be identified and analysed; and to decide between various possible courses of action. Such assessment should enable the CPN to clarify the 'problem' and its effects on individuals close to the situation, including, *inter alia*, members of the family, friends, neighbours and other professionals, any of whom may also be the referring agent.

Stage 2 (formulation)

This

> ... entails sifting out the relevant and significant features, both past and present,

> which in some way have adversely affected this functioning. It is essential for the CPN to analyse these factors ... and to come to an understanding of how the family relates, taking into account its strengths and weaknesses. It should be possible to recognise some of the dynamics linked with unresolved issues which are currently being acted out.

Once the relevant data have been identified, '... the treatment plan is formulated through negotiation between client, family and the CPN, with clearly defined and acceptable goals.

Stage 3 (implementation of nursing care plan, or intervention)

The purpose of nursing intervention is '... to bring about change (enabling clients to enhance) their coping, problem-solving capacity'. Here the Clinical Practice Group emphasises the importance of '... proper support and supervision in the model or models of care used, to enable the CPN to work towards the goals agreed with the client/family, while observing the highest standards of care'.

Stage 4 (review of impact of nursing intervention, or evaluation)

This stage '... provides opportunity for comparing expected with actual outcomes and for examining the original assessment, formulation, planning and related interventions'. In spite of its representation in process models as a discrete stage, evaluation '... takes place throughout care'; and '... without this information a CPN cannot improve clinical practice and quality of care'. The Clinical Practice Group considers that evaluation occurs at different levels within the care framework: that is during the interaction; following specific care interventions, both with the family and in individual reflections on nursing care; in preparation for withdrawal from care; and following discharge of the patient from the CPN's caseload.

Within the field of mental handicap nursing, notions or 'process' in care interventions find, if anything, a readier acceptance than has been the case in psychiatric nursing. This is attributable to two main factors: firstly, the degree to which behavioural psychology has contributed to a 'rebirth of hope' and an expectation of some measurable progress, however small, in social and educational programming of mentally handicapped people, both in hospital and in community contexts. The second factor is the close affinity existing between programming approaches in behavioural psychology, and the 'process' approach currently advocated as a basis for systematic care in nursing in all its specialties. Since the pioneering work of Pryor in the Child Development Research Unit of the University of Nottingham (Pryor, 1974), there has been a spate of literature designed to help caretakers, nurses and teachers of mentally handicapped children and adults to come to grips with the problem of 'programming' care more systematically and with better chances of a reasonably successful and rewarding outcome (Jeffree and McConkey, 1976; Jeffree, McConkey and Hewson, 1977; Cunningham and Sloper, 1978; Kiernan, Jordan and Saunders, 1978; Newson and Hipgrave, 1982). All are essentially concerned with what might be termed 'phenomenological behaviourism' - that is, with the use of behavioural techniques within the practical, everyday contexts of the home - and are designed to give parents, nurses and other caretakers the means both to contribute significantly to the developmental progress of their relative, patient or pupil; and - very importantly - to be aware, as a result of appropriate observations, that they are doing so.

NEEDS AND ROLES - CPN SERVICE

Preventive services such as those provided by the CPN/CMHN are frequently classified as

(1) primary: those services concerned with the prevention of newly occurring cases;
(2) secondary: those services concerned with the reduction of illness or handicap by early treatment or other suitable measures;
(3) tertiary: those services concerned with the reduction of disability and dependence in established cases (Caplan, 1964).

Professional thinking with regard to the needs to be met by emergent CPN services since their inception in Great Britain in 1954 can be seen to develop from an initial preoccupation with essentially secondary and tertiary aspects of nursing care in cases of chronic handicap and dependency, towards the slow evolution of a more extensive therapeutic role from the mid-1960s onwards (Hunter, 1974; Sladden, 1979). The earlier phase of 'continuing care' (that is, secondary and tertiary prevention) is summarised by Greene (1968), as follows:

(1) Provision of physical or psychological nursing care '... in accordance with the doctor's wishes', following discharge from hospital (for example, supervision of chemotherapy; observation of mental states in depressive illness).
(2) Liaison with doctors and social workers.
(3) Relatively limited interventions with patients and families, '... if such may reasonably be regarded as part of the nurse's work' (however, problems involving family dynamics were to be immediately referred to the social worker).
(4) Going to the aid of patients whose illness did not require treatment in clinic or hospital (tacitly at the referral of a consultant psychiatrist).
(5) Acting as consultant to non-psychiatric nurses experiencing problems with patients exhibiting symptoms of nervous or mental disorder.

Such descriptions are redolent of the earlier 'follow-up and after care' perceptions of CPN work, and of the almost exclusively nosological background of the work as a 'medical handmaid' service. More recently, the increased prominence given in the literature to educational and social-psychological aspects of primary prevention in psychiatry (Carstairs and Kennedy, 1978; CPNA, 1985a) and to the growing professional autonomy of the CPN/CMHN (Sladden, 1979; Carr, Butterworth and Hodges, 1980; Butterworth and Skidmore, 1981) have led to more progressive and therapeutic models of CPN care.

Educational aspects of this expanded primary preventive role are discussed by the Clinical Practice Group of the CPNA as follows (CPNA, 1985a):

> Mental health is concerned not with severe mental disorder requiring psychiatric treatment or conditions requiring remedial treatment, but rather with people's emotions, the way in which they behave, effects on feelings and the reactions by individuals or groups. The CPN has much to offer in providing a context for the expression of feelings through individual counselling or group work and in providing families with the opportunity to explore and

> understand their behaviour and its effect ...
>
> The CPN can (also) make a valuable contribution towards education in the home by helping the client and family to understand the nature of a specific illness ... and how to cope with the associated difficulties as and when they arise ...
>
> As a community worker, the CPN meets families, neighbours and others ... on a regular basis - and is, therefore, placed in an ideal position to work towards meaningful health change within a family or local community group ...

The discussion goes on to exemplify the various community situations in which this expanded educational role might apply: for example, in problem drinking; in stress situations associated with high-rise housing, redundancy or retirement; in school-based and college-based discussions on local community problems and life stresses. In addition (CPNA, 1985a)

> ... the CPN should become aware of the stress factors associated with transitional life events and could develop mental health programmes ... for clients at vulnerable stages of their lives - for example, adolescence, motherhood, career hurdles, bereavement ...

Social-psychological expansions of the CPN's preventive role are to be seen in some progressive services; and find their justification outside specifically nosological issues such as exact aetiology, or the validity of descriptive hierarchies in psychiatric diagnosis. Current psychiatric and social-psychological theory emphasises the less differentiated ways in which a great number of psychiatric patients differ from those who are 'well'. These differences may be inherent in various patterns of morbidity: for example, in personal perceptions of general illness; somatic symptoms; sleep disturbance and the like (Goldberg and Hillier, 1978). Alternatively, they may become apparent as one or more of the following general inabilities to:

(1) communicate with others;
(2) recognise or express personal feelings;
(3) perceive self or others accurately;
(4) solve personal problems;

(5) control feelings of debilitating anxiety.

Similarly, many mentally ill people encounter related difficulties in establishing stable interpersonal relationships (Yalom, 1975; Goldberg and Stanitis, 1977); and in developing or maintaining self-esteem (Goldberg and Stanitis, 1977). So-called 'generic' psychotherapy programmes, usually initiated while the individual is an in-patient in a residential psychiatric hospital or unit, are designed to help people to come to terms with, or to overcome, such difficulties (Remocker and Storch, 1982).

Within the practice literature, there are thus good pragmatic reasons for hypothesising that delivery of such programmes by nursing staff, with continuity before, during and after the critical 'bridge' phase in which a person returns home following an intensive period of assessment and psychotherapy as an in-patient, could be beneficial (Lancaster, 1976; Beard, Enelow and Owens, 1978; Cutler and Beigel, 1978; Towell and Harries, 1979; Mohamed, 1986). For example, recent studies discuss the potential benefits of a 'process' approach to the analysis and description of a patient's interactive needs; this is followed by the provision of individual social, creative and recreative programmes designed to help the patient improve his/her levels of social skills and resultant self-esteem (Langrehr, 1974; Loomis and Horsley, 1974; Manfreda, 1975; Butler and Rosenthal, 1978; Lewis, 1976; Goldberg and Stanitis, 1977; Trower, Bryant and Argyle, 1978; Ellis and Whittington, 1981; Mohamed, 1986). Other studies have demonstrated significant changes in levels of social competence and self-concept, ostensibly occurring as a result of carefully monitored programmes of individual social therapy implemented in various hospital and community contexts (Lancaster, 1976; Beard, Enelow and Owens, 1978; Cutler and Beigel, 1978; Towell and Harries, 1979).

The CPN's extended role must also take account of the stresses experienced by families in caring for their mentally ill members at home. Loss of social and leisure activities; disturbed domestic routine; disruption of work; loss of earnings; and fear of the possible effects on children, all take their toll (Grad and Sainsbury, 1968; Hoenig and Hamilton, 1969; Wing and Creer, 1980). Similarly, high levels of family dissension and criticism are associated with relapses in schizophrenia and depressive illness

(Vaughn and Leff, 1976; Wing and Creer, 1980). As previously noted, progressive CPN services now take a family approach, working with members from the outset, informing them and involving them in care and management (Priestley, 1979; Ekdawi, 1981). Taking this further, the CPN may function as a family therapist, examining with members '... whether any of the mismatches between expectations and performance can be resolved, or if some of the longstanding roots of critical comments can be explored' (Shepherd, 1984).

It would, however, be unwise to equate the contemporary 'ideal type' of progressive, therapeutic CPN service with reality. 'Medical handmaid' and 'progressive therapist' are simply extreme positions on a continuum of care practices; reflecting (inter alia) the extent of local commitment and local resources; local perceptions of needs and priorities within the preventive health service; local management structures and styles, both within, and contiguous to, the CPN team; and local philosophies of care. Beard (1984) writes:

> The contribution of the (CPN) nursing service is variable. In districts where the nursing service is strong, backed by nurses who can vocalise their patients' needs, articulate their contributions and gain the respect of their colleagues, initiatives other than medical ones are possible. The presence or otherwise of a 'open' referral system to the CPN service is a useful indicator of ... the level of nursing activity in planning and implementing a flexible range of services.

NEEDS AND ROLES - CMHN SERVICE

In the field of mental handicap, hospital/community nursing links were until recently both limited and scanty (Hodges, 1980). Although the principle of taking services to mentally handicapped people and their families was advocated by the White Paper, Better Services for the Mentally Handicapped (DHSS, 1971), and some early services established (Strong and Sandland, 1974) detailed recommendations were not made until the establishment of the National Development Group and the Development Team for the Mentally Handicapped in 1975 (DHSS, 1976; 1977a and b; 1978 a and b; 1980).

During the subsequent decade (1975-85) there

has been a ferment of criticism and self-questioning in mental handicap hospitals about the nature of their role. Traditional notions of the hospital and community nursing services as caring for 'patients' were vigorously attacked by some social scientists, who felt that mentally handicapped people are not 'patients', but are treated as such merely as an unsatisfactory means of social disposal, when in reality their problems are mainly educational and social - not medical at all, save in the case of a small minority. Thus within current social science there exists a tendency to reject any frankly 'nursing' input into mental handicap care: and to advocate its replacement by residential and social care inputs from social care workers whose training and preoccupations are supposedly more developmental than those of the mental handicap nurse.

However, this critique of nursing involvement in mental handicap care is based on a traditional, physically oriented 'bedside' stereotype of mental handicap nursing, which is far removed from modern practice (General Nursing Council, 1982); which equates 'nursing' with 'medicine'; and which seeks to perpetuate its limited, handmaid role. This view perhaps arises as a result of paying too much attention to the clinical origins of mental handicap nursing, which in its earlier phase could offer little beyond good general physical care; and too little attention to its evolving role as a developmental activity adopting a process or problem-oriented approach to analysis and solution of a wide spectrum of problems in mental handicap care. Something of this extended role is captured by the National Development Group in discussing the community role of the specialist nurse in mental handicap (DHSS, 1978a):

> The community nurse will offer special skills as a trainer/teacher of mentally handicapped children and adults, especially in relation to the development of self-help. He will also ensure that parents are helped to participate in the training programmes. Some parents will need advice about general management and physical care, especially if the mentally handicapped member is multiply handicapped. When behaviour problems are present, the CMHN will, in consultation with the team, be able to set up behaviour modification programmes and involve the parents as co-therapists ... The development of special interests by community

nurses should also be encouraged. Teams will develop their own particular way of working and must be able to respond in a flexible and sensitive way to the local situation.

Early types of services provided by CMHN teams were shaped by their hospital origins and by the perceived urgent need for 'dehospitalising' programmes in the wake of the 1971 White Paper. They included (inter alia) finding accommodation and employment for mentally handicapped residents in the community; liaison visits to inpatients' relatives; social education of residents; outpatient clinics; and liaison work with community agencies (Strong and Sandland, 1974). However, with the mid-1970s came increased awareness of the equally urgent need to offer continuing support to families in providing care for the majority of mentally handicapped people who have been at all times looked after in the community, by providing their caretakers with genuine alternatives to hospital care.

Current studies confirm the perennial relevance of the day-to-day management problems discussed by the National Development Group. Thus maximal stress occurs in families where the mentally handicapped member's hyperactivity reverses sleep patterns and severely disturbs the parents' rest; where behaviour disorders defy all attempts to maintain 'a nice home', and perpetual family vigilance is needed in order to prevent breakages and/or running away; where this and similar behaviour produces stress and tension between the parents, including possibly the threat of marital breakdown; where behaviour is perceived as interfering with the needs of siblings; and where parents live at a distance from extended family and are required to cope virtually unaided. Whenever parents are questioned regarding their support needs in order to go on looking after their child or grown-up family member, they stress problems of social isolation and lack of support (that is, they desperately seek temporary relief from incessant responsibilities of care); lack of knowledge of available facilities (frequently no one has informed them systematically regarding, for example, availability of attendance and mobility allowances; the existence of family support groups and/or of short-term care facilities in hospitals or community units; or of the existence of specialist psychological or community mental handicap nursing services); lack of knowledge of how best to help their child or grown-up family member (that, what ought to be their realistic short-term and long-term goals?; or with what aspects of social/educational development should they be seeking help, and from whom?); and fears for the future, especially as both they and their mentally handicapped son or daughter grow older (Hewett, 1972; Jones, 1980; Davies and Reed, 1982; Sewell, 1982).

Recently the Community Mental Handicap Nurses' Association (CMHNA) has produced a theoretical role-set which seeks to give priority to the tasks of the CMHN in attempting to meet some of these needs. In their 1985 document discussing roles and functions of the CMHN, the Association points out (CMHNA, 1985) that

> In the past, CMHNs have tried to fill the space left by the poor overall standard of community care for people with mental handicaps. They have fallen into the trap, like so many other services, of trying to provide for any and every need. In some instances, this has included doing jobs which do not require our skills; and in others doing jobs which require the skills of other professionals.

Following a discussion of 'past errors' (see role ambiguities (p.158), the document offers a role-set consisting of primary, secondary and tertiary roles (see Table 6.1). By far the most important of these are the so-called primary roles of 'educator'; 'health monitor', and 'caseload manager'. It is the performance of these primary roles which is seen as forming the basis of the daily work of the CMHN. The role of 'educator' has various target groups including the patient/client, who is taught various developmental and social skills and the basis of physical self-care; parents and caretakers, who may be taught realistic goal-setting with the patient/client, developmental needs, and techniques of behavioural programming and assessment and of working with mentally handicapped people; and members of the lay public, who may be informed of real issues in community care of mentally handicapped people, and possibly disabused of incorrect stereotypes.

The role of 'health monitor' is defined as '... doing for others the level of health monitoring that non-handicapped persons would do for themselves'. It is stressed that health monitoring as thus defined does not encompass traditional medical nursing care; but that it has close links with health teaching, and involves working in partnership with other professionals to ensure that mentally handicapped people have access to, and receive, services from the same sources as other members of the community. Finally, the primary role of 'caseload manager' supports the other primary roles, ensuring effective processing of referrals (with due regard to the requirements of the other primary roles); joint assessment visits with, and advice to, colleagues in other concerned professions; prioritisation and day-to-day management of work in connection with the caseload; and non-client meetings and routine administration. Secondary roles are those that complement the primary, client-centred roles and which tend to be natural developments of such roles (that is, 'key worker'; 'team worker'; 'advocate). Lastly, tertiary roles are those not necessarily involving face-to-face work with patients/clients. These include, inter alia, development of innovative projects; service planning and development; and teaching on a regular basis of professional, volunteer or parent groups. Such roles will reduce the amount of time available for client-centred work; and should, in the opinion of the Association, remain as relatively peripheral aspects of the CMHN's work.

Remarks made previously concerning the variability of CPN services (see page 151) may be applied with equal justice to present-day CMHN services. While some undoubtedly approach the 'ideal type' recently promulgated, it is also true that:

> Some are very institutionally-oriented, with a concentration on pre-admission, post-discharge visits, follow-up from outpatient clinics, depot injections (and with) making regular contact visits to iron out problems or offer short-term care (Hodges, 1980)

and in a number of cases, more than a decade after similar comments by the Hospital Advisory Service (Baker, 1972), it appears that short-term care services, though undoubtedly of great value, represent the sole contribution of the hospital to the needs of the mentally handicapped living in the community. In other cases, ill-considered or ambiguous role demands are seen by many CMHNs to vitiate their true role as supporters of the mentally handicapped and their families; and as needlessly attentuating an already tenuous service (CMHNA, 1985).

Table 6.1: Proposed Role-set for Community Nurses for the Mentally Handicapped (CMHN) (Based on a Discussion in CMHNA, 1985).

Role Type	Target Group(s)	Representative Role Content
A. PRIMARY ROLES: roles forming basis of CMHN's daily work, practised within a process model (assessment; planned intervention; delivery of nursing care evaluation of results)		
1. EDUCATOR	Client	Teaching early developmental skills (motor, cognitive, communicative, social, self-help); independence skills (travel around locality, familiarity with everyday signs, use of money); social, interpersonal, decision-making, communication skills; sex and personal relationships; methods of compensating for sensory/physical handicaps; health teaching (diet, self-medication, personal hygiene)
	Parents Caretakers Residential/ daycare staff	Realistic goal-setting; developmental needs; Behavioural programming and assessment of outcomes Working with client
	Lay public	Attitudes towards/knowledge of, mental handicap
2. HEALTH MONITOR	Client Parents/carers Residential/ daycare staff	Promoting awareness of client's general physical and psychological wellbeing. Observing for drug efficacy/side-effects (especially in epilepsy); fostering awareness of when medical or other help is needed, and helping client/carer to gain access to help
3. CASELOAD MANAGER	Referees Client/carers Professionals Care agencies	Day-to-day management of caseload; processing of referrals with due regard to requirements of primary role; advice regarding/promotion of access to, appropriate services and resources; joint assessment visits; establishment, prioritisation and review of waiting list in light of emergent needs/resources; non-client meetings and routine administration

Table 6.1: continued

B. SECONDARY ROLES: roles which complement the primary, client-centred roles; and which tend to be natural developments of such roles		
4. KEY WORKER	Client/carers Team colleagues Care agencies	Coordinative function between clients/carers and the various team colleagues/care agencies (NB: When CMNH's primary involvement with case ends, 'keyworker' role should pass to another professional)
5. TEAM WORKER	As above	Collaborative contribution of specific nursing skills to team care
6. ADVOCATE	Families/carers Service managers Statutory and voluntary bodies Specific social groups	Exposition of client's rights and needs
7. COUNSELLOR	Client/family Caretakers	Counselling on specific attitudes, problems or issues
C. TERTIARY ROLES: roles that are related to clients in that they concern service development; but which do not necessarily involve face-to-face work (NB: Such roles will reduce the amount of time available for client-based work, so should remain relatively peripheral)		
Systems-based research, development and educational activities		Development of innovative pilot projects Involvement with service planning Involvement in service development discussions at regional/national level Teaching professional, volunteer and parent groups

ROLE AMBIGUITIES AND ROLE PERFORMANCE

The nature of role demands placed upon the CPN are a management issue of the first importance. Here the basic question appears to be: should this role be generic in nature, with the CPN attempting to give 'total patient care' within a psychiatric frame of reference; or does his/her main contribution stem from more specific skills related to psychiatric nursing, which should serve clearly to delimit the role?

Some workers stress the ability of the CPN to operate relatively freely within medical, social and psychological frames of reference; a versatility which '... distinguishes him or her from other workers' (Sladden, 1979). Others indicate the more specific contributions of the CPN as assessor, clinician, therapist, manager, educator and consultant (Carr, Butterworth and Hodges 1980; Table 6.2); and deplore the somewhat ad hoc service development which has resulted from CPNs striving to fill '... a vacuum created by the genericism of the social worker' (Carr, 1985).

In situations where organisational patterns lead to considerable overlap of disciplines working in the community, problems associated with discontinuity of care may arise and adversely affect the patient and his family. In such situations:

> ... there should be a commitment at organisational level to bring fieldworkers from the various disciplines together, by encouraging shared learning for shared care. (Only) if an organisation is committed to the disciplines working together, (will) the staff see each other as facilitators of an effective and coordinated plan for a particular family or patient. (Beard, 1984).

Such shared care need not, and should not, obscure the specific contribution of the CPN as a skilled professional, performing the specialist nursing roles previously discussed. Following a careful review of the evidence, the Social Services Committee of the House of Commons (1985) state:

> The idea of the CPN giving 'total patient care' is disturbing. We believe that such use of the specialised skills of CPNs would be a waste. The general merging and blurring of skills (implied in a generic 'community health worker' role)

Table 6.2: Proposed Role-set for Community Nurses for the Mentally Ill (CPN) (Adapted and Expanded from Carr, Butterworth and Hodges, 1980).

Role-Type	Target Group(s)	Representative Role Content
1 Assessor	Patient, family, carers	Assesses nursing requirements of potential patients; subsequently evaluates outcomes of nursing care
2 Clinician	Patient	Performs clinical nursing involved in care process; this may be <u>basic</u> (such as monitoring diet, self-care) or <u>technical</u> (such as injections, monitoring chemotherapy)
3 Therapist	Patient, family	Delivers individual psychotherapeutic and family therapy programmes (see pp.148-51 above)
4 Manager	Patient, family, carers, referees, professionals, care organisations	Processes referrals; organises work priorities, establishes effective communication network with community agencies, carries out day-to-day management of caseload
5 Educator	Nurses, other professionals, lay public	Teaches preventive, curative, and potentially hazardous aspects of mental illness
6 Consultant	Nurses, other professionals	Advises concerning type/level of psychiatric nursing care required in specific cases

would be unfortunate. What is required is greater cooperation with other community-based staff and allocation of skilled social worker resources to match the development of the CPN service. CPNs are in the community to provide expertise in psychiatric care equivalent to the best nursing care available in hospitals.

Problems of role definition are also discussed in relation to the CMHN service, where a tension exists between the clearcut professional role-set identified in Table 6.1, and the less differentiated roles which CMHNs have often felt compelled to enact as a result of the general dearth of community services for mentally handicapped people and their families - a situation that closely parallels that confronting the CPNs. Elements of past and current services which CMHNs feel to be jobs not requiring their specific skills include:

(1) convenience transportation of clients and families;
(2) medical nursing care (including, for example, physical nursing, depot injections);
(3) crisis intervention (as opposed to genuinely preventive care);
(4) befriending (purely, that is, for its own sake);
(5) 'handmaid' services to psychiatrist, psychologist or social worker;

and the common role of the social worker manqué (CMHNA, 1985).

Conversely, the views of the Social Services Committee (1985) regarding the 'particular function' of CMHNs leave aside such 'basic tending' skills, which it is felt may be employed with equal facility by other professionals; and approximate closely to the primary 'educator' role advocated by the CMHNA (1985), including the provision of

(1) 'professional advice and support to parents, residential care staff and daycare staff;
(2) long-term management and training;
(3) services in particularly difficult cases rather than a generic service for all mentally handicapped people';

and ending with a strongly worded caveat against the potential wasting of such skills as a result of inappropriate role expectations (Social Services Committee, 1985).

While it is to be hoped that such unequivocal opinions will help both CPNs and CMHNs in clarifying and implementing their modern roles, it is also true that role ambiguity may be perpetuated by factors other than traditional working and restrictive ideologies. There is, for example, the massive organisational and communicative investment required to establish and maintain such services. Thus although the majority of CPN/CMHN practitioners questioned are in no doubt where their professional priorities lie (that is, in face-to-face work involving patients and families), the results of the small-scale study summarised in Table 6.3 are illustrative of how much of their time is probably spent otherwise. Here 23 experienced practitioners in the final stages of ENB course no. 805/810 were asked to rank-order their professional tasks in community nursing in terms of the perceived amounts of time necessarily spent in each activity. In both groups the nurses perceived themselves as spending most of their time in activities which they regarded at the best as merely supportive to their true professional roles: that is, travelling; 'administrative work'; meetings with other care workers; and liaison with other agencies.

EDUCATION AND SKILLS

Many problems surround methods of preparing CPNs/CMHNs for their community roles. These are mainly to do with the provision, nature and content of preparatory courses. Training beyond basic statutory qualification in psychiatric nursing (RMN) or in mental handicap nursing (RNMH) is so far non-mandatory for practising community nurses in these specialties; though both the professional associations and the ENB are committed in principle to mandatory post-basic training (CPNA/RCN, 1982). For more than ten years now, post-basic training courses have been outlined and approved by the Joint Board for Clinical Nursing Studies (JBCNS) and latterly by the new controlling national boards for nursing, midwifery and health visiting. Currently, nine establishments are approved by the English National Board (ENB) for courses 805 (mental handicap option) and 810 (psychiatric option), with approximately 164 course members in the year 1984-85 (Social Services Committee, 1985).

However, at the present time only 22.4 per cent of practising CPNs have completed a post-

Table 6.3: CPN/CMHN Perceptions of Personal Time Utilisation Within Their Current Services. (NB: Higher ranks indicate activities in which greater amounts of time are perceived to be spent)

Rank	CPN Group (n=16):	CMHN Group (n=8)
13.0		Meetings with other care workers
12.0		Liaison with other agencies
11.0		'Administrative work'
10.0	Travelling	
8.5	'Administrative work' Meetings with other care workers	Travelling Teaching student nurses and other care workers Offering support to group homes Supporting/carrying out teaching programmes with families
6.5	Liaison with other agencies Individual and family counselling and support	
5.0	Administering depot injections	
3.5	Teaching student nurses and other care workers Outpatient clinics	'Standing-in' Outpatient clinics Liaison with mental handicap hospitals concerning discharge to community Counselling clients Arranging short-term care Carrying out individual programmes with clients living independently
2.0	Ward rounds with consultant psychiatrist	
1.0	Long-term supportive work with patients	

registration course in community psychiatric nursing (that is, JBCNS Courses 800, 810; ENB course 810), representing an increase of only 60 CPNs per year achieving such a qualification during the period 1980-85 (CPNA, 1985b). Clearly these numbers are derisory even in terms of coping with the existing demand for places, let alone when they are seen in terms of the rapidly escalating demand for highly qualified community nursing staff resulting from current moves towards community care (Skidmore, 1985). The dearth of training places has recently led to urgent recommendations by the Social Services Committee (1985) '... that funds be earmarked by health authorities and by the ENB for the future training of CPNs; and that the Government undertake to find the funds necessary over a period of years'.

While action to increase the available number of training places is important, so, too, is the type of course which is to be provided: since clearly the quality and character of community nursing practice will relate closely to the skills and training content developed and experienced by the individual nurse (Beard, 1984). Arguments in favour of mandatory post-basic training rest upon the fact that it is not realistic to assume that basic RMN/RNMH training will enable the nurse instantly to undertake the wide range of therapies and professional activities implicit in the expanded role-sets (Tables 6.1 and 6.2 above). Of equal concern are some preliminary research indications that even CPNs who have undertaken post-basic training may still lack the necessary skills to carry out their job effectively (Skidmore and Friend, 1984); and that the acquisition of such skills may require the nurse to resort to '... trainings which do not lead to a specific nursing qualification', such as counselling courses (Beard, 1984), courses in family casework and in interpersonal teaching skills (CPNA, 1985a)

The Clinical Practice Group of the CPNA has recently re-emphasised the urgent current need to develop '... appropriate and realistic training programmes' for CPN practitioners; which it sees as a joint function of schools of nursing and institutions of higher education within specific catchments (CPNA, 1985a). Similary, while the CMHNA feels that the basic RNMH course:

> ... should have equipped nurses to carry out the primary roles ... if nurses are to get involved in the secondary roles they need training in counselling and psychotherapy; theory and

> practice of normalisation; family therapy; service and community knowledge; ethical and legal aspects of community care; the nature of organisations and how to achieve change; interpersonal skills; and personal development and independence training, especially in coping with stress; and in developing confidence in their roles, skills and independent decision-making (CMHNA, 1985).

Related to this emphasis on practice needs are indications of a growing practitioner dissatisfaction with what is perceived as the relatively static and academic manner in which some training institutions interpret syllabuses of post-basic CPN/CMHN training. There is now widespread consensus among nurse managers and some educators that such courses should be skills-based (Ellis and Whittington, 1981); that they should reflect the living and dynamic contexts in which community psychiatric and mental handicap nursing is practised (CPNA, 1985a); and that they should be the product of closely integrated joint planning and delivery by service staff and educators (Skidmore, 1985). This would, it is felt, help to overcome the current overemphasis on academic content at the expense of practice skills: 'CPNs require training for the job they do, not for what they are thought to be doing ... While the theory in the present course is important, the course should be more practice-oriented' (Skidmore, 1985).

The view here expressed is that practitioners should increasingly be called upon to evaluate their own training needs, possibly in a manner similar to that indicated in Table 6.4, summarising a study in which 28 field supervisors were requested to rank 40 practice skills which they would wish to see developed in new team members during their post-basic training course. These 40 skills identified as important by experienced CPNs/CMHNs formed the basis of the field placement report to be completed by members of the 1983-84 CPN/CMHN field supervisors' course at Sheffield City Polytechnic, on members of the then current ENB courses 805/810. In aggregate these skills provided a fourfold functional analysis of the performance skills required by a CPN/CMHN, as seen by practitioners, in social-interactional, educational, organisational and professional areas. Course members were asked to rank-order these skills in order of importance. The total positive correlation between CPN/CMHN field supervisor responses was high (Spearman Prho = 0.728, $t = 6.557$, d.f. = 38, $p < 0.001$, two-tailed). Such skill-statements would then be content-analysed as a foundation for a skills-based curriculum, employing casework both as a focus for the theoretical material drawn from the contributory disciplines (for example, psychology, sociology) (Hodges, 1985); and in formative evaluation of the student's progress. In such a skills-based approach, it is of considerable interest to note how closely the policy statements of the two professional associations regarding desirable educational content are paralleled by the empirically derived practitioner statements set out in Table 6.4. The acquisition of such skills is not necessarily related to the 'inert' treatment of academic content that occurs in some existing courses; and their acquisition by practitioners '... can pose major problems for those districts where there is little or no commitment, financial or otherwise, to ongoing education and training of (community) nurses' (Beard, 1984).

Despite the recent revision and replacement of ENB course 810 in an attempt to reflect more closely current issues in community psychiatric nursing care (ENB 811, CPN (83)2), numerous practitioners and educators feel the present post-basic training to be rather tenuously related to the realities of practice: in that, for example, it sets out to teach as if students were totally inexperienced, whereas in fact very few have less than two years qualified experience (Skidmore, 1985); and in one recent intake of students at Sheffield City Polytechnic (n = 22), the mean qualified experience of the student group was as high as 10.5 years. Some nurse practitioners and informed colleagues from other professions are concerned that '... further expansion and more effective use of the CPN service are hamstrung by the lack of training facilities and by uncertainty as to the sort of qualification which should be required'; and that '... there is no way at all in which the present training facilities for CPNs are going to match the increased burden placed upon that particular group' (Social Services Committee, 1985).

Such comments refer to the current rapid expansion of CPN teams in which more and more registered psychiatric nurses are being 'pushed into' community roles without appropriate post-basic training (Skidmore, 1985): and to a situation in which the present post-basic training does not always appear to prepare CPNs to offer a good comprehensive service to clients (Skidmore and Friend, 1984); and

Table 6.4: Functional Analysis of 'Common Core' Skills: Ranking by Field Supervisors of 'Upper Quartile' Skills. (NB: Higher ranks indicate skills which are perceived to be more important. The number in columns 2/5 refers to the location of each skill in the checklist of 40 relevant skills. SI = social-interactional skill; ED = educational skill; ORG = organisational skill; PR = professional skill. These four types of skill represent the areas of the fourfold functional analysis)

CPN Supervisors (n = 15)			CMHN Supervisors (n = 13)		
Rank	Number	Skill	Rank	Number	Skill
10	3	Establishes effective relationships with clients/families (SI)	10	3	Establishes effective relationships with clients/families
9	33	Explains clearly when teaching family members to cope with specific problems of care (ED)	9	35	Shows skill in personal/social counselling with clients (ED)
8	11	Has knowledge of assessment skills and when to use them (PR)	8	23	Shows ability to assign priorities appropriately in problem situations (ORG)
7	23	Shows ability to assign priorities appropriately in problem situations (ORG)	7	33	Explains clearly when teaching family members to cope with specific problems of care (ED)
6	19	Maintains a calm, rational but caring approach to problem-solving (PR)	6	4	Shows a flexible and suitable empathic style with clients of differing age/socioeconomic/clinical groups (SI)

Table 6.4: continued

Rank	Number	Skill	Rank	Number	Skill
5	35	Shows skill in personal/social counselling with clients (ED)	5	16	Can appreciate need for prompt action and forsee implications of delay (PR)
4	4	Shows a flexible and suitable empathic style with clients of differing age/socioeconomic/ clinical groups (SI)	4	19	Maintains a calm, rational but caring approach to problem-solving (PR)
3	13	Displays ability to select/apply appropriate therapy (ies) (PR)	3	34	Shows ability to communicate special knowledge and experience to other members of staff (ED)
2	2	Displays a good communicative style with colleagues and other members of staff (SI)	2	11	Has knowledge of assessment skills and when to use them (PR)
1	14	Shows realistic appreciation of own/other role limits within the team (PR)	1	2	Displays a good communicative style with colleagues and other members of staff (SI)

in which practitioner skills and expertise are challenged by rapid change in the presenting problems of community psychiatric nursing care (Butterworth and Skidmore, 1981; Skidmore, 1985).

Similar issues affect CMHN training, where the preparation is largely hospital-based and a sizeable majority of practitioners have yet to receive substantial post-basic training for their community roles. Here, arguably to an even greater extent than is the case with CPNs, training needs would be clarified and their fulfilment facilitated by firmly agreed role definitions such as those recently offered by the CMHNA (see Table 6.1). The basic professional qualification (RNMH) has recently undergone a syllabus change to reflect the general pattern of recommendations regarding unified community nursing/social care training advocated by the Jay Committee (1979) which are currently being pursued collaboratively by CCETSW and the nursing national boards, with the aim of developing '... mutually compatible programmes in mental handicap care' (Social Services Committee, 1985). With regard to skills-based learning and practitioner involvement in the planning, implementation and evaluation of post-basic courses for community nursing practitioners, similar considerations apply both to CPNs and to CMHNs. There is a consensus that greater liaison is required between educators and practitioners; that more emphasis should be placed on the role of practitioner-supervisors in peer preparation and assessment; that training institutions and CPN/CMHN services should together explore more effective ways of training community nurses to cope with the accelerating demands being made on such services. In summary, there is in both specialties a feeling abroad that '... a radical alternative to the present system of training is needed, with the practitioner taking a more active role in the training of his peers' (Skidmore, 1985).

ORGANISATION AND RESOURCES

Though differences occur as to detail, there are now basically two organisational patterns for the provision of CPN/CMHN services in the United Kingdom. The first, historically older, pattern regards such services as an offshoot of the mental illness/mental handicap nursing services, and administers them as such (Figure 6.2, model A). Such teams are normally hospital-based either in a psychiatric hospital (37

Figure 6.2: Representative Schemata of Two Alternative Organisational Patterns for Delivery of CPN/CMHN Services (see Text). (NB: Double lines represent direct line responsibility for organisation and delivery of nursing elements of the service. Single lines represent interactive communicational and collaborative links)

MODEL A: A hospital-based CPN/CMHN Team

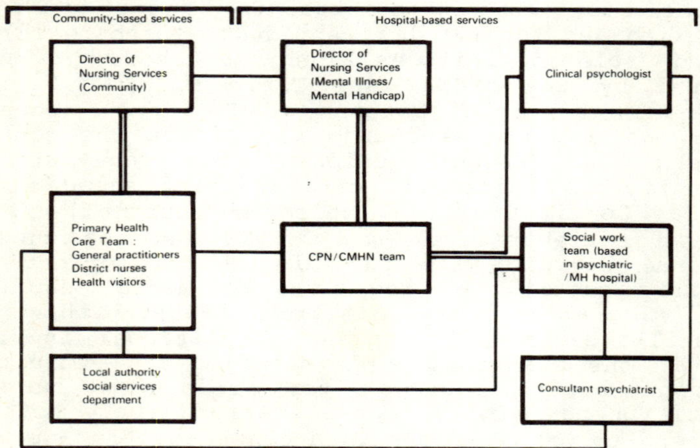

MODEL B: A Community-based CPN/CMHN Team

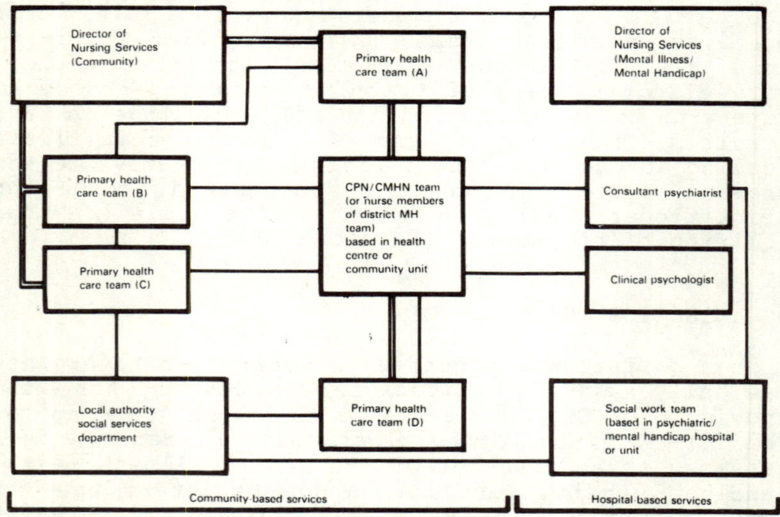

per cent); a psychiatric unit of a district general hospital (19 per cent); or in a day hospital (10 per cent). (These and other statistical details in this section are drawn from the CPNA National Survey Update (CPNA, 1985b)). Typically, day-to-day management of the community nursing team is delegated either to a senior nurse grade 7 or a senior nurse grade 8 (72 per cent); reporting to a Director of Nursing Services (69 per cent); though in almost one-quarter of cases the immediate service manager reports to an assistant director or other intermediate service manager (24 per cent).

The Director of Nursing Services normally administers a district-wide CPN/CMHN service, communicating laterally with the Director of Nursing Services (Community) regarding community service needs. The main source of referrals for a model A team is the geographically based consultant psychiatrist. The CPN/CMHN team operates an advisory and practical service to primary health care teams (PHCTs) on a district-wide basis, accepting some referrals from general practitioners and other PHCT members. Acceptance of referrals from other agencies and longer-term therapeutic involvement by members of the CPN/CMHN team are normally at the discretion of the consultant psychiatrist.

By contrast with the traditional model A team, there has recently been a steady increase in the number of model B teams having health centres and general practitioner practices as their main base (Figure 6.2, model B). This 'community-oriented' shift represents an increase of almost 10 per cent in model B teams during the period 1980-85, with a corresponding decrease in the number of teams having psychiatric hospitals or psychiatric/mental handicap units as a main base. Such teams are normally located in a health centre (CPN/CMHN) or community mental handicap unit (CMHN). The team is normally administered by a Director of Nursing Services (Community), communicating laterally with a Director of Nursing Services (Mental Illness/Mental Handicap) regarding specialist nursing needs. In other situations, line management responsibilities are retained by the Director of Nursing Services (Mental Illness/Mental Handicap). Whichever organisational pattern is adopted, the referral pattern in such community-located teams is generally radically different from that of the model A team. Its main source of referrals is the general practitioner and other members of the extended health care team, including district nurses, health visitors, social workers and relatives. This contrasts markedly with the normally consultant-oriented pattern of referrals in model A teams. The shift in team location and organisation is discussed in the CPNA National Survey Update, with the conclusion that over the past five years:

> ... CPN service resources are being diverted from traditional hospital bases (change, minus 20.55%) to locations that are more community orientated (change, plus 23.15%). However, the largest group of CPNs (n = 962) is still to be found (located) in psychiatric hospitals (CPNA (1985b), p. 14)

There is no doubt that members of the emergent model B teams spend much more time working in areas of primary and secondary promotive and preventive psychiatry/mental handicap than do their model A counterparts: and that general practitioners tend to refer to them cases which would not be adequately dealt with in other circumstances (Carr, Butterworth and Hodges, 1980). In ideological terms, the newer team pattern de-emphasises the consultant psychiatrist as controller of the service, and stresses the relative autonomy of the CPN/CMHN as a professional colleague and resource for other workers in the extended health care team. One important issue concerns the supposed increased epidemiological relevance of the new-style services. Workers in the Mill Hill experimental CPN service became aware (Feinmann, 1985):

> ... that the time span on which the (more traditional) team was focusing its attention was several years too late. We realised that people rarely come to the attention of hospitals when the crises occur that start the process of emotional damage. But professionals such as the clergy, teachers and GPs know when people are going through transitions that make them vulnerable. We decided that helping these professionals to give help themselves could be the basis of a system of preventive psychiatry.

and the policy of model B teams is generally to avoid the conventional CPN role of 'taking-on' 40 or 50 severely damaged clients, in favour of the relatively flexible, innovative role of PHCT resource member.

Such redeployment of relatively scarce resources is not without its problems and its critics. Thus the relocation of CPNs in primary care bases has recently been criticised for its supposed deleterious effects on the care of chronic psychotic patients; by implication, for its tendency to fragment district-wide CPN services (Beard, 1984); for the possible professional isolation it may produce in some CPNs working for a relatively unsympathetic community division; and for the career insecurities produced by loss of mental health officer status as a result of moving to the community division (Carr, Butterworth and Hodges, 1980). One pragmatic solution suggested is that CPNs should continue to be employed by the psychiatric nursing division, irrespective of their team location; and that they should continue to accept at least some referrals from hospital sources.

CMHN/CPN services remain a slender, though rapidly growing, community resource. One current estimate of the number of CMHNs practising in the United Kingdom is 400-500 (Social Services Committee, 1985): and of CPNs so practising 2758 (CPNA, 1985b). The rate of growth of such services is indicated by the CPNA National Survey Update, in which it is seen that, during the period 1980-85, the total pool of CPN nursing manpower has increased by 1091 WTE (that is, by 65.5 per cent). The mean regional population ratio per CPN (1:23800) is still much greater than the current recommended rate of 1:10000; and displays wide regional variations ranging from 1:17800 (in Wessex) to 1:34500 (in Yorkshire), although during the last five years the ratio has been reduced by a mean 26200 in the 14 regions studied. Projecting from current service growth rates, this indicates a likely mean population/CPN ratio which will be at or near the current recommended level by the year 1990.

Bearing in mind the considerable potential for community psychiatric nursing interventions in general populations (see page 148 above), it is interesting and somewhat surprising to note that almost two-thirds (that is, 64 per cent) of CPNs are currently specialising in work with the elderly;with a further 9 per cent specialising in established cases of drug/alcohol abuse. By contrast, only one-quarter give their specialisms as acute or crisis work (12.6 per cent); rehabilitation (5 per cent); children/adolescents (4.5 per cent); behavioural and/or family therapy (4.7 per cent). These are clearly areas requiring substantial development if justice is to be done to the promotional/preventive role of the CPN so much discussed as an essential element of a modern community psychiatric nursing service.

DEVELOPMENT

Clinically, future developments of importance both to CPN and to CMHN services concern clarification of the precise nature of the roles to be performed having regard both to the needs of local communities and to the national debate on roles outlined on pages 147-61. Organisationally, it will be necessary for employing authorities to experiment flexibly with alternative modes of service delivery, basing such experiments on local needs and seeking to work with social partners to overcome bureaucratic constraints leading to frustration, uncertainty or insecurity among CPNs/CMHNs. In particular, if the CPN service is to perform its promotional/preventive role effectively, there is much scope for development in acute specialisms; in rehabilitation; in work with children and young people; and in behavioural and family therapies. Educationally, many problems concerning provision, nature and content of preparatory courses for CPNs/CMHNs remain to be solved (see pp.161-68 above): and the ultimate efficiency and effectiveness of both services will be critically dependent on the theoretical and practical calibre of the resultant courses.

Finally, there is a dearth of good, systematic research into all aspects of these services. To date, evaluations in clinical, organisational and educational aspects incline to the anecdotal. There is a need for relatively rigorous, action-oriented studies, locally based and involving (inter alia) evaluation of outcomes of various therapeutic methods with specific client groups; analyses of the evolution and organisational pattern of new services; and studies of local educational initiatives for the preparation of community nurse practitioners, both in regard to the contexts and the contents of such courses, and their outcomes for the specific services and practitioners involved.

REFERENCES

Altschul, A. (1978) 'A Systems Approach to the Nursing Process', Journal of Advanced Nursing, 3, 333-340

Baker, A.A. (1972) Annual Report of the Hospital Advisory Service (DHSS, London)

Barton, R. (1958) Institutional Neurosis (John Wright and Son, Bristol)

Bateson, G. (1972) Steps to an Ecology of Mind (Granada Publishing Limited, St Albans)

Beard, P.G. (1984) 'The Nursing Element in an Ideal Service', in Reed. J. and Loomis, G. (eds) Psychiatric Services in the Community - Developments and Innovations, pp. 114-120, (Croom Helm, London)

Beard, M., Enelow, C. and Owens, J. (1978) 'Activity Therapy: A Reconstructive Plan on Social Competence of Chronic Hospitalised Patients', Journal of Psychiatric Nursing and Mental Health Services, 16(2), 33-40

Blackham, G.J. and Silberman, A. (1975) Modification of Child and Adolescent Behavior, 2nd edn, (Wadsworth Publishing Company Inc., Belmont, California)

Butler, R. and Rosenthal, G. (1978) Behaviour and Rehabilitation, pp.165-188, (John Wright and Sons, London)

Butterworth, C.A. and Skidmore, D. (1981) Caring for the Mentally Ill in the Community (Croom Helm, London)

Caplan, G. (1964) Principles of Preventive Psychiatry (Basic Books, New York)

Carr, P.J. (1985) 'CPNA President's Evidence to the Social Services Committee of the House of Commons', in the Second Report from the Social Services Committee, p. xcviii, (HMSO, London)

Carr, P.J., Butterworth, C.A. and Hodges, B.E. (1980) Community Psychiatric Nursing (Churchill Livingstone, Edinburgh)

Carstairs, G.M. and Kennedy, P.F. (1978) 'Social Science in Relation to Psychiatry', in Forrest, A.D., Affleck, J.W. and Zealley, A.K. (eds) A Companion to Psychiatric Studies, pp. 13-29, (Churchill Livingstone, Edinburgh)

Chapman, C.M. (1974) 'Nursing Education - Curriculum Content', Queen's Nursing Journal, October

Clarke, A.M. and Clarke A.D.B. (eds) (1974) Mental Deficiency: The Changing Outlook, 3rd edn, (Methuen, London)

CMHNA (1985) 'Community Mental Handicap Nursing and Management - Roles and Functions' (Community Mental Handicap Nurses' Association, Bolton)

Conolly, J. (1973) 'The Psychiatric Nurse and the Adult Neurotic (The Psychiatric Nurse as Therapist, 5)' Nursing Times, 69 (39), 153-156

CPNA (1985a) The Clinical Nursing Responsibilities of the Community Psychiatric Nurse (Community Psychiatric Nurses Association, Bristol)

CPNA (1985b) The 1985 CPNA National Survey Update (Community

Psychiatric Nurses Association, Bristol)
CPNA/RCN (1982) The Way Forward: A Joint Statement on Mandatory Training for CPNs (CPNA/RCN, London)
Cunningham, C. and Sloper, P. (1978) Helping Your Handicapped Baby (Souvenir Press Limited, London)
Cutler, D. and Beigel, A. (1978) 'Church-based Community Activities for Chronic Patients', Journal of Hospital and Community Psychiatry, 29 (8), 497-501
Davies, T. and Reed, V. (1982) Education for Community Care: a taxonomic approach to the in-service needs of NHS residential workers with the mentally handicapped - a preliminary report. Department of Health Studies Occasional papers No. HS/3/82, Sheffield City Polytechnic
Davis, D.R. (1946) 'Neurotic Predisposition and the Disorganisation Observed in Experiments with the Cambridge Cockpit', Journal of Neurological Psychiatry, 9, 119-124
DHSS (1971) Better Services for the Mentally Handicapped, Cmnd 4683/71 (HMSO, London)
DHSS (1975) Better Services for the Mentally Ill, Cmnd 6233/75, (HMSO, London)
DHSS (1976) NDG Pamphlet No. 1, Planning Together (DHSS, London)
DHSS (1977a) NDG Pamphlet No. 2, Mentally Handicapped Children: A Plan For Action (DHSS, London)
DHSS (1977b) NDG Pamphlet No. 3, Helping Mentally Handicapped School Leavers (DHSS, London)
DHSS (1978a) Development Team for the Mentally Handicapped: First Report, 1976-1977 (HMSO, London)
DHSS (1978b) Helping Mentally Handicapped People in Hospital (DHSS, London)
DHSS (1980) Mental Handicap: Progress, Problems and Priorities (DHSS, London)
DHSS (1981) Standards of Nursing Care: The Nursing Process - A Systematic and Problem-solving Approach to Nursing Care. DHSS CNO(SNC) (81) 2, June, (DHSS, London)
Eccleston, D. (1978) 'Neuropharmacology', in Forrest, A.D., Affleck, J.W. and Zealley, A.K. (eds), A Companion to Psychiatric Studies, pp. 109-127 (Churchill Livingstone, Edinburgh)
Ekdawi, M.K. (1981) 'Counselling in Rehabilitation', in Wing, J.K. and Morris, B. (eds) Handbook of Psychiatric Rehabilitation Practice (Oxford University Press, Oxford)
Ellis, R. and Whittington, D. (1981) A Guide to Social Skills Training (Croom Helm, London)
Feinmann, J. (1985) 'An Experiment Paying Dividends', Health and Social Services Journal, 3 October, 1228-1229
General Nursing Council for England and Wales (1982) A New Syllabus for Nurses for the Mentally Subnormal (GNC, London)
Goldberg, D. and Hillier, V. (1978) 'A Scaled Version of the GHQ', Journal of Psychological Medicine, 9, 135-145

Goldberg, D. and Stanitis, M. (1977) 'The Enhancement of Self-esteem through the Communication Process in Group Therapy', Journal of Psychiatric Nursing and Mental Health Services, 15(12), 5-8

Grad, J. and Sainsbury, P. (1968) 'The Effects that Patients Have on their Families in a Community Care and a Control Psychiatric Service', British Journal of Psychiatry, 114, 265

Greene, J. (1968) 'The Psychiatric Nurse in the Community', International Journal of Nursing Studies, 5, 175-183

Hall, V. and Russell, O. (1982) 'The Community Mental Health Nurse: A New Professional Role', Journal of Advanced Nursing, 7 (1), 330-341

Haque, G. (1973) 'Psychosocial Nursing in the Community', Nursing Times, 69 (2), 51-53

Hayward, J. (1975) Information - A Prescription Against Pain (Royal College of Nursing, London)

Hewett, S. (1972) The Need for Long-term Care, Occasional Paper 3, Institute for Research into Mental Retardation (Butterworths, London)

Hodges, B.E. (1980) 'Emergence and Development of the Community Mental Handicap Nursing Team', in Carr, P.J., Butterworth, C.A. and Hodges, B.E. Community Psychiatric Nursing, pp.50-62 (Churchill Livingstone, Edinburgh)

Hodges, B.E. (1985) The Health Career Model (Harper and Row, London)

Hoenig, J. and Hamilton, M.W. (1969) The Desegregation of the Mentally Ill (Routledge and Kegan Paul, London)

Hunter, P. (1974) 'Community Psychiatric Nursing in Britain: A Historical Review', International Journal of Nursing Studies, 2(4), 223-233

Jasmin, S. and Trygstad, L. (1979) Behavioral Concepts and the Nursing Process (The C.V. Mosby Company, St Louis)

Jay Committee (1979) Committee of Enquiry into Mental Handicap Nursing and Care. Cmnd 7468 (HMSO, London)

Jeffree, D. and McConkey, R. (1976), Let Me Speak (Souvenir Press, London)

Jeffree, D., McConkey, R. and Hewson, S. (1977) Let Me Play (Souvenir Press, London)

Jones, E. (1980) 'Assisting the Families of the Mentally Handicapped' in Simon, G.B. (ed.) Modern Management of Mental Handicap (MTP Press, Lancaster)

Jones, K., Brown, J., Cunningham, W.J., Roberts, J. and Williams, P. (1975) Opening the Door: A Study of New Policies for the Mentally Handicapped (Routledge and Kegan Paul, London)

Karoly, P. and Steffen, J.J. (1980) Improving the Long-term Effects of Psychotherapy (Gardner Press Inc., New York)

Kiernan, C., Jordan, R. and Saunders, C. (1978) Starting Off (Souvenir Press, London)

Kratz, C.R. (1979) The Nursing Process (Baillière Tindall,

London)
Laing, R.D. (1960) The Divided Self (Penguin Books, Harmondsworth)
Laing, R.D. (1961) The Self and Others (Tavistock, London)
Lancaster, J. (1976) 'Activity Groups as Therapy', American Journal of Nursing, 76 (6), 947-949
Langrehr, A. (1974) 'Social Stimulation', American Journal of Nursing, 74 (7), 1300-1301
Leopoldt, H. and Hurn, R. (1973) 'Towards Integration', Nursing Mirror, 136 (22), 38-42
Leopoldt, H., Hopkins, H. and Overall, R. (1974) 'A Critical Review of Experimental Psychiatric Nurse Attachment Schemes in Oxford', Pratice Team, 39, 2-6
Leopoldt, H., Corea, S. and Robinson, J.R. (1975) 'Hospital-based Community Psychiatric Nursing in Psychogeriatric Care', Nursing Mirror, 141 (25), 54-56
Lewis, L. (1976) Planning Patient Care, 2nd edn (William C. Brown Company, Dubuque, Iowa)
Lonsdale, S., Flowers, J. and Saunders, E. (1980) Long-term Psychiatric Patients: A Study in Community Care (Personal Social Services Council, London)
Loomis, M. and Horsley, J. (1974) Interpersonal Change: A Behavioral Approach to Nursing Practice (McGraw-Hill, New York)
Manfreda, M. (1975) Psychiatric Nursing, 9th edn, pp. 277-285 (F.A. Davis Co, Philadelphia)
Marais, P.A. et al. (1976) 'Community Psychiatric Nursing: Alternative to Hospitalisation', Nursing Times, 72 (44), 1708-1717
Marks, I.M., Conolly, J. and Hallam, R.S. (1973) 'Psychiatric Nurse as Therapist', British Medical Journal, 3, 156-160
Mittler, P. et al. (1970) The Psychological Assessment of Mental and Physical Handicaps (Tavistock/Methuen, London)
Mohamed, N.A. (1986) Behavioural Outcomes of Systematic Bridging Therapy in Hospital - and Community-based Psychiatric Nursing Care, Department of Health Studies, unpublished PhD thesis, Sheffield City Polytechnic
Newson, E. and Hipgrave, A. (1982) Getting Through to Your Handicapped Child: A Handbook for Parents, Teachers and Carers (Cambridge University Press, Cambridge)
Parnell, J.W. (1978) Community Psychiatric Nurses: A Descriptive Study (Queen's Nursing Institute, London)
Penrose, L.S. (1949) The Biology of Mental Defect (Sidgwick and Jackson, London)
Priestley, D. (1979) 'Schizophrenia and the Family, Part II: Helping a Self-help Group', in Wing, J.K. and Olsen, R. (eds) Community Care for the Mentally Disabled (Oxford University Press, Oxford)
Pryor, C. (1974) Working with Parents: A Behavioural Approach, unpublished PhD thesis, Department of Psychology, University of Nottingham, Nottingham

Royal College of Nursing (1981) Towards Standards: Second Report of the RCN Working Committee on Standards of Nursing Care in England and Wales (RCN, London)
Remocker, A.J. and Storch, E.T. (1982) Actions Speak Louder (Churchill Livingstone, Edinburgh)
Sewell, G. (1982) Reshaping Remedial Education (Croom Helm, London)
Shepherd, G. (1984) Institutional Care and Rehabilitation (Longman, London)
Skidmore, D. (1985) 'More than Chalk and Talk', Community Outlook, September
Skidmore, D. and Friend, W. (1984) 'Muddling Through', Community Outlook, May
Sladden, S. (1979) Psychiatric Nursing in the Community: A Study of a Working Situation (Churchill Livingstone, Edinburgh)
Social Services Committee (1985) Community Care, with Special Reference to Adult Mentally Ill and Mentally Handicapped People. Second Report of the Social Services Committee of the House of Commons, Session 1984-1985 (HMSO, London)
Strong, P.G. and Sandland, E.T. (1974) 'Subnormality Nursing in the Community', Nursing Times, 7 March
Szasz, T. (1962) The Myth of Mental Illness (Secker and Warburg, London)
Tough, H., Tingerlee, P. and Elliot,P. (1980) 'Survey-attached Psychogeriatric Nurses: An Evaluation of Psychiatric Nurses in the Primary Care Team, Journal of the Royal College of General Practitioners, 30 (211), 85-89
Towell, D. and Harries, C. (1979) Innovation in Patient Care: An Action Research Study of Change in a Psychiatric Hospital (Croom Helm London)
Trower, P., Bryant, B. and Argyle, M. (1978) Social Skills and Mental Health, pp.70-102 (Methuen, London)
Vaughn, C.E. and Leff, J.P. (1976) 'The Influence of Family and Social Factors on the Course of Psychiatric Illness', British Journal of Psychiatry, 129, 125-138
Wing, J.K. and Creer, C. (1980) 'Schizophrenia at Home', in Rollin, H.R. (ed), Coping with Schizophrenia (Burnett Books for the National Schizophrenia Fellowship, London)
Yalom, D. (1975) The Theory and Practice of Group Psychotherapy, 2nd edn (Basic Books, New York)
Zeal, B. (1973) 'Psychiatry or People?', Nursing Times, 69 (15), 513-514

Chapter Seven

FAMILY PLACEMENT SCHEMES: CASE STUDY 1

Gina Armstrong

INTRODUCTION

During the past 20 years there has been an increasing awareness of the rights, needs and expectations of mentally handicapped people and their families. The move away from large-scale residential provision, the growth of pressure groups among parents and the voluntary services, and the development of the 'normalisation' principle, have all helped to create a shift away from providing services by group definition 'the elderly', 'mentally ill', 'mentally handicapped', and so on and towards a service based more on individual assessments and consumer needs. The history and philosophy underlying these changes can be found elsewhere in this book, and this chapter is concerned only with one small area of service - the provision of short-term care for handicapped children. This is only a minor element in the total spectrum of day, residential and community care, but the growth and development of short-term, family and respite care provides a model of how attempts are being made to put theory into practice.

THE DEVELOPMENT OF FAMILY PLACEMENT SCHEMES IN THE PAST TEN YEARS

During this time information was being more widely circulated about alternative types of care, and there was also a dramatic increase in the number of family placements for handicapped people. In 1975 Leeds and Somerset Social Services Departments began special short-term fostering schemes to provide regular holiday breaks for children with multiple handicaps. These schemes were set up under section 12 of the Health Services and Public Health Act 1968 (now section 21 and schedule 8 of the National Health Services Act 1977) which meant that the children did not have to be taken into care and the parents did not lose their rights as they would if they were fostered under the Chlidren's Acts.

The idea of providing care in ordinary family homes in the community rather than in separate residential institutions was adopted by other local authorities, hospitals and voluntary organisations such as the Church of England Children's Society, the Spastics Society and Dr Barnardo's. All the schemes differed somewhat in organisation, scale, type of care and range of clients, but they all had the same underlying aim which was to provide family care individually matched to the needs of the child and his/her family.

THE GROWTH OF RESPITE CARE IN SHEFFIELD

Before 1976 short-term care for mentally handicapped children in Sheffield was provided mainly by the Education Department and sometimes by hospitals. In 1976, however, the Area Health Authority (AHA) and Family and Community Services (F and CS) took over this service and both the amount and type of care changed.

Previously short-term, or 'respite care' as it came to be called, had tended to cover block periods of one or two weeks either to help in an emergency such as hospital admission of the mother, or to enable parents to take a holiday. In 1976 F and CS opened its first children's unit specifically designed to provide short-term care for the mentally handicapped and this was to prove instrumental in developing the idea of 'phased care' whereby families could have a more flexible and regular type of care covering weekends or one day each week. The AHA also provided a flexible system of care in a residential unit which was part of a new purpose-built complex incorporating a day care centre and assessment unit for handicapped children.

Between 1978 and 1981 the number of admissions to short-term care doubled, and although the average length of stay fell the number of people using the facilities increased dramatically. It was obvious that as more people were becoming aware of the availability of respite care, so the resources were being correspondingly stretched.

THE SHEFFIELD 'PARTNERSHIP WITH PARENTS' SCHEME

In Sheffield the pressure on existing short-term care facilities and the growing emphasis on community care indicated a need for some form of more locally based service which would extend the choice available to parents of handicapped children. Many parents were concerned to keep their children at home and out of long-term residential care, and it was considered that if a child could enjoy a reasonable quality of life in his own family he would benefit from substitute care in another family, rather than in an institution such as a hospital or children's home. In 1980 a pilot project was launched to explore the possibilities of working with parents and establishing 'partnerships' by matching specially recruited caregivers with families requesting respite care. Initially six carers were recruited and children were placed for one or two weeks during the holidays. The placements were largely successful and in August 1981 proposals were put forward to extend and consolidate the scheme.

At the same time a working party of the Joint Consultative Committee for Sheffield AHA and the Metropolitan District Council was preparing a report on the Strategic Planning of Services for the Mentally Handicapped. This stated that

> if mentally handicapped children and adults are to remain in the ordinary community by living in the homes of their parents or other relatives, it is essential that very much more be done than at present to provide these families with readily available, acceptable and nearby sources of relief.
>
> Short-term care should cover a wide spectrum of provision for short periods during shopping hours and evening relief to overnight, weekend and longer periods of planned cover, as well as emergency arrangements made necessary by illness or accident affecting the caring household.

This statement summarised the philosophy underlying the family placement scheme, and over the past four years it has tried to put the strategy into practice.

Administration

The scheme was set up under joint funding and for the

first 18 months, from April 1981 to October 1982, was run by the Senior Principal Assistant, Homefinding Unit. This Unit provides a citywide service responsible for placements ranging from adoption and long-term fostering for teenagers to respite care for the elderly, mentally ill and mentally and physically handicapped. In 1982 a full-time social worker was appointed to the scheme, and funding was made available for 30 children to receive six weeks of care each throughout the year (a total of 1260 bed-nights).

The scheme was set up under Section 21 and Schedule 8 of the NHS Act 1977 which meant that the children were not received into care, and parents neither lost their rights over them, nor were they liable to pay contributions. Carers were paid a special fee plus the boarding-out rate appropriate to the age of the child. The adminstrative procedure was kept as simple as possible to enable parents and carers to make arrangements between themselves regarding care, which often had to be both flexible and immediate.

The Partnership

From its small beginnings in 1980 the scheme has grown and developed in many ways and the following sections attempt to give some idea of the scope and type of provision available.

The scheme was called 'Partnership with Parents' because it was felt that any family placement would be very much a two-way working arrangement. Both the parents of the children and the families registered on the scheme are 'caring families' but, for simplicity's sake the parents are referred to as 'the families' and the people providing the short-term care are called 'the carers'. The central pivot of the whole partnership, however, rests on the child, and it is the children who are considered first.

The Children

When the scheme began its official description was 'for children with mental and multiple handicaps', and it was envisaged that the majority of children would attend either one of the three Sheffield schools for severely mentally handicapped children, or the school for physically handicapped children.

'Multiple' was defined as 'more than one' handicap rather than mental plus physical, and children with solely physical handicaps such as blindness, deafness, spina bifida or muscular dystrophy were accepted.

Between 1981 and 1985 approximately 200 children were referred to the scheme, all varying tremendously in age, type and degree of handicap, and the sort of care they needed. In April 1985 109 families were registered as using the scheme on a regular basis and a more detailed analysis was made of these children to monitor the development of the scheme and try to evaluate its usefulness for both families and carers. The figures used in Figures 7.1 and 7.2 thus refer to this group of 109 children, but some of the examples quoted are taken from other families who have used the scheme at some time during the past four years.

Figure 7.1: Age and Sex of the Children

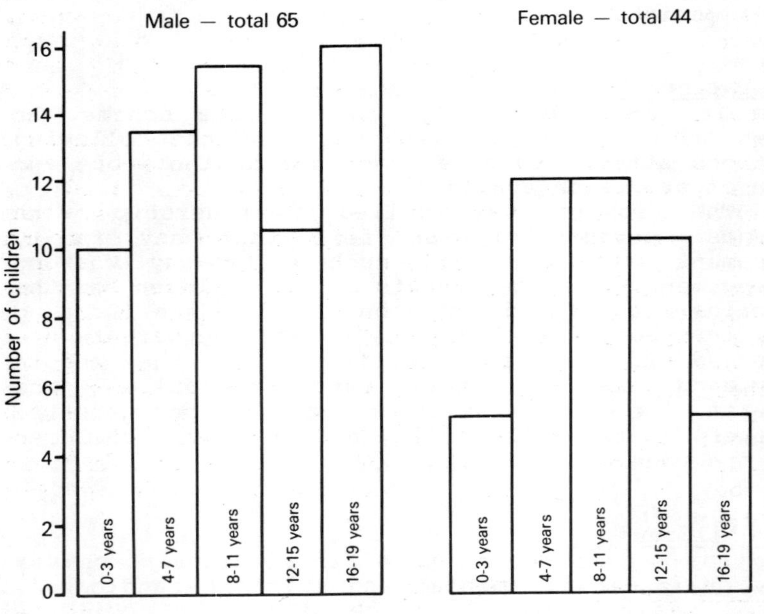

As can be seen from Figure 7.1 slightly more boys than girls used the scheme, and this is also the case in admissions to other types of short-term care in Sheffield (Short Term Care, 1975-83, Case Register, Sheffield AHA). In the age group 16-19 years there are significantly more men than women requiring family placements. This highlights the difficulties faced by some parents as their sons become physically larger and emotionally more demanding and also reflects the lack of appropriate placements for older boys. An example of this was Andy, a 17-year-old mentally handicapped boy who was cared for occasionally by his grandmother when he was small, but as he developed she found it increasingly difficult to cope with his outbursts of temper. His mother was reluctant to use residential care, but felt he needed someone younger and stronger than his grandmother.

At the other end of the spectrum, it was assumed when the scheme began that children under 5 years would not require placements. As the scheme widened to incorporate daycare and babysitting placements, however, parents with children only one or two years old began to make enquiries. Parents of newly born handicapped babies often wish to hear about services which they may not use at once, but will consider for when the child is older. Although the scheme originally only took children under the age of 19 years it was felt by all those involved, children, parents, carers and social workers, that it was wholly wrong to cut short a service for which there was no suitable alternative simply because of an age limit. 'John' a severely physically handicapped young man was already 18 when the scheme began. A family living nearby cared for him for a few hours two evenings each week. Both John and his widowed mother enjoyed this contact and wanted it to continue when he reached 19. Using this as a test case a request was made to extend the scheme to older children who had established placements, and in October 1984 a parallel scheme was set up for people of all ages.

Type and Degree of Handicap

Every child using the scheme is very much an individual and the range of abilities and behaviour is extremely wide. The chart below thus gives only a very general breakdown of the number of children who are mentally as opposed to physically handicapped, have multiple problems or behavioural difficulties.

Children with Down's syndrome form the largest single identifiable group of mentally handicapped children and are shown separately in Figure 7.2.

Figure 7.2: Type and Degree of Handicap

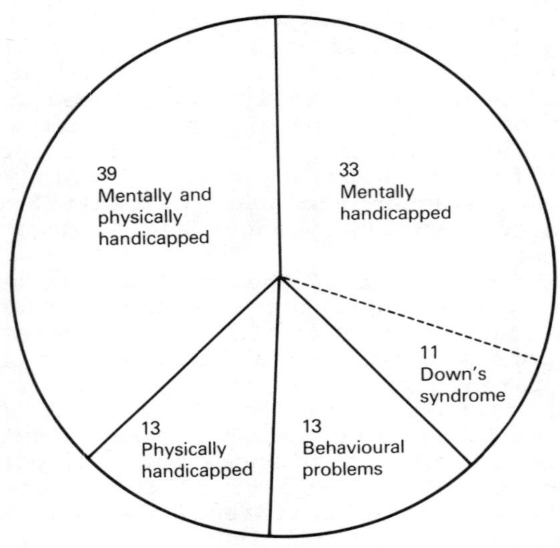

It can be seen that 76 per cent of the children have some degree of mental handicap, and almost half of these have an additional physical handicap. Many are unable to walk or can only manage a few steps unaided. Approximately a third are doubly incontinent and many more are enuretic at night. Some suffer from additional problems such as epilepsy, heart disease, deafness or blindness, and over a third have little or no speech.

It was envisaged that there could be problems placing profoundly mentally and physically handicapped children. Parents would be understandably reluctant to trust an inexperienced family unfamiliar with their child and few carers would have the nursing skills and facilities required, unlike hospitals and residential homes which are equipped and staffed to cope with bathing, feeding and toileting problems.

However, the majority of children are cared for

in ordinary homes, often with stairs and narrow doorways, and their parents have devised ways of caring which they can pass on to carers. 'Alison' is ten and apart from some movement in her left arm cannot control any part of her body. She needs to be washed, fed and changed and the alternating rigidity and floppiness of her muscles make all these tasks difficult. She has no speech, very little vision and suffers constant fits. When she first joined the scheme the carers spent some time at her home learning how to handle her, and also visited the hospital and physiotherapy department for advice. There is regular and frequent communication between the two families and any new problem or development is discussed together. Despite her handicap Alison is a happy, loving child who responds to affection and the smallest improvement is shared and greeted with delight by both parents and carers.

Children who are solely physically handicapped have mainly spina bifida, cerebral palsy or muscular dystrophy. While it is not difficult to place these children while they are young and relatively small, problems can arise as they become older. Teenagers who have learned to bath and toilet themselves in specially adapted bathrooms at home do not want to take the retrograde step of being carried in a home where there are stairs or no room to turn a wheelchair.

The scheme can provide some help to carers regarding bath aids, rails, special beds, etc., but for some children the problem of finding a suitable placement highlights the more general problem faced by all handicapped people of coping in a society geared to non-handicapped living.

In a few cases where the children have been so disabled that it has not been possible to place them in someone else's home, carers have been able to stay in the family home. One of the first placements on the scheme was when a young married couple stayed in the specially designed bungalow of three handicapped children for two weeks.

The third very general category of children which have 'behaviour' problems, covers hyperactivity, autism or emotional disturbances in addition to learning difficulties. 'Pam' is a seven-year-old severely autistic child. She has no speech and is subject to violent irrational outbursts when she will bite and scratch herself or bang her head against the wall until it bleeds. On one occasion she accidently broke her carer's nose and because of her inability to appreciate any sort of danger she cannot be left unsupervised for any length of time.

Some of the behaviour difficulties can be linked to medical conditions, such as the after-effects of meningitis or syndromes such as Prader-Willi, but for many children there is no known cause and problems can range from minor obsessive behaviour to major physical and verbal aggression.

The range of handicap is also reflected in the type of daycare the children receive. As previously stated, it was envisaged that referrals would come from the four main schools in the city specifically designed for handicapped children. Of the 109 children currently using the scheme, however, only half (53 children) attended these schools. Of the remainder 40 received a wide range of services including hospitals, adult training centres, day nurseries and special units within mainstream schools, and 14 did not attend any form of daycare.

'Mental and multiple' handicap has thus been fairly liberally interpreted, and a more appropriate description would be 'children with special needs'. Families are accepted on the scheme on the basis of individual need and no one would be refused because the child either had too many problems or was insufficiently handicapped.

It is important to note that the need for respite care does not vary in direct proportion to the child's degree of disability. A profoundly mentally and physically handicapped child may be seen by both parents and carers as less demanding than a more able but very lively child with Down's syndrome, and the strain of caring for a deaf three-year-old can be as taxing as looking after an older mentally handicapped child.

The two types of handicapped children for whom it has proved most difficult to find placements are the extremely hyperactive, and older children who have severe mobility or behaviour problems. Finding the right placement however does not depend solely, or even primarily, on the child's disabilities. There are many other factors to take into consideration, of which the most important one is matching the families' needs with what the carers are able to offer.

The Carers

Just as the children differ greatly in their needs, abilities, ages and home backgrounds - so the caregivers vary both in themselves and in what they can offer. The first two caregivers offered their services in 1980 in response to a local radio talk on the proposed scheme. Since then the need for carers has spread mainly by word of mouth, and in 1985 a total of 49 carers were registered and matched with at least one family. Some caregivers have joined the scheme and left after a year or two, but the majority, including the two original ones, have remained faithful to the scheme and their families for five years.

Recruitment

The scheme was advertised in the local press, on radio, and in talks given to interested groups of parents and professionals including the Society for Mentally Handicapped Children, schools, training centres and hospitals. The first carers tended to be people who had had some experience of handicap either in their family or through work, but as the scheme became more widely known people who were quite new to the field of handicap expressed interest. Occasionally advertisements are used for a specific child, but there is a constant stream of enquiries from people who have heard about the scheme from others already involved. All the enquirers are prompted by a genuine interest and desire to help, but less than half complete the assessment and training procedure and are registered as carers on the scheme.

Assessment

Although the children are not received into care, and the carers are neither registered, nor acting as foster parents, applications are processed in the same way as fostering applications regarding references and interviews.

Families have proved to be extremely trusting of anyone recommeded by the social services, and the local authority has a clear responsibility to ensure that all necessary checks have been made regarding the health, medical, social, educational and police records of would-be carers. This does not mean that someone who is not 100 per cent fit or has been fined for a traffic offence would be refused consideration, but it does mean carers have to be honest about their strengths and weaknesses and realise their responsibility in caring for someone else's child. The parents of a handicapped child who were interested in becoming carers were delighted when they were asked for references as 'we wouldn't want our child to go to someone who hadn't been properly checked'.

Training

The assessment and training as a whole aims to help applicants view the scheme not in terms of 'caring for the handicapped' but rather with regard to the principles of child care and the effect on all those involved of caring for someone in their own home.

The training sessions, which are now an integral part of the assessment, have developed over the past three years. They consist of one evening a week for four weeks and have been described by one carer as 'a crash course in putting people off the whole idea!'

Since it would be impossible to cover all aspects of care or problems which might arise, the course does not even try to teach people how to deal with every single situation. Instead it encourages potential carers to use their own knowledge and experience to consider what is involved from the child and his/her parents' point of view. Through films, role-plays, decision mazes and small group discussions, the applicants are able to listen to other people's ideas and try to formulate their own. Often many people in the groups have experiences that they can use to illustrate why they would deal with a problem in one particular way, and sometimes a fresh outside view can give a new slant to an old problem.

Some carers may not have fully considered the problems posed by an incontinent child, the effect on their own children, or how far a stranger in their home will upset their way of life. During the course people gain a clearer idea of what they can offer, or may at this stage decide to drop out altogether. On completion of the course, the social worker responsible prepares a report on the carers. This covers the carers' reasons for applying, details of all family members and their views, the family's strengths and weaknesses, practical details of housing and the age and type of child they feel able to care for. This report, plus all their references are presented to a panel consisting of social workers and managers involved in family and residential care. The majority of carers who reach the panel are accepted, but in a few cases where there may be doubts as to the carers' capabilities approval can be given for a short-term trial placement with a further review at the next panel.

The Range of Carers

The above procedure is the same for all applicants, but there all similarity ends. When asked 'what sort of people become carers', there is no single definition. The 49 carers currently registered range from young single people in their early 20s to retired couples in their 60s. Table 7.1 gives some idea of the variety of carers, but even within categories the families differ greatly from one another.

Table 7.1: Age of Carers

Years	18-34	35-49	50+
Number of carers	14	26	9

NB: Where a married couple were of widely differing ages the average of their combined age was taken.

Since the registration process closely parallels that of fostering, applications are not accepted from people less than 18 years of age. Young people can offer a great deal in terms of energy and enthusiasm, but their situation often changes quite rapidly and they may find it difficult to combine caregiving with the early years of marriage, particularly if they wish to have a family of their own.

Ann and Dave were a young couple who had a lot of experience of working with handicapped people and were registered on the scheme early in 1981. They provided excellent care for two children and hoped to continue working with the families after they had children of their own. However, the wife became pregnant with twins and it proved impossible to combine caring with the needs of their babies.

Sue and Jim, another young couple, were quite happy to continue providing respite care after the birth of their first child, but the mother of the handicapped boy who had visited them previously was reluctant to send him as she felt she was 'putting on the carers' and 'they would be too busy to look after him'.

Some couples however have succesfully combined caring with their own families, and a baby in the home can be added attraction for the child who is coming to stay.

The majority of carers tend to be people aged between 35 and 49 years with well-established jobs and families. There are several couples in their 60s, however, who have a great deal of life experience to offer, and provided that families are carefully matched they have proved invaluable to the scheme. Older people have to consider carefully the implications of becoming involved with a family who may require help for several years during which time the child will become larger heavier and possibly more demanding as they themselves are becoming more frail.

Family Composition

Out of all the families 41 are couples, the remaining eight being either unmarried, widowed or divorced. Five of the families (four couples and one single person) have no children of their own, 33 (32 couples and one single person) have children living at home with them, and the remaining 12 (nine couples and three single people) have children living away.

Although the majority of carers are married couples, a significant number of people who live alone have proved excellent carers. Mrs J is a widow with a severely handicapped long-term foster child, and in addition provides respite care for two young handicapped children on alternate weekends and during school holidays. She is an extremely practical and organised lady who thoroughly enjoys looking after children, and now that her own family have grown up and married she can devote all her time and energy to the young children in her care.

The largest group of carers, who have children of their own still living at home, combine their caring and parenting roles in different ways according to the ages of their children. Table 7.2 below shows the ages and total number of children living with parents and thus involved in the scheme.

Table 7.2: Age Distribution of Carers Children Living at Home

Years	0-5	6-10	11-15	16+
Children	17	12	15	16

Some families find their own children a great help in caregiving. Mr and Mrs T have three children aged 12, 15 and 18, all of whom enjoy having different children to stay and like the variety of sharing their bedrooms with a six-year-old one week and a 14-year-old the next.

Other families find that their children, especially as they become teenagers, are not really interested in helping on a practical basis, but will offer moral support to their parents. Where there are young children in the family they often play on an equal basis with the children who come to stay, and parents feel there is a real benefit for both parties in teaching children of different abilities to share with and understand each other. Mrs G, when first applying to the scheme, expressed the view that 'it is only through children learning about handicap when they are young that we can hope to change society's attitude'.

In some families where the children are older and living away from home, they are concerned that their parents are taking on too much, and should have a rest from the rigours of child care. Mrs B was told by her married daughter that she was 'crazy' joining the scheme and Mrs D said 'all my family think I'm mad'. Other parents have to make a special effort to show they are not neglecting their own children or grandchildren.

The Carers' Experience of Handicapped People

The original carers tended to be people with some knowledge of handicapped people, and it has remained true that the majority of carers have some expertise as parents, teachers, doctors or nurses, as shown in Table 7.3 below.

Table 7.3: Carers' Experience

	Teacher				
Family Member	Handi-cap	Main-stream	Doctor/ Nurse	Social services employee with handicap	Foster parent/ child-minder
7	7	4	12	10	11

Parents and brothers and sisters of handicapped children knew at first hand how beneficial respite care can be, and they saw how they could use their own expertise to help people in a similar position to themselves. Some families were at first users of the scheme and went on to become carers. Mr and Mrs C were among the first families to place their 12-year-old Down's syndrome son with carers for a week's holiday. When he was 15 they enquired about becoming carers themselves and the fact that they had a handicapped child and used the scheme themselves proved a great encouragement to other parents who were nervous of letting their child go to someone else. Mrs C's personal knowledge of handicap and her familiarity with the schools and facilities in Sheffield has enabled her to give support and advice to young parents, and empathise with their fears and worries about the future.

Other carers are parents whose handicapped children have died, and who feel that their experience can be used to help others. These parents often feel that they would have appreciated help and can now offer it to others.

Carers who are working as teachers or nurses of handicapped people often see at first hand the stresses on families. Mrs D, a teacher in a special school, became concerned about the elderly parents of a teenage child and enquired about the possibility of offering occasional overnight stays to give the child a change of scene, and the parents a good night's sleep. They were registered as carers initially for this particular child, but went on to help many other families.

The fact that carers have some experience, and in particular medical training, can be very reassuring to parents whose children may be prone to illness or have chronic congenital conditions such as spina bifida, epilepsy or heart disease. Mr and Mrs E have a severely handicapped little girl who suffers violent convulsions. She had received some respite care in hospital, but it was felt a family placement might be more appropriate. The parents were understandably reluctant to consider anyone who would be unsure about dealing with their daughter's fits, but were willing to consider a couple where the wife was an experienced children's nurse.

Many carers are also involved with the social services either as employees working in residential or daycare with handicapped children and adults, or as foster parents/childminders. Care assistance in hostels and instructors in adult training centres are in a similar position to nurses and teachers as regards helping parents to care for their children.

Foster parents have sometimes become interested in the scheme through having a handicapped child placed with them; in other cases they have felt after several years of 'ordinary' fostering that they were ready to undertake a new challenge.

Combining fostering and respite care can be problematic but given good communication and flexibility it has worked well in several instances. Mr and Mrs S are short-term foster parents of many years standing who felt they would like to do something for a handicapped child. They were introduced to a ten-year-old multiply handicapped girl whose parents requested occasional weekends, which they could manage in addition to fostering. Gradually they met other families who wanted daycare or help in the holidays, and with careful planning they devised a timetable to accommodate all the referrals while continuing to foster.

Although there is a wealth of experience among the carers, as the scheme has grown people with no previous knowledge of handicap have become interested and discovered the problems and rewards of caring. Mr and Mrs W have seven grown-up children of their own, and felt that once they retired they had time to help other people in some way. Although they had no specific knowledge of handicap, their experience as parents had given them a good understanding of the needs of children and they were prepared to 'try anything once'.

It can be seen that there is no 'blueprint' for the 'ideal carer' - what is perfect for one family may be totally wrong for another. A lot of emphasis has been given to the needs of the children and the abilities of the carers - but the most important aspect of any placement is how successfully it meets the overall needs of the families concerned.

THE NEED FOR CARE

To return to the strategic plan quoted at the beginning of this chapter (p.181), it defined short-term care as a 'wide spectrum of provision' covering 'short periods during shopping hours and evening relief, overnight, weekend and longer periods of planned cover as well as emergency arrangements made necessary by illness or accident'. It also had to be 'available, acceptable and nearby'. To establish a scheme which would offer such a diversity of care required an open and flexible approach by families, carers and social workers, and could only be achieved over a period of time. The pilot scheme placed children for one or two weeks during the holidays. Once this type of care was established, weekend and regular placed care were introduced. Babysitting, daycare, occasional overnight and emergency placements developed as the need arose. Figures 7.3 and 7.4 below show the increase in care over the past four years and how demand varies at different times of the year.

It can be seen that while overnight stays are the most popular form of care, day care has shown a

Figure 7.3: Overnight Stays

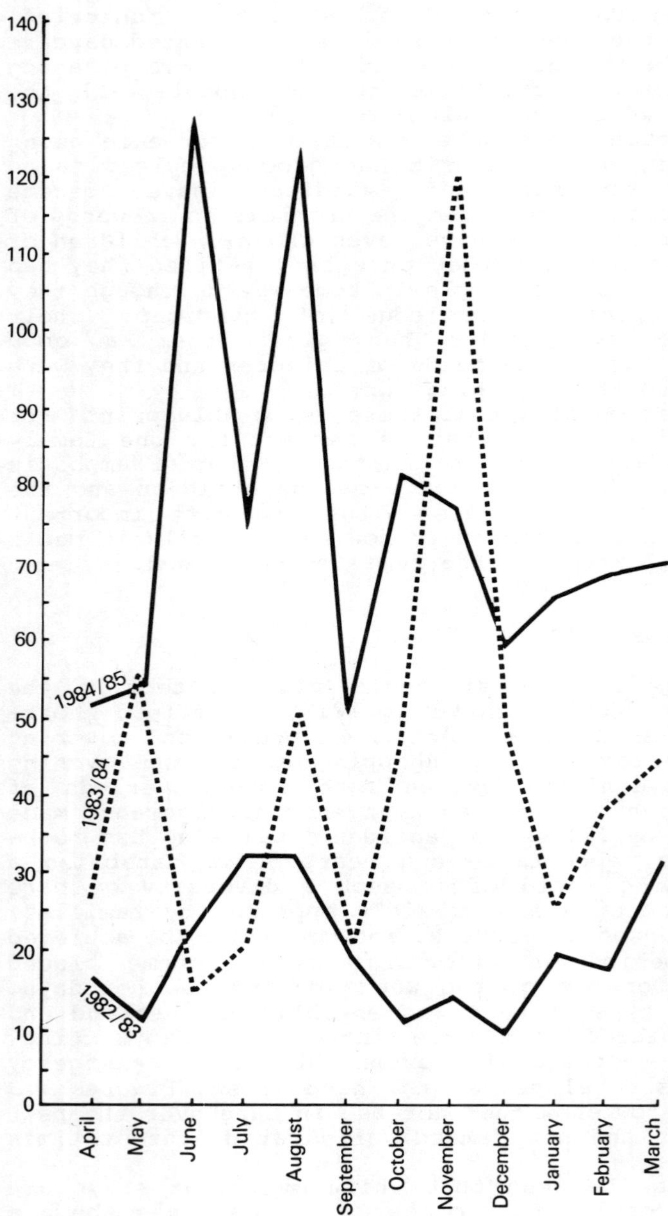

Figure 7.4: Daycare (Including Babysitting)

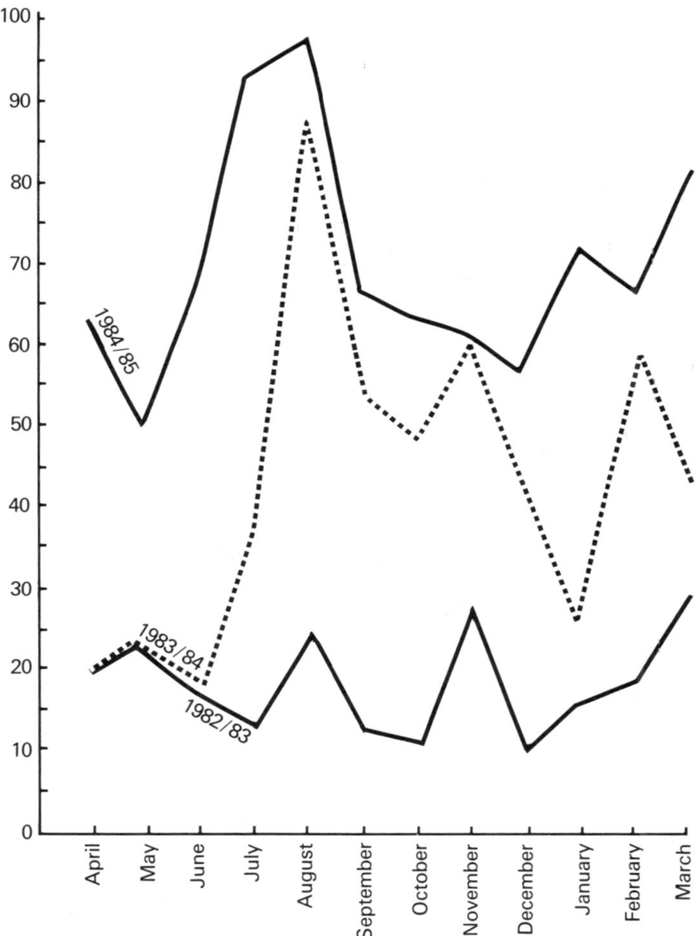

steady increase and remains a fairly constant demand throughout the year.

Parents of very young preschool children, who feel unhappy about the child spending a night away from home, appreciate a regular break of a few hours one day a week, and often spend this time taking their children out, or doing jobs which are difficult with a handicapped child.

Daycare is also used as a method of gradually introducing a child to carers either with a view to a longer overnight stay when he/she is older, or against the possibility of an emergency placement. Parents can gain reassurance from the knowledge that the child will be staying with a familiar carer and the carers will have gained confidence in their ability to look after the child.

Some families use overnight stays on a regular basis throughout the year, but demand increases sharply at holiday times.

All the carers on the scheme can offer overnight, daycare or babysitting, but some are more flexible than others. Mr and Mrs A both have full time jobs and three young children of their own. They initially offered to provide daycare to see how this fitted in with their own commitments, and were introduced to a little boy who visited them on a regular basis one day a week after school for tea. After several months both families felt ready for an overnight stay, and because the carers felt happy in what they were doing, they decided not to take any more children, but to concentrate their energies on this one placement. Mr and Mrs B on the other hand began with one family and as their confidence increased were gradually introduced to others who required different sorts of care. They currently have one little boy on a regular basis alternate weekends, a 14-year-old girl one weekend a month, a 16-year-old boy for two weeks' holiday each year, a ten-year-old one evening a week and an 11-year-old girl whenever her mother has a driving lesson. Organising these caregiving sessions has to be done very carefully to ensure that every family receives the service they need without the carers becoming too over worked. The number of children each family is linked with is shown in Table 7.4 below.

Table 7.4: Number of Children Cared For

Children	1	2	3	4	5+
Carer	15	15	10	6	2

Each family is allowed approximately six weeks of care per year, to be apportioned as they and the carers wish. Some only use the scheme very occasionally such as three or four evenings babysitting during the whole year. Others request one night per week plus occasional weekends and holidays. If a family requires more than six weeks, as happened in one case where a mother was taken into hospital for two months, this can usually be arranged. Once two families are linked, they can decide between themselves how they would like the care to be arranged. How far this develops into a genuine partnership depends to a large extent on how successfully the families are matched.

MATCHING

In considering the needs and means of both carers and families there are many factors to be considered, including where the families live, the age and handicap of the child, the sort of care required and both families' background, ideas and beliefs. Matching for all aspects is not always possible, but attempts are made to ensure that care is available, accessible and nearby.

Geographical Matching

Carers on the scheme come from all over the city, and six live outside the city boundary. Families also come from a very wide area, and distance between the two homes can be a psychological as well as a physical problem.

Parents do not usually want the carer to live too close to home as this might confuse the child if, for example, he was out shopping with the carers and met his parents. However it is equally important that parents have quick and easy access to the carers in case of an emergency, and carers can gain confidence from the knowledge that parents are nearby if the child is ill or homesick.

Babysitting and daycare are simplified if families live fairly close together, and parents feel happier about asking for a few hours' help if they know the carer does not have far to travel. Problems can arise over transport when neither family has access to a car (especially as some of the children find travelling on public transport very difficult). The special schools have been extremely helpful in taking and collecting on their transport, but they cannot operate outside the city or carry children not attending their schools.

Having said this, some placements work extremely well even if the two families are at opposite ends of the city, providing that in all other respects the families are well-matched.

Family Background and Composition

Some families express a preference for carers 'like us', meaning from similar backgrounds and with the same outlook in life. In terms of race, religion, occupation, housing and education, both carers and families cover a wide spectrum, and if two families have similar backgrounds this can help initially in getting to know each other. However, these factors are not necessarily a good guide to the type of care available, and the families' attitude to children and handicap in general is more important than income or type of housing.

Families and children are often fairly specific about the sort of carer they feel would be most appropriate. Mrs G's son, a lively 14-year-old wanted a carer with 'other teenagers' who enjoyed outdoor activities and sports. Mrs R was concerned that her very dependent six-year-old daughter did not go to a carer with young children as she felt it would not be fair to them. The reasons for care and the child's own family composition also determine the sort of care required. A single parent mother with a boisterous teenage son may request a young couple or single man who would provide some alternative adult company. An only child may benefit from the company of others and enjoy playing with the carers' children, and a child from a large family could gain from the individual attention of an older couple whose children had grown up and left home. The carers themselves may have definite ideas about what sort of child would be happiest with their family, and consideration should be given to the needs of everyone involved. Age, sex, type of handicap all have to be thought about carefully - but the most important feature in matching is that both family and carer agree on the care of the child and have confidence in each other.

THE FEARS AND REWARDS OF SHARED CARE

Parents will feel nervous about leaving their children, and need to be sure that the carers are both able and willing to cope in an emergency. Handicapped children are sometimes subject to unkind or thoughtless comments, and their families may be sensitive to criticism.

Children themselves are very aware of other people, and the most profoundly handicapped child will know if he is being looked after by someone who really does care about him. Richard has no speech, movement or sight, but his face lights up at the sound of his carer's voice and his mother speaks with real pride of how much his carers enjoy his company. To know that your child is lovable and loved is a great boost to parents who may have seen their child treated with fear and suspicion. The fact that your child's company is not merely acceptable, but genuinely wanted, can help overcome parents' reluctance to accept care.

Parents can also feel guilty about imposing on other people. Most families with a handicapped member have evolved their own methods of coping and feel that the child is their responsibility. They do not like to feel that they are 'putting people out' or 'causing any trouble' and they need reassurance often over quite a long period.

Parents may see using caregivers as a reflection of their own abilities and an indication that they have difficulty in looking after their child. When this happens they need to be helped to understand that shared care is not a replacement of what they are doing, but an additional resource to help them to care. They may fear that the caregivers will be 'better' than them in some way, and that their handling of the child may be criticised. Mrs O, whose hyperactive daughter has kept her awake at night for years, said she was secretly relieved when the carers returned her child after a weekend stay and reported 'she's kept us up all night, how do you cope with her?' As Mrs O said 'if she had slept all night for them I would have wondered where I was going wrong'. Carers need to strike a balance between reassuring parents they are happy with the child, and yet not give the impression that they are miraculously going to resolve all the problems parents have been struggling with for years.

Relatives of the child may feel that asking for help from a caregiver is a criticism or rejection of the help they often give the family. They also need to be reassured that carers are an addition to the network of support, not a replacement.

Carers are also nervous of how they will cope, and need advice from the parents on what to do if the child is homesick, unhappy or ill. Often the children are unable to articulate their needs and carers may be at a loss to understand what is wrong. Familiarity with the child over several visits can help overcome this, and as the two families get to know each other they will feel more at ease about discussing problems and finding mutual solutions.

Carers can also worry about how a handicapped child will affect their own family, whether friends and neighbours will raise any objections, or whether their own children will resent the visitor. In the majority of cases the children have to quote Mrs B 'fitted like an old shoe'. Others describe children as being 'one of the family' and 'like our own'. Friends and neighbours have often proved to be supportive, and as their knowledge of handicap has increased, so has their understanding. All the carers felt that their children had gained something. Mrs T felt that her daughter's involvement had not only benefited her, but had also influenced her friends and made them more positive towards handicapped people.

There are obviously rewards for the carers both in terms of pleasure to be gained from the children, and self-fulfilment in doing a useful job. The main aim of the scheme however is to provide a service to families and their children, and how far this has been successful can only be measured by whether parents continue to ask for the service. All the indications are that families are coming back for more care, and that as knowledge of the scheme spreads demand will continue to rise. Mrs L who has used the same carer one night a week, every week for over two years, summed up the feelings of many parents when she said 'it's such a relief just to know someone is there.

Not every family wants or needs a regular carer. Some want help in an emergency, others may view the scheme as a last resort if all else fails. There are over 1200 registered mentally handicapped children in Sheffield, and many more with physical handicaps or behavioural problems. Many of these will never request help outside of their own circle of friends and relatives, but for all those who do, the ultimate aim of the scheme must be to provide a carer for every child.

REFERENCE

Short-term Care (1975-83) (Sheffield Area Health

Authority Case Register)

Chapter Eight

FAMILY PLACEMENT SCHEMES: CASE STUDY 2

Malcolm May

INTRODUCTION

The past few years have seen a healthy development of short-term fostering schemes for mentally handicapped children. Such schemes are given various titles including Family Placement Schemes, Respite Care and Give Mum a Break. All aid to provide regular or occasional short-term care for mentally handicapped children or adults in the homes of foster carers or substitute families. One such scheme in Sheffield is described in Chapter 7.

The social services departments of Leeds City Council and Somerset County Council pioneered this idea almost simultaneously about eight years ago and since then many similar projects have been developed throughout the country, mainly by local authorities. The provision of joint funding has greatly enhanced this development.

Most would agree that short-term fostering schemes have been one of the more exciting developments in the past few years in the field of mental handicap and a substantial number of children have benefited enormously from such a service. However, one gets the occasional feeling that in the almost 'evangelical' fervour to promote such schemes, many agencies have tended to forget some of the potential problems which might arise when a child is regularly removed from home. Perhaps this particular service is now sufficiently mature to bear examination with an occasional critical eye and this chapter attempts to do this. Most of the new developments in the field of social care have undergone this period of critical analysis including such services as intermediate treatment, group homes for mentally disordered people and core and cluster schemes. Maureen Oswin in her recent book, <u>They Keep</u>

Going Away, takes a very objective view of a whole range of short-term care schemes for mentally handicapped children.

The benefits of short-term care in a substitute family setting are obvious and have been recounted on numerous occasions in the past few years: the child's uniqueness is retained, it is non-institutional and 'domestic' in nature; it enables such a service to be developed locally; the child and family have a realistic opportunity to develop a personal relationship with the carer; it is more flexible and cheaper than most forms of residential care.

BACKGROUND TO FAMILY PLACEMENT SCHEMES

It is interesting to note that until seven to ten years ago the vast majority of local authorities had access to only a few short-term places in homes administered by voluntary organisations, or a handful of places in their own residential homes and some short-term places in hospital for mentally handicapped people. This was pitiful. There was an obvious demand for more short-term care provision, particularly in the holiday period, but the resources were clearly inadequate or, in the case of hospital care, unacceptable to most parents. Because the level of provision was so poor, most parents had either never considered requesting short-term care or had simply given up asking in sheer desperation. At a recent seminar, one parent graphically stated 'there was no point in asking because there was nothing available'. Because of this, the evidence of need for more short-term care provision was kept artificially low and the full extent of the real demand never emerged. An additional factor influencing this rather distorted picture was the considerable number of parents who were never given the opportunity to 'let go' of their child and trust someone else to care for him or her. Such a parent recently stated

> I knew that I needed a break every now and again - I was getting to breaking point - but nobody was around to help me take the first step. Ten years ago there was no point in even thinking about it because there were no places available. When the family placement scheme started, it was offered to me but, again, nobody seemed to have the time to help me to hand over my child to somebody else and I didn't take up the offer. It was only when I talked to some parents using the

scheme that I finally took the plunge.

There is a vigorous grapevine amongst many parents of handicapped children, and the most effective form of publicity for short-term fostering schemes has been through this network of social links. Naturally, some parents were, and still are, reluctant to hand their children over to a 'non-expert' as they see it. It is important, therefore, that other forms of short-term care are also offered in the traditional residential setting, preferable in small houses.

It was clear then that, ten years ago, nobody knew the full extent of the demand for short-term care and this made the task of 'selling' the idea to the local authority a rather difficult task. Naturally local authorities tend to respond more sympathetically to overt evidence of need. For example, with a considerable waiting list for places in homes for elderly people, one builds more homes. Faced with an articulate demand for more long-term places for mentally handicapped adults, additional homes are built. But such evidence for short-term care for mentally handicapped children was never really clear. It was kept artificially low by the number of factors including those mentioned earlier. Things are different now. Most local authorities readily acknowledge the demand for more short-term care places as a result of increasing pressure from parents and professionals within the local authority or from the evidence for such a service manifested in other parts of the country. It is much easier to establish projects when other agencies have revealed the need and paved the way.

For the first time the writer can recall the department of social services had to sell the rather unconventional idea of a family placement scheme to parents, professionals and voluntary organisations. Initially, there were quite substantial pockets of resistance to the idea, particularly from a number of voluntary organisations and parents. Parents and local authorities feel safe with 'more of the same' developments, and this was even more apparent ten years ago. 'Hostels seem to work so we shall build more hostels' was the tempting philosophy. Leeds demonstrated a healthy willingness to pioneer this idea and has reaped the benefits of this.

The widespread developments of short-term fostering schemes has created an increasing number of parents in many parts of the country who have acquired quite sophisticated expectations. One of these is that short-term care should be reasonably available outside a hospital or hostel setting, and many local authorities are now having to cope with this additional and quite substantial demand.

PROBLEMS

But what sort of problems can arise?

There are times when frequent short-term fostering can cover up deepseated problems within the family. On occasions, an inability to cope or the existence of strong parental rejecting attitudes may be around but not detected or dealt with by the support worker on the assumption that short-term care is meeting all the needs of the family in their task of rearing a mentally handicapped child. Likewise, the parents may feel that they should be able to cope with regular breaks and this may inhibit the request for additional help. On one occasion, a decision to receive a child into care was deferred fairly regularly until a major crisis arose. One wonders if regular short-term care was not being provided, whether this matter would have been dealt with much earlier and difficult but important decisions taken. Similar problems arise in the field of long-term residential care for many client groups including mentally handicapped people. Much has been written about the apparent abandonment of the problem of the client once he has been received into residential care. Occasionally, the same dynamics seem to take place when short-term care is provided.

Short-term fostering as a solution may be interpreted as a general assumption that the child is the major problem, and if he is removed from the home occasionally then things will improve. Regular respite care may perpetuate this assumption and mask the need for the family or support worker to examine relationships in a different light rather than using the child as a scapegoat. It seems to be a common assumption that mentally handicapped children are a perpetual burden to parents who need frequent breaks from the seemingly eternal task of rearing such a child.

Sometimes, the support worker may wish to establish some immediate credibility with the newly referred family and succumb to the temptation to offer short-term fostering as a 'gift' without first assessing the needs more carefully. This reflects the difficulties which support workers may experience in trying to establish the role with a family, particularly when there are no major presenting problems at the time of the referral. Offers of short-term fostering or such services as aids and adaptations can often enable the worker to be seen as a useful person right from the start.

On the whole, places on short-term fostering schemes seem to be more readily available than residential short-term care (this is one of the obvious benefits of such schemes). Referrals for this service often request quite frequent periods such as one week in five and more. It occasionally begs the question whether this is absolutely necessary in many cases. There is some concern at times that this frequency of care is regarded as the norm and a pattern of respite care is established which does not always reflect the real needs of the family and their child. It is important that this issue is not overplayed, but it behoves the support worker to be at least aware of this temptation.

The problem of homesickness is another issue which does not seem to have been considered very carefully. It is significant that when a non-handicapped child is admitted to hospital, attempts are made to encourage one of the parents to maintain daily contact with their child. Indeed, many hospitals have developed sleeping rooms for parents. It may be an interesting reflection of our different attitudes that we arrange for mentally handicapped children to be removed from home regularly without giving much thought to his needs and response to separation. However, short-term fostering schemes are much more successful than residential care in dealing with the problems of homesickness and separation.

The needs of the carers can also be forgotten in our enthusiasm to provide a vital service to parents. Because of their close relationships with the child and his family, carers can occasionally face considerable difficulties. The carer may undergo serious pressure to take a child when they may have problems within their own family or might take the child so frequently that their own quality of life is damaged. Some carers often find it difficult to refuse the requests of a rather tired mother of a handicapped child. Consequently, things can get a little out of hand when arrangements for the frequency of care is left solely to the parent and carer. It is important for the social worker to be involved for many reasons not the least being the need for the carer to be protected from the danger of overuse. Some agencies are tempted to leave the support of the substitute family to the social worker of the child on placement. This is a move fraught with dangers and it is vitally important that a worker is assigned to the very special task of supporting the carer and acting as mediator. One of the obvious consequences of not doing this results in exhausted and disillusioned carers who quickly burn out and feel that they are constantly being manipulated.

CONCLUSIONS

When the family placement scheme began it was assumed that most carers would undertake this task for many years. Time has shown that the average period of contract with a carer is about four years. They leave the scheme for many reasons, including a change in family circumstances, starting full-time employment, a relative moving into the household, or they may leave the district. A parent and child can find this a difficult experience and have enormous difficulty in accepting a new carer. It is hard for parents not to make comparisons with the previous carer and this can lead to difficulties on all sides. The growth of short-term fostering schemes has been part of a healthy shift toward a more comprehensive range of community services for mentally handicapped people. At a time when more and more parents are expressing a wish to care for their children at home the demand for this and other services is likely to increase.

Short-term fostering projects have clear implications for many ordinary unqualified people. No longer are we placing the onus of care and training solely on the professionally qualified person. Instead an increasing number of women and men, both married or single, are taking on board this task with support from the caring professions. This interesting trend can be seen as part of the process of the 'normalisation' of services for mentally handicapped people in the community. This process is having an enormous effect on the planning of such services in the field of community, residential and daycare. Alongside short-term fostering schemes we now see the development of long-term fostering, ordinary housing, alternatives to training centres, Manpower Services Commission (MSC) work projects and an increasing use of volunteers with people who are mentally handicapped. All these developments reflect a shift away from major capital projects toward the use of existing community resources.

REFERENCE

Oswin, M. (1984) They Keep Going Away (King Edward's Hospital Fund, London)

Chapter Nine

DAY SERVICES

Kevin Teasdale

This chapter analyses the development of day services for adults in both the mental handicap and mental illness fields. It examines the mainstream services, and makes no attempt to survey specialist facilities for children or for the elderly. It has been a useful discipline to compare developments in mental handicap and mental illness, since research and debate on the developing pattern in one sheds light on what is happening in the other. The writer's own background is in mental illness nursing; he has worked in day centres for mentally handicapped people but all his recent clinical experience is in working in a mental illness day service.

HISTORICAL DEVELOPMENT

Day services in both the mental handicap and mental illness fields preceded the detailed philosophy of community care which underpins the two influential White Papers, Better Services for the Mentally Handicapped (DHSS, 1971) and Better Services for the Mentally Ill (DHSS, 1975). This is important because there is a tendency for writers to ask about the aims of day services, or about the extent to which the reality of these services conforms to the philosophy and pattern of development outlined in the White Papers, but not to acknowledge that day services have developed over time in an individual, localised and 'organic' fashion. Moreover despite the formal impetus to extend day services which the White Papers certainly gave, this varied pattern of development has continued, and partly explains the confusion over the aims and value of day services which is such a dominant feature of the literature on the subject.

To the extent that day services can be regarded

as the bricks and mortar of day centres and day hospitals, they have an institutional life of their own. In the mental handicap field the first day services were the 'occupation centres' which came into being as a result of the 1913 Mental Deficiency Act, and were established as a local authority provision to give training, occupation and supervision. They were the precursors of the adult training centres which expanded as a result of the community care movement and the more liberal climate of public opinion reflected, for example, in the 1959 Mental Health Act. The approach in these centres was to provide training and occupation based on the methods of commerce and industry. More recently attempts have been made to change this design to a model that will emphasise assessment, education and skills for living.

In the mental illness services, the first separate day unit in Britain was the Social Psychotherapy Centre, or Marlborough Day Hospital as it was later known, opened in 1946 by J. Bierer. Gradual development from isolated, experimental day hospitals continued until the 1962 Hospital Plan for England and Wales (Ministry of Health, 1962) which officially countenanced the expansion of day services at the same time as the slow run-down of the old mental hospitals began. Every mental hospital came to have some sort of day provision, although that provision might take many different forms.

In some places, for example, purpose-built day hospitals were created because of the interest of one particular consultant in this type of service. But in other places, day services began as chance developments, consequent on the building of occupational therapy or industrial rehabilitation units in the 1950s and early 1960s. When these facilities were opened, and if they had spare capacity, some former patients who had left the hospital were allowed to return during the daytime and work in these new departments until they found paid employment in the community. As the big hospitals began their slow run-down, so the numbers of day users grew, until separate staff, dining facilities, and eventually separate day units themselves came into being. These units were very often housed in old villa-type wards standing apart from the main body of the hospital. Further examples of this very varied pattern of growth could be found in day centres run by social services or by voluntary agencies.

PRINCIPLES

The principles behind the development of day services are based to some extent upon rationalisation from an existing service. As far as they can be deduced, they derive from a basic belief that mentally disabled people ought not to be segregated from the rest of the community, but have a right to lead lives which are as 'normal' as their disability permits. But given the fact of disability, whatever its cause, they have particular needs. Day services have come to be seen as the most appropriate means of providing for these needs while allowing the person to continue to live in the community.

As regards mentally handicapped people, the 1971 White Paper defines their needs as education, training and support. It argues that the service set up to meet these needs should be a local authority provision, thus implicitly acknowledging that a medical model is not appropriate for this group of people. The brief of day services for mentally handicapped people is to assess, prevent, modify and compensate for the disabilities of individuals. The official view also places a secondary emphasis on spreading the burden of caring and providing some relief for the families of the disabled.

The needs of the mentally ill which day services are officially deemed to meet are defined less clearly. Thus Better Services for the Mentally Ill (DHSS, 1975) recommends a division of day services between day hospitals run by health authorities and day centres run by social services departments. It states that: 'Day centres like day hospitals have a broadly therapeutic role but their orientation is social - unlike that of the day hospital where the activity and therapy form part of a therapeutic programme under medical supervision.'

If this means anything, it must be that day hospitals will treat the illness and day centres will cater for social needs. Viewed objectively this is an awkward division of need, which papers over the equally awkward division of the helping services into separate hierarchies for health and for social services consequent on the National Health Service Act of 1946. However it further reflects and is reinforced by the ideological division between a medical or 'illness' model and a social or 'deprivational' model.

There is a sense in which to ask 'Why community care?' is a redundant question. To take groups of people, label them rightly or wrongly as mentally ill or mentally handicapped, and send them away to institutions isolated from the areas where they and their families live, is unjust and unjustifiable. Therefore there is no further need to justify community care. It is the only moral way to provide help, treatment and support.

This view has not always been as self-evident as it now appears, and indeed there are only certain sections of opinion, mostly people in positions of power and responsibility in government, health and social services, who presently hold this view. Large sections of the general public still see the old asylums as necessary for their protection. Educated opinion in favour of community care has been moulded by books which have condemned the old institutions, but have not usually presented proposals on how a future service should be organised. Goffman (1961) described the damaging effects of institutional life; Scheff (1966) proposed an influential labelling theory which to some extent discredited psychiatrists, the medical model, and consequently the institutions which provided treatment using this model; in Britain investigations such as the Normansfield Report (DHSS, 1978) exposed scandalous abuses in the treatment of mentally disabled people in some of the old hospitals.

Thus community care, and day services themselves, derive at an official level from a change in attitude towards the mentally disabled which was fuelled by a body of evidence and theory which presented the old institutions in a very negative light. This idea - that the places we have now are so bad that anything else must be better - goes far to explain the lack of clear positive principles on which a community-based service for the mentally disabled should be founded.

A further issue of principle is exactly how one defines a day service. It is easy to fall into the view that those needs of the mentally disabled which can be met during the daytime are fully and best catered for by units - places that patients or clients attend and in which staff work. Patmore (1981) argues that to view day services in this way, and consequently to begin to think in terms of 'places' which may 'silt up' is to perpetuate the values of institutional care. Patmore defines a day service as encompassing all those activities and aids to living available in any community. In this view a further education college offering classes in adult literacy, a Citizens' Advice Bureau, or a community nurse with an open referrals policy are all part of a day service.

In this book these areas are discussed by other writers, and the bulk of this chapter is focused on day centres and day hospitals. However, the point to bear in mind is that if planners neglect the broader view then a day unit may come to be seen as a nine-to-five institution which will look inward rather than outward, segregate rather than integrate and control 'abnormal' behaviour rather than promote 'normal' behaviour.

The present provision for the mentally disabled is in the middle of a transition from a largely hospital-based service to a largely community-based one. We do not yet know how day services will fare if they are to become the focal point of provision, as Bennett (1981) suggests they may become. The large hospitals continue to mask any deficiencies of the future service by providing a back-up facility. Most day units offer a five-days-a-week service. Almost by definition it is <u>not</u> an evening, night, or weekend facility. Presumably those who will use the service are the less dependent, less disturbed, better supported and more physically or intellectually able groups. The two White Papers imply that the majority of the mentally disabled will be able to benefit from this service and that adequate inpatient or supervised hostel accommodation, as well as support for the families, will be provided for those who do not fit the pattern. They also argue that this transition from a hospital-based service must be modulated by the response of the general public. And yet there is no evidence of a determined policy to inform and educate the general public, and only isolated local initiatives to pacify it.

The thrust of this argument is therefore that the 'disordered development of day care' described by Vaughan (1983) is true in both the mental handicap and the mental illness fields; that its origins lie in its organic development, and have been influenced more by a reaction against the old institutions for the mentally disabled than by any clearcut vision of the benefits of the future service; that there is therefore a risk of a narrow view of the new service prevailing, and that this may lead to the development of 'community institutions', which force users and their families to define their needs in terms of what the service can provide, rather than supporting flexible facilities which are able to adapt to the changing needs of users. The negative view is the extreme case. In practice, the adequacy and responsiveness of local services will vary greatly.

It is possible to discern some of the salient trends in the future pattern of services, and the remainder of the chapter will attempt to do this, but the wide local variations in day services, as well as the masking effect of the old hospitals, continue to make firm judgements hard to arrive at.

TRENDS

Any attempt to evaluate a service as diverse as day provision for the mentally disabled must use as its database two national surveys of the services. Whelan and Speake (1977) collected data from 305 adult training centres (ATCs), 78 per cent of the total number in England and Wales. During the same period, Edwards and Carter were conducting a large-scale survey of all types of day service in England and Wales, published in tabulated form - Edwards and Carter (1980) - and summarised with discussion - Carter (1981). In the time that has elapsed since these publications it is possible to clarify some of the trends that they discerned.

TRAINING AND OCCUPATION

It has already been noted that the principles behind day services are obscure, and it is no surprise to learn that both surveys showed that staff and users were far from agreed on the aims of individual day units. Moreover the stated aims were by no means always reflected in the activities of the units themselves. However the idea of work, both as training and occupation, was frequently mentioned among the aims of day units, and particularly of the ATCs.

The ATCs developed out of the old occupation centres with a brief to provide training in skills and work-discipline which would make it possible for some mentally handicapped people to find either open or sheltered employment. The DHSS (1971) White Paper also acknowledged that permanent daily occupation was part of the function of the ATC when sheltered employment was not available. Both staff and users interviewed in the Edwards and Carter survey thought that training and practical services (company, food and occupation) were the main aims of the ATCs. But Whelan and Speake (1981) pointed out that although about one-third of all trainees were capable of either open or sheltered employment, their survey estimated that only 3.9 per cent actually entered such employment. They argued that the high general level of unemployment was not a sufficient explanation of this state of affairs. They quoted studies which suggested that the staff in ATCs have consistently underestimated the abilities of trainees. They also questioned the extensive use of industrial contract work, on the grounds that the majority of those who entered open employment were employed in job categories unrelated to industry. They suggested that the likely categories of job available in each locality be assessed, and types of training be provided on the basis of this assessment. One further criticism was that there was a distinct lack of opportunity for graded progression towards more demanding types of work, while the wages limit before loss of supplementary benefit kept average weekly earnings below £2.

While it is clear that expectations of future levels of employment have altered drastically during the period in which ATCs have become the major provision for the mentally handicapped in this country, it is also apparent that ATCs are offering an unduly restricted service to mentally handicapped people who are too often treated as a homogeneous group, rather than as individuals with diverse abilities and disabilities.

These criticisms are well-known, but to produce change in established institutions is very difficult, and there are many who are angry and frustrated at the lack of progress. There is a new trend in the mental handicap field for the run-down of the old hospitals to spawn local units sponsored by the health authorities which combine some residential places with a day unit on the same site. In these newer units, an emphasis on education and social skills training has replaced the idea of contract industrial work. This is a recognition of the inadequacy of statutory education, which is not to be faulted on account of its quality so much as its quantity - and in particular the lack of provision beyond the age of 16, which is the time when many mentally handicapped people are capable of much further progress, given a suitable environment. Even in these new services there is a shortage of trained staff capable of undertaking this highly skilled work. The solution proposed by Whelan and Speake - the development of learning packages to be implemented by care staff of all grades - needs to be accompanied by a programme designed to give care staff confidence in their own skills, in the value of such programmes, and in the possibility of producing worthwhile change in the lives of the users of the service. There is a desperate need for a complete new training programme for those who work with mentally handicapped people in ATCs, perhaps developed along the lines of the 1982 RNMH syllabus for nurses. To make full use of modern communications technology, in the form of videos and computer-assisted learning, could also become a powerful public statement on the degree of priority accorded to these ideas, and to mentally handicapped people in our society.

On the positive side, the surveys show that day services do attempt to occupy the time of their users. On examination, the activity programme of an average day centre, day hospital or ATC, will compare favourably with that of most hospital wards, and indeed with what can feasibly be provided within the average family. The users, whether mentally handicapped or mentally ill, in the Edwards and Carter survey saw practical services as an important aim of their units. However, these same users also saw plenty of scope for improvements to the programme. Locker and Dunt (1978) note that it is notoriously difficult to elicit critical views from the users of any health or social services provision. Therefore the statements by some mentally handicapped people in the Edwards and Carter survey that they found the work part of their programmes tedious and boring, and that they felt that they were being financially exploited, must carry a great deal of weight.

Users and staff expect day units to be active places. This mutual expectation is something which can be developed as a force for change. It is in itself a change on what went on before in many hospitals, but the question to ask is whether it is being channelled in the 'best' direction. Any programme, whether oriented towards work, leisure or social skills, needs to offer options to the users and to include some system whereby an individual's potential and interests are assessed and used to determine the programme. The high levels of unemployment in Britain in the 1980s have led some writers such as Bender (1983) to argue that day services may deflect concern from political action, by keeping the mentally disabled out of the public view, and, through institutional provision, emphasise the disabilities of the individual rather than that person's potential.

Again it comes back to what is seen as the aim or the function of an individual unit. It is possible, particularly in day hospitals for the mentally ill, to develop a treatment programme which focuses upon overcoming a particular medical problem, or developing a certain range of social skills, but which excludes the issue of training for work. Patmore (1981) argues that in the present economic climate many day units should provide long-term, but low key, support for their users. There could also be a valuable role here for volunteers in helping users to integrate into the community and to transfer the social skills practised at the day unit back into 'normal' settings.

However, 'work' is still seen as the 'normal' occupation for the great majority in our society, during at least a part of their lives. It gives the benefit of self-respect, the respect of others, and an income which confers a degree of freedom and control over one's life. If this is permanently denied to the mentally disabled, partly because of the stigma attached to the group by employers, and partly because unemployment has particularly affected those job categories which are considered most suitable for mentally disabled people, then no matter how much activity is provided within a day unit, for many users it can be no more than a second-best solution. Whelan and Speake (1977) argued that by establishing advanced work sections within ATCs, by offering employers ATC staff to work alongside mentally handicapped trainees in enclave schemes, and by taking a broader view of suitable job categories, many more mentally handicapped people could find open employment even in the present economic climate. This is probably true also of the mentally ill, where it is rare to find a day unit which sees placing users in open employment as a major part of its brief. There is a very real sense in which day services, often with highly organised activity programmes, are actually providing a second-best substitute for the sort of activity which our society regards as the norm for 'normal' people.

TREATMENT

Whereas the avowed emphasis in day services for the mentally handicapped is to provide training, in the mental illness service Edwards and Carter found that the most common aim expressed by staff was to keep users out of hospital. The users themselves emphasised the more positive aspects of giving them help in living in the community. It may be that this division reflects the institutional training and background of many of the staff. Whereas the majority of day units for the mentally handicapped were provided by social services, the opposite is true of the mentally ill - with 75 per cent of units in the Carter and Edwards survey being health authority day hospitals.

The literature on day hospitals includes a few attempts to evaluate the effectiveness of these units in providing treatment for illness. Most of the studies either compare day hospital treatment with inpatient care, or compare one day hospital with another. Most attempt to evaluate change in users through standard measures of clinical state or social behaviour. However, the great diversity of hospitals and their user groups reduces the confidence with which one can generalise from such inevitably small-scale studies. Moreover, as Vaughan (1983) points out, studies would be more useful if they sought to identify the user groups who can most benefit from day care and the specific aspects of the treatment programme which are producing benefit. There has been a tendency to regard a day hospital as a specific form of treatment, and then to evaluate it <u>against</u> hospitalisation. This clearly reflects the effects of thinking in terms of institutions as treatments in themselves, rather than trying to evaluate the specific treatments which are offered within the care environment.

A British paper by Hirsch <u>et al</u>. (1979), and an American one by Herz <u>et al</u>. (1977) suggest that hospital inpatient admission can be shortened with no disadvantage to the patient if day hospital follow-up is given. With the building of day hospitals within small district general psychiatric units, the transition from inpatient to day-patient care will be eased, and the trend towards shorter inpatient stay should become more general.

A study by Ferguson and Carney (1970) sought the opinions of users about their day hospital, and also used a standard test to evaluate clinical improvement. They found that an enthusiastic attitude towards the unit correlated with good clinical outcome. An incidental feature of a study by Turner-Smith and Thomson (1979) was that the part of the day hospital programme which was criticised by a significant number of users was group work, and particularly formal group work. This was a small-scale study of one unit and it would be unsound to generalise widely from it. However, given that critical opinion is hard to elicit, and that group work was part of the previous week's activity programme for 58 per cent of those interviewed in day hospitals in the Edwards and Carter survey, it is a finding which might merit further investigation, especially if users' enthusiasm about the service is significantly related to clinical improvement, as Ferguson and Carney suggest.

A study by Milne (1984) attempts to compare clinical outcome in two day hospitals. The author argues that the greater clinical efficacy of one of the day hospitals can be explained by the activity programme which was weighted towards directive social skills training using a behavioural model. However, as the author himself admits, the study does not attempt to identify or control variables other than the activity programme, and this again means that the results must be interpreted with great caution in the absence of other studies.

The work of Vaughn and Leff (1976) on the connection between emotional atmosphere in the home and recurrence of florid symptoms of schizophrenia has suggested that if the amount of face-to-face contact between a person suffering from schizophrenia and a critical or overinvolved relative can be reduced to under 35 hours per week, this will act as a buffer against relapse into florid symptoms of the illness. This buffer function could usefully be undertaken by a day service and its therapeutic value for this particular group of users would be quite independent of the programme offered in the day unit.

In an investigation of users' views of a day hospital which I am currently undertaking, many people value the day hospital as a place where they are kept 'busy'. They also appear to equate being busy with feeling well, and being bored with feeling ill. Given that day units in general seem to be active places, it may be that a full programme is what is required, rather than any one specific activity.

The literature on treatment in day hospitals for the mentally ill contains much opinion, but little by way of well validated theory. The studies are small scale, and few in number. Perhaps the same could be said of treatment in psychiatry in general. One interesting trend in evaluation of day hospitals, and indeed of community services in general, is that towards taking account of the views of the users or consumers of the service themselves. This is consistent with a trend towards seeing the users not as passive receivers of a service, but as people who know their own needs better than the professional experts themselves.

DAY HOSPITALS AND DAY CENTRES

The 1975 White Paper (DHSS, 1975) advocated the division of day services for the mentally ill between day hospitals run by health authorities and day centres run by social services departments. However, the Edwards and Carter survey found that the types of programme and of client in day hospitals and day centres were broadly similar. They found a similarity of stated aims and of qualifications of the staff. The only major difference that they noted was that those users who were attending day centres had spent longer periods in psychiatric hospitals - over 50 per cent had been inpatients for more than two years, whereas 87 per cent of day hospital users had spent less than two years as inpatients. Day centres also allowed users to attend for longer than day hospitals. More than half the users of day centres who were interviewed said they had attended for over two years, whereas only one-third of those interviewed at the day hospitals had attended for so long. Despite the similarity in user groups, referral to the two types of unit showed strict demarcation. Social workers referred to day centres, while hospital doctors and general practitioners referred to day hospitals. In one of the few areas in the survey where both types of unit existed in close proximity, referral and follow-up agencies remained quite separate. In the late 1970s, therefore, it was hard to justify this nominal division of a service between two types of agency. The survey merely highlighted the often very poor relationships between health authority and social services employees. Prejudices and stereotypes exist as keenly as ever, and it is easy to extend these to the users of the services, characterising certain people as suitable, or more likely unsuitable, for one's own particular type of day unit.

The survey did also illustrate a dangerous trend for day centres to become units for 'chronics', with all the problems of maintaining standards and morale which used to be found on the back wards of the old hospitals. It may be that this is the result of a medical model, with its emphasis on assessment of illness, treatment and discharge, being contrasted with a social model which is not offering the hope of progression or permanent solution to problems, perhaps because the unemployment situation blocks the natural path to progression beyond a day centre. This is only at the level of speculation, and is not to suggest that those who are discharged from day hospitals are 'cured' or even clinically improved. Many day hospitals will operate a policy of offering people an opportunity to attend the unit on a limited time contract. If the person improves he is discharged because of the improvement; and if he fails to improve he is discharged because he is failing to profit from a service which should therefore be offered to others who may be more likely to benefit.

It may be that in the next few years the differences between day hospitals and day centres will become more marked. In the Edwards and Carter study, 74 per cent of day hospitals for the mentally ill stood within the grounds of an institution, presumably mainly old psychiatric hospitals. Many of these had started in chance fashion, meeting a need for a degree of support, or for sheltered occupation in people newly discharged as a result of rehabilitation programmes. Thus in many cases these units had developed their own user group, separate from those who were admitted to the short stay wards of the main part of the hospital.

However, in the years leading up to the Edwards and Carter survey, psychiatrists and psychiatric nurses had become aware of the potential of day hospitals as a means of easing the transition back to home life for people who had spent a comparatively short period as inpatients. Although there is little research evidence to prove the efficacy of this policy, it is a frequent assertion in the literature, and a common attitude among the professionals. A tendency has also developed to use day care as a long-stop device to keep people out of hospital. Thus instead of offering immediate hospitalisation, a doctor will often offer day care as a less drastic and perhaps more acceptable alternative.

These new trends have come at a time when plans for closing the old mental hospitals are being pushed forward with great determination. Large numbers of small psychiatric units are springing up in the grounds of district general hospitals. In these, there is invariably a day hospital which, following the Better Services (DHSS, 1975) pattern, is designed to provide a treatment milieu for the majority of the inpatients of the psychiatric unit, as well as for people living in their own homes and attending as true day-patients. The 1975 White Paper recommended that at least 50 per cent of places in these new day hospitals should be for the use of inpatients.

This will produce a very different day hospital from the ones surveyed by Edwards and Carter. In 1977 many functioned as units separated by all but geography from the rest of the hospital, and with very few inpatients attending. The hospital wards had large day rooms, and the hospitals themselves had occupational therapy and industrial rehabilitation departments which functioned independently from whatever was offered at the day hospital. But part of the purpose of the new day hospitals is to replace these formerly separate departments, and so meet the needs of the inpatients in the smaller new psychiatric units.

It may be that many of the day hospitals in the Edwards and Carter survey were functioning more along the low-key support lines of day centres, perhaps with a philosophy of care emphasising a people-with-problems approach, as distinct from a strict medical model. This difference may have occurred precisely because the day hospital was not seen as fitting in with the design of the rest of the hospital service. However a day hospital in a small psychiatric unit may well come much more closely under a medical, or at least a treatment model, because it will be seen as the focus of the whole unit, rather than as an appendage on the periphery of the service.

Medical input in the new pattern of day hospitals will be greatly increased. Very often a consultant will use the day unit as his base for outpatient clinics, and inpatients are also likely to meet their consultant there, since the day hospital rather than the ward is the place where they will be found during the consultant's normal working hours. In contrast, Edwards and Carter (1980) found that in more than one-third of day hospitals, the consultant never visited, and in one-fifth he attended less than once a month. Consultants will be more familiar with the new day hospitals, will probably conduct more frequent reviews of their day-patients, and this will almost certainly lead to quicker discharges and less long-term support.

This new type of day hospital also coincides with the implementation of the 1982 Syllabus for Registered Mental Nurses (General Nursing Council, 1982). In many respects this radical revision of the training of psychiatric nurses moves away from a medical model, and certainly strongly emphasises the role of the nurse as a therapist skilled in counselling and group work, and with a sound knowledge of psychology and sociology, as well as psychiatry. The National Boards, which are the governing bodies in nursing, are using their Education Advisers to ensure that this syllabus is far more than a paper document. In consequence the day hospital will see a much more active treatment programme, involving counselling, group work and behavioural approaches undertaken by the nurses who form the largest of the professional groups.

One further change, the effects of which are more difficult to predict, will be the atmosphere of a day hospital where the true day-patients mix with the inpatients. Although the more disturbed inpatients will remain on the wards, the definition of 'more disturbed' will doubtless include the over-active and unpredictable patients, but may exclude the moderate or even severely depressed, or indeed anyone who does not present a major management problem. Severity of illness will not in itself be a determinant of whether a patient stays on the ward or goes to the day hospital. This is speculation based on personal observation in the absence of research. But it seems plausible that true day-patients will meet some acutely ill people, which might not have been the case in the older type of day hospital. In consequence they will have to come to terms with how they see themselves - are they suffering from an illness of the same type as the inpatients? If they decide they are different from the inpatients, will they feel uneasy about mixing with them? No doubt there will be some who will choose not to make use of the day service precisely because of these ambivalent and uncomfortable thoughts and feelings.

The result of these trends may be that the day hospitals of the future will come to meet the treatment needs of mentally ill people and develop aims focused on this treatment model, but will no longer give the sheltered occupation and social support which the day hospitals in the old psychiatric hospitals to some extent provided. This is merely to say that the division mapped out in the 1975 White Paper (DHSS, 1975) will become more of a reality. But the problem is that social services provision for the mentally ill is not keeping pace with these major developments in the health service. Edwards and Carter found that social services provided only one-fifth of day units for the mentally ill, and there is no reason to think that there has been any sudden increase in this proportion since then, with financial restrictions tighter if anything than in the 1970s.

On a small scale there is an exception to this trend, to be found mainly in large rural counties. Here some health authorities are setting up peripheral day hospitals in towns which are distant from the psychiatric unit which forms the base for the service. Such day hospitals often occupy old health authority properties in residential areas. They are small-scale units, staffed by nurses, and because of their isolation from the base hospital are more likely to resemble day centres than the new type of day hospital. They also illustrate a more general tendency in the mental illness field for health authorities to develop autonomous community-based schemes, rather than to divert money into social services facilities.

DAY SERVICES AND THE COMMUNITY

Among the folklore values of a day service is the idea that it can help users to maintain contact with their own communities, and because of this the transfer of new skills into real-life settings is improved - especially when there is close contact between day units and the families of users. While day services undeniably have this potential, the Edwards and Carter data do not suggest that any great effort is presently being made to capitalise on these possibilities. Their survey revealed that 40 per cent of mentally handicapped users had made no visits to the homes of friends or relatives in the preceding fortnight, and a further 27 per cent had made only one to two visits in that fortnight; of the same group 34 per cent had received no visitors in that time, and 26 per cent had received a maximum of two visitors in this period. The same general pattern held true for the mentally ill. This isolation may be no more than a measure of the degree of disability or of deprivation of the mentally disabled in general, but it must also raise the question as to whether day units are providing users with social support which is acting as a substitute for the more varied social networks used by other members of the community. On this evidence, day services have a long way to go before they can claim that they are assisting users to broaden their social networks in the community.

Again the figures for the frequency of use of outside facilities made by the various units are not especially encouraging. For example, Edwards and Carter (1980) found that 12 per cent of social services day units for the mentally handicapped admitted to making no use of outside facilities during the previous month. A visit to the shops was the only activity undertaken more than ten times a month on average by units for either group of users. Also the survey showed very little use of volunteers, with more than 70 per cent of all units actually admitting to never using volunteers at all!

Moving from contact with the community in general, to contact with the families of users, it must again be said that very little is known, and that local practices will certainly vary widely. Vaughan (1983) quotes one Irish and one American study which suggest that families of the mentally ill often prefer day care over inpatient care for their relatives. However the figures given by the heads of units in the Edwards and Carter survey indicate that day services themselves have comparatively little formal contact with the families of users. Only 10 per cent of day units for the mentally handicapped could claim regular monthly contact with most families about the problems of their relatives, and only 23 per cent of all units for the mentally ill claimed the same. This may imply that the professionals do not regard it as part of their responsibility actively to seek contact with the families of users, and certainly not to the extent of offering the day unit as a place to which family members can come regularly and talk about how they can help the user to capitalise on the skills and knowledge acquired within the unit.

It is possible that other professionals, such as social workers and community psychiatric and mental handicap nurses are maintaining regular contact with the families of at least some of the users. There is, however, a risk that the extension of day services could actually lead to less contact with families of users than for example during inpatient care, when visiting time can become a regular and useful contact. This is not to imply that day units never do useful work with families. But there is little evidence at present that day units in general are building contact with relatives systematically into their programmes.

STIGMA

Achievement of the ideal, that a mentally handicapped person should be able to lead as 'normal' a life as possible, depends not only on the skills and understanding of the professionals, but also on the attitude of the general public. Community care for the mentally ill also depends either on the acceptance by members of the public that their stereotyped views of 'mental patients' are unjustified, or on former inpatients concealing their contact with the psychiatric services. The literature on stigma of all kinds is large, but it suggests that any form of mental disability is a master status, one which leads outsiders completely to redefine their views of the individual in terms of the label 'mental'. Moreover, it should be remembered that many lay people do not distinguish between the mentally ill and the mentally handicapped, attributing to each a compound stereotype made up of the most feared or despised attributes of both groups.

The advent of day services was envisaged both as part of a caring system which reflected the more tolerant values of at least some sections of our society, and also as a system which would in itself promote greater tolerance. However, day services in themselves present some particular and little-understood problems for users and their families in stigma management.

Mental illness units provide the clearest example. Miles (1984) showed that even attendance at an outpatient clinic at a psychiatric unit in a district general hospital can present attenders with problems as to how to explain this to family and friends. Regular attendance at a day unit will increase the need to find some way of managing the stigma. In the past, many patients in psychiatric hospitals defined themselves as 'ill' when in hospital, and 'well' as soon as they were discharged home. Relatives and friends accepted this in the same way that they would accept discharge from a general hospital, with the reassuring claim 'I'm cured now', implied at very least. But how can a user explain attendance at a day unit, especially if it immediately follows a period of inpatient care? If the person is 'cured', why does he have to go to a day unit? The uncertainty about aims of day services adds to the problem, since even the staff may present ambivalent views about the function of the unit, the nature of illness, or the degree of control which the unit seeks to exercise over the behaviour of users. Even a social services day centre with a clear non-medical approach may still be known locally as a psychiatric unit, with all the stigma that entails. If the day service is still situated in the grounds of an old hospital, then those users who reject the 'illness' label will consequently be placed in a difficult position when explaining attendance to relatives and friends.

The dilemma of true day-patients mixing with inpatients in the new psychiatric units has already been described. The extent to which a user's view of himself corresponds with the official day unit view can be an important influence in acceptance of, and benefit from, whatever help is offered. It is something which needs to be discussed when the idea of attendance is first suggested.

Some users in an especially difficult position are those who have attended a large day unit at one of the old hospitals, and are now expected to use a day hospital or day centre in their own locality. One user I talked to vividly described the problem:

> They've put a big piece in our local paper saying that they're dreading us going there and that we would be prying in the windows and take the value of the houses down and they were frightened for their children. They all think it's a lot of wild people running about.

In the past such users had the option of trying to conceal attendance at a distant day unit. However with a day unit in their own small town it will be much harder to keep it secret. The option of being open about attendance will also present new problems. Many people are ready to make exceptions for one or two individuals from a stigmatised group. However, these attitudes quickly harden when the prospect of contact with a larger group in a day unit closer to home becomes apparent. There is no reason to doubt that mentally handicapped people and their families are faced with the same problems.

The conclusion is not that day units are therefore 'bad things', but rather that staff and users together need to be fully aware of this problem and to negotiate options acceptable to each user, and to the local community. The therapeutic potential of a day service will in part depend on the resolution, or at least the acknowledgement, of these problems. The comparative lack of contact with local communities previously noted suggests that this is another area where day services need clear guidance and purposeful action.

REFERENCES

Bender, M. (1983), 'For What and For Whom?' Community Care, 445
Bennett, D. (1981) 'What Direction for Psychiatric Services?', in The Mental Health Year Book 1981-82 (MIND, London)
Carter, J. (1981) Day Services for Adults: Somewhere to Go (George Allen and Unwin, London)
DHSS (1971) Better Services for the Mentally Handicapped, Cmnd 6233 (HMSO, London)
DHSS (1975) Better Services for the Mentally Ill, Cmnd 4683 (HMSO, London)
DHSS (1978) Report of the Committee of Inquiry into Normansfield Hospital, Cmnd 7337 (HMSO, London)
Edwards, C. and Carter, J. (1980) The Data of Day Care, 3 vols (National Institute for Social Work, London)
Ferguson, R. and Carney, M. (1970) 'Interpersonal Considerations and Judgements in a Day Hospital', British Journal of Psychiatry, 117, 397-403
General Nursing Council for England and Wales (1982) Training Syllabus, Register of Nurses, Mental Nursing and Training Syllabus, Register of Nurses, Mental Handicap Nursing (GNC, London)
Goffman, E. (1961) Asylums (Doubleday, New York)
Herz, M. et al. (1977) 'Brief Hospitalisation: A Two-year Follow-up', American Journal of Psychiatry, 134, 502
Hirsch, S. et al. (1979) 'Shortening Hospital Stay for Psychiatric Care', British Medical Journal, 1, 442-6
Locker, D. and Dunt, D. (1978) 'Theoretical and Methodological Issues in Sociological Studies of Consumer Satisfaction with Medical Care', Social Science and Medicine, 12, 283-292
Miles, A. (1984) 'The Stigma of Psychiatric Disorder', in Reed, J. and Lomas, G. (eds) Psychiatric Services in the Community (Croom Helm, London)
Milne, D. (1984) 'A Comparative Evaluation of Two Psychiatric Day Hospitals', British Journal of Psychiatry, 145, 533-537
Ministry of Health (1962) A Hospital Plan for England and Wales, Cmnd 1604 (HMSO, London)
Patmore, C. (1981) 'Day Centres, Unemployment and the Future', in The Mental Health Year Book 1981-82 (MIND, London)
Scheff, T. (1966) Being Mentally Ill (Aldine, Chicago)
Turner-Smith, A. and Thomson, I. (1979) 'Patients' Opinions', Nursing Times, 19 April, 675-679
Vaughan, P. (1983) 'The Disordered Development of Day Care in Psychiatry', Health Trends, 15, 91-94
Vaughn, C.E. and Leff, J.P. (1976) 'The Influence of Family and Social Factors on the Course of Psychiatric Illness', British Journal of Psychiatry, 129, 125-137
Whelan, E. and Speake, B. (1977) Adult Training Centres in England and Wales: Report of the First National Survey

(National Association of Teachers of the Mental Handicapped, Manchester)
Whelan, E. and Speake, B. (1981) Getting to Work (Souvenir Press, London)

Chapter Ten

FRIENDS AND NEIGHBOURS: RELATIONSHIPS AND OPPORTUNITIES IN THE COMMUNITY FOR PEOPLE WITH A MENTAL HANDICAP

Dorothy Atkinson and Linda Ward

INTRODUCTION

The material on which the first part of this chapter is based is drawn from a series of interviews with mentally handicapped people living in towns and villages in Somerset. The respondents were interviewed in a study which followed up a group of 50 people who left long-stay mental handicap hospitals to live in different parts of Somerset, in a variety of domestic housing - flats, cottages, bungalows and houses - and household arrangements - living alone, or with one, two, three, four or more companions.

RELATIONSHIPS AND THE QUALITY OF LIFE

A common theme emerged in interviews with these 50 people - that the quality of their lives was, to a great extent, determined by the range and type of their social relationships. They described their lives and lifestyles in terms of the people they knew - the people they shared house with, members of their family, their friends and workmates, and people in their neighbourhood.

Not surprisingly, individuals vary in how they rate the quality of their lives. At one extreme, Edgar describes himself as 'very very happy'; at the other extreme, Geoffrey describes himself as 'very very lonely'. Their lives, and lifestyles, are indeed very different. Edgar has regular and positive contact with his family, he shares a house with two congenial companions, he has a job which brings him into contact with workmates, and he has made friends in the neighbourhood. Geoffrey, on the other hand, has lost all contact with his family, lives alone, has no job, no friends, and is on bad terms with his neighbours.

Although Edgar and Geoffrey's lives and lifestyles are very different, they share areas of common interest - with each other, and with everyone else in the study. They are interested in social relationships; their lives can be compared across the different sorts of relationships in which they are involved:

(1) Family relationships
(2) Household relationships
(3) Job-based, or role-related, relationships
(4) Friendships
(5) Neighbourhood relationships.

Edgar does particularly well on this checklist, and Geoffrey does particularly badly. There are one or two others who fare nearly as well, or nearly as badly. However, most people in the study have mixed experiences of community living. They can tick at least one item on the checklist. The challenge for those of us who are involved in community services for people with a mental handicap is to help create opportunities for them to develop and sustain relationships in all five categories if they so choose, and thus enrich the quality of their lives. In the second part of this chapter we look at practical ways of addressing this challenge, but first we look in more detail at the actual experiences of the people in the Somerset study.

LIVING IN THE COMMUNITY - PEOPLE'S EXPERIENCES

People's views about their lives are presented under the five headings from the checklist above.

Family Relationships

The 'family' was often the starting point in a general discussion about relationships. Everyone had something to say about their family, some comment to make on their present degree of contact, or lack of contact. Those people with no contact at all were often in this position because of earlier geographical separation from their families. For some people it was the ageing process in themselves, and/or their relatives, and the consequent loss or lessening of mobility which led to decreasing contact.

Only Douglas stated in starkly simple terms, 'I haven't got anybody'. Other people were in the same position, but they did not state it in Douglas's words. For example, Edward admitted 'I've got no-one', but went on to explain his planned trip to a relative's grave in a country churchyard - 'There is someone from the family in North Cadbury churchyard. The social worker is going to take me there sometime.'

Other people had no contact but, like Arthur, put a brave face on it: 'I've got a sister at Clevedon. Sometimes I generally go there now and again. It's difficult to get there. Sometimes she generally writes to me.' (These claims were fiercely contested by other members of Arthur's household.) Others settled for letters, like Philip, who said, 'My brother writes sometimes, but never comes. I'm waiting for a letter now.' Nigel balanced his admission of no contact with family with a claim to some with distant friends: 'I haven't got no family, but I've got friends in Bridgewater, and sometimes, if they're not busy they might come'. Mabel lives in hope of seeing her favourite nephew again - and she is encouraged in this by her friend Joan, who explains, 'Mabel hasn't heard from him in years, and doesn't know where he is. I say to her, "You never know, one of these days he might turn up", and she keeps an eye open for him.'

Many people were in contact with their families, though the degree and nature of the contact varied between individuals. The contact with his sister is extremely important to Alan, but he has no control over, or say in, the regularity and frequency of the visits she makes to his home. Alan lives alone in a flat 45 miles from his sister's house. He has no telephone, and cannot read and write. He describes one of his sister's unexpected appearances in his life:

> She came on the off-chance, not knowing if I'd be in or not. I'd just had my dinner and gone to the toilet. I heard someone at the door, but thought to myself, 'It's nothing to do with me, I'm not expecting anybody. It's probably someone for upstairs.' I came out of the toilet, and opened the door and of course it was her. I said, 'Oh it's you!' She had her husband with her, and a cake she'd baked for me, and some sandwiches for tea.

Many people do have regular and frequent contact

with their families. The meaning of this contact varies according to individual needs, and personal circumstances. Three examples illustrate the spread of meaning for individual people - Bruce has a good time when he is out and about with his sister; Agnes and Doreen make a contribution towards the wellbeing of their respective elderly parents; and Richard finds relief from group-home tensions when staying with his sister.

> **Bruce**. My sister comes up once a fortnight and takes me and my wife out. We go to the shops and have lunch out, usually on Tuesdays. On our wedding anniversary she takes us out for a special lunch, and the same for our birthdays. She's my favourite sister. They're all nice but she's my favourite.

> **Agnes**. I go on the bus every Thursday to see my dad. He's 91. I clean up for him and that. I get his pension for him and do his shopping. I bring his washing back home to do, his hankies, socks and shirts.

> **Doreen**. I go to my mum's place every week. I'm going tonight. She lives in Victoria Road, not far from here. I take the dog out for a walk. She can't get outside the door now, and has to have trolley meals taken in. If it gets late, like half past nine, and it's dark, I'll come back in a taxi. It's only 60p from mum's house. I go on Saturdays too sometimes.

> **Richard**. I go to my sister's now and again, and my aunty's. I'm going to Guernsey with my sister for a holiday, she says it'll be nice if I come along. I try to keep my pecker up, and make the best of it here. I don't like letting myself down. We try to make an effort to get on. When I go home to my sister's house, it's nice.

Household Relationships

Four people live alone. They do not, therefore, have home-based relationships. Although Geoffrey chose to live alone, he now feels the absence of company: 'It's very difficult being a handicapped person. A handicapped person shouldn't live alone. How do you expect a handicapped person to live outside?' Two people left their group homes in order to live alone. They feel positively about leaving behind the tensions of group home life, and concentrate their energies on building up outside contacts. Maurice, for example, comments on his approach to living alone: 'I don't stay here all weekend, I go out. I go on my bike to see Doreen and them, or to have a drink in the pub.'

There are four married couples in the study. The marital relationship seems to provide a special sense of security, and ensures ready companionship for the people involved. Everyone took pride in referring to 'my wife' or 'my husband'. Thus, Ada and Vincent describe their home life together:

> **Vincent**: My wife gets the breakfast ready while I take the dog out. I'm in charge of the house. I'm the manager, but she sticks to it. If anyone calls, she tells me who it was.
> **Ada**: Me and my husband go shopping in the town every week. I cook the meals, and he dishes it out. He looks after the garden, and I've put flowers in the tub at the front. Mr Jameson came from the council one day and said to my husband, 'Oh tell Mrs Watts that's the first time I've seen that flower tub used!' He was pleased because the people before us never bothered.

In group homes, fortunes are more mixed. As seen earlier, Richard's group home is not a happy supportive environment and he takes refuge with his sister and aunt. Another member of that four-person group, Edward, expressed his views of domestic life thus: 'I've been thinking for a long time that I'd like to make a move. Four in a house is too much. They can't agree, and can't get on. Young Colin plays up. I'd like a little house, one up, one down.'

In Edgar's group, however, the three householders are good friends. Edgar and Robert were friends for years in hospital, and now Norma has become a friend too. They go together when Edgar visits his family in another town: 'All three of us go. We go together. I always take them with me, I don't like leaving them behind. They go and see Charles and them while I see Mum and Dad. I don't like going on my own, it's not nice leaving Norma and Robert back here.' The principle of sharing is well-established in this group home. They share the decisions ('we talk it out between ourselves'), they share the budgie ('he belongs to all of us'), and they share the chores ('we all help'). This companionship serves them well, and each member of this threesome seems to enjoy a full and active life both at home, and out and about in the community.

Job-based or Role-related Relationships

Only Edgar and Robert are in paid employment, although Maurice is a full-time volunteer with Riding for the Disabled. A job offers opportunities for making relationships, as Robert explains: 'I work at The King's Head doing general odd jobs. I work there mornings and weekends. I have lunch with John and Margaret, who own the pub, and the bar staff. They give me birthday and Christmas presents, and sometimes call in.'

Many people discussed employment opportunities. People recalled the jobs they had done in the past. Bridget, for example, had worked in a domestic capacity in a hospital, a convalescent home, an old people's home and a school; Carol used to work in a factory; and Bruce 'used to work in a gentleman's garden'. Many people, although currently unemployed, would like to have a job, in order to earn money and to meet people. For example, Rita, who attends an adult training centre (ATC) full-time, said: 'I'd like to work at an old people's home, it's more in my line. I'd really like an outside job. I used to work in a hospital years ago, and enjoyed it.' Isabel attends an ATC part-time but would really rather work in a shop, and Dennis, also part-time at an ATC, is making systematic enquiries at all the pubs in town to find a job washing up glasses.

Some people are not going to an ATC, nor are they seeking paid work; they have settled for socially acceptable roles outside the job market, such as housekeeper, housewife, or retired person. Each of these roles entails certain tasks and responsibilities, and certain sets of relationships. Doreen describes herself as 'the housekeeper' in her group home: 'I'm the housekeeper here. I'm not going on holiday because I'm staying here to look after the house. I stay back to do the housework, and I go to the shops for everyone else, and have their meals ready when they get in.'

Helen, Bruce's wife, describes herself as a 'housewife'.

> I get up when my husband says it's time to get up, and I bring his breakfast upstairs. I do the

> jobs in the morning, and cook dinner for us. We wash up together. My husband works in the garden, and I do the shopping at the post office and the co-op round the corner. We sit together after dinner. I do a puzzle, or some knitting, and I might watch TV. I watch whatever he's watching.

Roland, now in his 60s, is retired. He 'potters' through his days. 'I hoover the downstairs rooms, and clean the sinks. I call in at The Wheatsheaf for a drink at lunchtimes when I'm out shopping. I might have a cup of tea in the cafe with Isabel later in the day.' Out on his daily rounds, Roland has made contact with local tradespeople and with some of their other regular customers.

Friendships

Most people in the study have friends - at home, at work, or at the ATC. Sometimes people have friends belonging to their past lives, for example a friendly nurse from hospital days or a previous social worker now reclassified as a personal friend. These friendships are important. They are relaxed and informal relationships in which both parties participate. They are usually reciprocal relationships.

One particular sort of friendship is important in the context of living in the community, and that is a companion - someone with whom to go around. Use of community facilities, and participation in leisure activities, may depend on having a friend to go with - to boost confidence perhaps, or just to share the experience. Some people have home-based friends, or marital partners, who are household companions and community companions in this way.

For example, Ralph and Enid, a married couple, spend a lot of their time out and about together: 'We go shopping together. In the summer, on Sundays, we sometimes go for a walk in the park together. We've got some friends where we used to live, called Mr and Mrs Armstrong, and we pop round there sometimes. Mr Armstrong answers the door and says "Hello, come on in." We go in then and stay for a chat.'

Edgar, Robert and Norma enjoy drinking at their local pub. Edgar explains: 'On Saturday nights we go down the pub to see Dave, the landlord. We walk down and get a taxi back. If its raining, and we're wearing our suits, we don't want to get wet. On Sundays, Norma and me have dinner here then go to The

Hare and Hounds. Robert has his dinner at work then joins us at the pub. I put one behind the bar for him ready for when he comes.' This easy companionship for regular visits to The Hare and Hounds has led to other friendships. The landlord, David, is now a friend, and provides food and the skittle alley for their birthday parties. The captain of the pub pool team, Pete, is also a friend nowadays - and Edgar is a member of the team.

Laura, now widowed and living alone, retains the friendship of a nurse from her hospital days. She describes a day out with her friend, Jean: 'We went to Longleat, we see some lovely roseydendroms, all colours, a real picture. The dog went on the lake, right in the middle of the pond. He liked the water. We had some fun with him. We had a ride out, and stopped at a cafe for dinner. Then we went shopping. Jean likes secondhand shops, picking up stuff, seeing if she can buy anything cheap.'

Other people do not have companions of this sort, and feel this keenly. Geoffrey lives alone and has not made any friends: 'Sometimes I long for a visitor, for someone to knock on my door, and ask me to go for a walk'. Richard lives in a group home with three people, but still feels the need for a companion of his own: 'I like to go out when I've someone to go with.I like to have somebody with me. I've asked my aunty but she's too busy. I have to go on my own. I go to bingo on Friday nights. I go alone. I felt I'd like to go, it would be nice and it would be fun. I go for a bit of fun. There's more women than men - nine men, and all the rest is women. They're quite friendly up the bingo.' But although people are 'quite friendly', Richard still goes alone, sits alone and returns home on his own.

Neighbourhood Relationships

Being accepted by local people is an important consideration for most people in the study. They describe neighbours as 'nice' or 'very friendly', and comment favourably on those who stop to speak to them, or chat across the garden fence. Thus, Daniel says of his neighbours: 'They're friendly, and say "hello" to us', while Laura says of hers: 'Mrs Williams is nice, she talks to me in the garden. Marjorie, who lives on the other side, calls in every day for a chat.' Dennis describes his neighbour Betty as 'very nice. If we're going out we give Betty the milk money and she'll pay the milkman. When we get home we go round for the change.' Arthur comments:

'Plenty of people round here talk to you and all that. They're nice and friendly.'

Often good neighbourliness extends beyond saying hello and chatting together. People gave many examples of good neighbours who follow up kind words with kind deeds. Neighbours alter clocks, write letters, change light bulbs, provide emergency candles, lend money, mend fuses, repair televisions, tend the sick, unblock drains, stop floods and put out fires.

Not everyone, however, found themselves with kind neighbours. Geoffrey's experience is entirely negative: 'I can't ask them for help if I'm ill because they are hard liners. They put rubbish through my letter box, and they bang on the walls when I make a noise.'

Some people reported mixed experiences - some neighbours were kind but others were not. A married couple, Beryl and Keith, describe mixed experiences of this kind. 'Some of the children call us "bastards" and "effing this" and "effing that". They're all quite small, about 7 or 8 or 9. The people next door don't even say "hello" to us, so we try to keep out of their way. We've got friendly with the people upstairs, they're ever so friendly and they bring their grandchildren in to see us.'

Ada and Vincent, too, described mixed experiences when they moved into a village and tried to make contact with their neighbours.

> The neighbours round here, especially next door, they aren't worth living with. She's terrible! You know what country people are! My husband was out there, and he said "Good afternoon madam", and she went inside, slamming the door. On the other side, in no. 8, one minute she'll speak, another minute she won't. We might say 'Hello Mrs Fisher' or 'Good afternoon Mrs Fisher' - then bang goes the door! We have got a very very dear friend up there in no. 14. Mrs Walters is a good friend, and helps us. We took her a bunch of daffodils last week, and she was thrilled.

Some people have moved on from simple acceptance in the neighbourhood, to becoming part of the web of neighbourhood relationships. Such participation in local events, and involvement with local people, brings with it a special reward - a sense of belonging. Only a few people have succeeded in making these inroads, and they have done so in two ways -

through making a contribution to the welfare or wellbeing of others, and through developing relationships which are reciprocal.

Ralph and Enid, a married couple, help elderly and handicapped people in their neighbourhood. Ralph explains: 'I call on Mrs Harris every morning to see if she's all right, beause she lives on her own. If she wants anything down the shops I'll get it for her.' Enid says: 'I do Marjorie's washing, and the old man's washing. They can't do their own, so we help. I do Marjorie's bath towels and hand towels for her, and put them outside on my line. I took some clean dry washing over to her the other afternoon and found her fast asleep by the fire. I didn't want to wake her, so I put the things in a pile on the settee.' Ralph and Enid between them spent 47 years in long-stay hospitals, as recipients of services. Now they have become dispensers of care and kindness to others. Their role as voluntary helpers in their neighbourhood has given them a sense of belonging, and a sense of purpose to their lives.

Edgar, Robert and Norma participate in local events, and frequent local places. They enter the carnival, drink in the pub, and invite neighbours and friends to birthday parties, and in for Christmas drinks. They do football pools with neighbours, an activity which involves reciprocal house calls. Edgar remembers the time they all won: 'A friend of ours, Pauline, she won at the same time as we did. You should have seen her face, she nearly fainted on the floor. I had to pick her up and put her on the sofa.' Edgar, Robert and Norma are part of their neighbourhood, they are on first name terms with people in their street and nearby streets, and with the people they meet in the pub. They have developed reciprocal relationships not only with Pauline, but with John, Daphne, Dave, Pete and others.

The five people who have moved beyond community acceptance to the next stage of community participation are exceptions. Most people in the study have settled for far less.

DEVELOPING OPPORTUNITIES FOR RELATIONSHIPS

The checklist of relationships used here is based on the real-life experiences of the people followed up in the Somerset study. Their experiences are rich and varied. Some people describe their achievement in keeping old friends, and in making new ones. Others, however, describe the disappointment, sadness or loneliness which accompanies their 'failure' to extend their personal set of relationships. The 'failure' is, of course, not primarily their own. By and large it is a 'failure' on the part of those of us who are involved in setting up and supporting residential services in the community for people with a mental handicap. Sometimes, we have been slow to realise that helping people settle into ordinary houses in ordinary streets does not of itself bring integration into 'the community' or a high quality of life. For that, we have to look beyond bricks and mortar, to ways of encouraging the development of social relationships in community settings. The rest of this chapter looks at practical steps which can be taken to this end by those involved in residential services - staff, families, volunteers, friends and residents themselves - including services catering for people with a more severe degree of handicap than the participants in the Somerset study.

Rebuilding Family Relationships

Moving into the community from a long-stay hospital may bring with it the chance for easier and more frequent contact with families. Experience shows, however, that rebuilding family relationships before, during and after such a move may take as much sensitivity and careful planning as the development of any other relationships. Many parents, not surprisingly, view the imminent closure of the local hospital and/or the resettlement of their relative in the local neighbourhood with disquiet, and are not slow to voice their opposition. Some may not believe that their relatives can possibly survive in an ordinary house in the community, given that they were once told that they would be 'better off' in hospital. They may have real doubts about the amount of staff supervision and support available, the availability of long-term funding for the home and of monitoring of the quality of life inside it, the reaction of their relatives to a new life of this kind and the outlook for their long-term future. In particular, they may have anxieties - especially if they are themselves elderly - about the new responsibilities that may descend on them with the move. Will there be pressure on them to 'take back' their relative if this new community placement fails?

Some families may, of course, welcome a move into the community for their relative: 'It's an opportunity for her to have a home of her own ... We might see more of her.' Most will probably have a mixture of positive and negative feelings of these kinds (Hannam, 1985; Carruthers, in Allen et al., 1983).

So what can be done to help families - and their relatives - in these circumstances? Recent experience in community services suggests that the following will help:

(1) involving parents in the planning and development of new community services from the outset;
(2) involving families in individual programme plans with and for their particular relatives (alongside professional and other staff);
(3) time and space for families to talk through anxieties and reservations about plans (with a social worker, community nurse or whoever else seems appropriate) to ease worries and help alleviate past guilt ('Did we do wrong in letting him go originally?');
(4) talking to other parents whose relatives have already made the move;
(5) clear information about practical issues - for example, how and where their relative will spend their day; how they will be helped to learn new skills (crossing roads, handling money); in particular, contingency plans if 'things go wrong';
(6) an early chance to meet staff who will be working in the new home, plus other residents (and their families if appropriate).

Recent research shows - encouragingly - that although parents frequently do initially oppose plans for their relatives to move into the community (because they believe them to be happy where they are), once the move is made they are very happy with the result (Rudie and Reidl, 1984).

Of course, assistance may also be necessary to help those who are making the move as they redevelop family ties. For some, guidance on regulating social contact may be needed so that relatives are not immediately overwhelmed with constant phone calls or visits. Help in using a diary or calendar to fix appointments, outings and visits may pay dividends. Once a balance agreeable to both sides is found, then picking up family relationships may bring other spinoffs, beyond the security of being an active part of a family again. For one resident of a new community service, attendance with a married brother at a local church has re-established other social links in the neighbourhood which were severed during the years in hospital; for others, family relationships have brought the pleasure of reciprocity to their lives for the first time, as people 'with a handicap' are encouraged by staff and others to themselves adopt a 'caring' role towards elderly or frail parents.

Help with Relationships at Home

Just as relationships with families may need sensitive attention in order to flourish, so too may relationships in the new home. In good services which have been carefully planned and tailored to the individual needs of particular, known clients, residents will hopefully be settling in with others who are already known to them as friends. They will have been involved together in preparation for the planned move for some time. Even so, guidance will be needed from staff - whether staff working full-time in the home or professionals supporting the residents on a popping-in basis, like a social worker, community nurse or home help - to help iron out the differences and difficulties inevitable in group living. At a basic level, advice on practical issues like sharing responsibilities for shopping, cleaning, cooking and so on, may be needed. Guidance may also be required on appropriate behaviour when sharing a home: for example, the need to put on a dressing gown before going downstairs in the morning in a mixed household; the inappropriateness of walking into other people's rooms when they are not there or of regularly wandering around the house in the middle of the night. Most difficult of all to resolve may be problems and tensions between different members of the group, and acceptable ways of dealing with them.

Most of these difficulties will be familiar to anyone who has experienced group living, whether or not they have a 'mental handicap' label. The difficulties will be aggravated, however, where households are not set up to accommodate the needs and wishes of particular individuals who seem compatible and want to live together, but are established in accordance with some predetermined plan. Fitting people to houses ('we need another person for that four-bedded house') leads to greater relationship difficulties in the long run than starting the other way round. ('Peter and Brian get on well together. We need to look for a three-bedroomed house for them and a staff member').

Difficulties may also reduce as planners begin to 'think small', as individuals may live more happily with just one chosen companion than in the groups of five or six deemed desirable in the recent past.

A striking lesson now emerging from community services which have been in operation for a number of years is that - not surprisingly - people with handicaps, like their 'non-handicapped' peers, sometimes like to make changes and move on. From group home to shared flat, from bedsit to married life - once someone with a handicap is settled in the community they are not necessarily settled in that particular domestic situation for life. Moving home within the community, and adjusting to the changes in relationships and lifestyles involved, may require just as much support and advice from families, friends and professional staff, as the original move from hospital to community living.

Developing Friendships at Work and in the Neighbourhood

People who have a 'mental handicap' label develop friendships in the same way as the rest of us - that is, primarily through getting to know people at work, or in the course of other daytime activities, or through involvement in shared interests and activities during leisure time. Work (or unpaid work-experience) provides a particularly good environment for making contact with new people, which may develop over time into friendships, based on shared coffee and lunch breaks and out of work social activities. Thus, one man interviewed in a recent study commented of his work: 'I've got good friends here. We go to football, play darts. I went to the Christmas dance.' Another woman explained: 'In work experience you get out and mix with people. It makes you feel more grown up. It's not the money, it's the independence. I want to be part of the people' (Porterfield and Gathercole, 1985).

Once fellow employees have been helped over any initial apprehensions or misunderstandings about their 'handicapped' colleagues (and they, in turn, have been helped to learn how to behave appropriately in different work situations), relationships can develop well and people can be accepted on an individual basis. Staff (in either the home or employment-finding service) may then be able to help a preliminary acquaintance develop into a deeper relationship or friendship by hints on how to move forward socially - for example, going to the pub after work (and learning how to buy a round of drinks), inviting a colleague back home for a meal one evening, or suggesting a shared trip to the cinema. The ATC offers opportunities for friendship in the same way - albeit only within the 'handicapped' world.

For those not in full-time occupation in the day, opportunities for making relationships can be fostered through other kinds of activity, for example, involvement in local conservation projects, attendance at Women's Institute meetings, belonging to a local 'good neighbours' scheme - all with whatever help (from volunteers or paid staff) is needed to make participation possible. Some individuals may have a clear idea of the activities in which they would like to engage: the task for staff may simply be to find a volunteer or befriender to help them do this until such time as independent relationships with other participants in that activity may develop. Many more individuals will have little idea of the huge possible range of activities available in the community. Again, 'leisure volunteers' or, in some areas, 'neighbourhood workers' employed through the Manpower Services Commission's community programme, may have an important role to play in introducing individuals to new experiences and activities on a one-to-one basis, and gradually helping them to become integrated into the social club or leisure pursuit of their choice (Hutchinson and Lord, 1979; Gathercole, 1981; Lord, 1981; Gaskell, 1985). In this way, Sean has become an accepted member of the local Catholic Club, where he regularly goes for a drink. Martin has become an indispensable member of an informal football team which meets to play every Sunday in the local park - the youths who make up the team value Martin, who has limited communication skills, for the much more important skills he has with the ball.

A similar principle may apply in the field of adult education classes. People may need initial help in deciding on the class of their choice - whether it be cookery, literacy, pottery, yoga or keep-fit - and further help from a volunteer (either specially recruited for this purpose or found from amongst existing students in the class) to understand and keep up with the class from time to time (Billis, 1984). Again, from a shared interest or evening class, relationships and friendships with non-handicapped peers may blossom.

Within the locality, good relations with neighbours may be encouraged by the exchange of surplus garden produce over the fence, by participation in neighbourhood schemes and events and by the employment of local staff (and volunteers) who are already accepted in neighbourhood life. Sensible measures at the outset of a community service - for example, only moving two or three people with handicaps into any one house in a street; making sure their homes look neat and presentable on the outside and in keeping with other houses in the area; not holding public meeting to advertise the planned move - will increase community acceptance and participation and the possibility of warm neighbourhood relationships (Atkinson and Ward, 1985).

CONCLUSIONS

Not everyone with a handicap is new to the community in which they are now living. Many have lived all their lives at home with their families and will continue to do so for the foreseeable future. A few of these have flourishing networks of relationships based on family and other contacts and activities in the area. Many more lead much more restricted lives with limited social opportunities (Wertheimer, 1981; 1983) and welcome the chance of developing activities and friendships offered by some new community services. Others now have the chance with the support of these services to move away from the family home into their own home in the neighbourhood, as their non-handicapped brothers and sisters have done. In these families, especially where there are elderly, lone and frail parents, support for the change may be needed as much by parents as by son or daughter. Residential staff, social workers and others may need to invest as much time, sensitivity and energy in developing alternative systems of support, social activities, contacts and friendships for parents left on their own after years of caring as they do for the handicapped relative who is moving out. It is, after all, not just for people with handicaps, but for their parents and indeed their professional helpers as well, that friendships make all the difference to the quality of life.

ACKNOWLEDGEMENTS

Thanks are due to Somerset social services department, and to Somerset health authority, for supporting the follow-up study of people living in the community. Thanks are due, too, to the consumers in this study, for giving their time and for sharing their views. Thanks are also due to the Joseph Rowntree Memorial Trust for financing the research into the Wells Road Service on which part of this chapter is based, and to all those involved in the service for sharing their experiences.

REFERENCES

Allen, P., Brown, F., Carruthers, P. and Robson, I. (1983) 'Getting Severely Handicapped Children and Young Adults out of Hospital to Live in Ordinary Housing', in Association of Professions for the Mentally Handicapped, Mental Handicap: Care in the Community (APMH, London)

Atkinson, D. and Ward, L. (1985) 'A Part of the Community: Social Integration and Neighbourhood Networks', in Heginbotham, C. (ed.) Aspects of Residential Services (Campaign for Mentally Handicapped People, London)

Billis, J. (1984) From Theory to Practice. Adult Education Integration Project. (MENCAP, London)

Gaskell, E. (1985) Link-up. An Integrated Leisure Service for Mentally Handicapped Teenagers and Young Adults Living in the Community (Barnardo's, Ilford)

Gathercole, C.E. (1981) Residential Alternatives for Adults who are Mentally Handicapped. 4: Leisure, Social Integration and Volunteers (BIMH, Kidderminster)

Hannam, C. (1985) 'A Cake for David', New Society, 72, 1165

Hutchinson, P. and Lord, J. (1979) Recreation Integration: Issues and Alternatives in Community Involvement and Leisure Services (Leisurability Publications, Toronto)

Lord, J. (1981) Participation: Expanding Community and Leisure Experiences for People with Severe Handicaps (Canada, National Institute of Mental Retardation, Toronto)

Porterfield, J. and Gathercole, C. (1985) The Employment of People with Mental Handicap. Progress towards an Ordinary Working Life (King's Fund Centre, London)

Rudie, F. and Reidl, G. (1984) 'Attitudes of Parents/Guardians of Mentally Retarded Former State Hospital Residents Toward Current Community Placement', American Journal of Mental Deficiency, 89 (3), 295-7

Wertheimer, A. (1981) Living for the Present. Older Parents with a Mentally Handicapped Person Living at Home (Campaign for Mentally Handicapped People, London)

Wertheimer, A. (1983) Leisure (Campaign for Mentally Handicapped People, London)

Chapter Eleven

HOMES AFTER THE HOSPITALS CLOSE: ACCOMMODATION AND THE MENTALLY ILL IN THE COMMUNITY

Jim Monach and Phil Thomas

INTRODUCTION

The rhetoric of community care for the mentally ill has been heard for over 25 years, since the days of Enoch Powell's 'watershed' speech in 1961 (MIND, 1961), whilst action has been slow to follow. Suddenly, however, the pace of change is quickening, very dramatically. Those large Victorian buildings that for the last 100 years have been homes for so many people are finally to be phased out. It is now planned that before the end of the century they will be closed down, to be handed over, in many cases, to the land developers to be used for very different purposes than housing those who were judged to be insane. This is surely an event that should be eagerly welcomed, that we should be planning for with enthusiasm. It is certainly an event that we have been told many times is long overdue. As one commentator wrote some ten years ago (Meacher, 1976):

> When 71000 people in this country have between them spent fully one and a half million years in our outdated and isolated mental illness hospitals, the rest of us cannot simply sit back and say how good it would be to bring these people back to life in the community, if only we had the resources and staff to do it.

Since this was written the atmosphere has radically changed. Now, at a time when hospital administrators are actively planning the closure of mental hospitals, few people who work in the field of mental illness can sit back and make wistful comments about community care.

Despite this, however, the atmosphere is hardly one of optimism, except perhaps amongst those in the profit-making private sector eager to fill the gaps they know will increasingly exist. The reasons for pessimism are clear enough. In the 15 years that followed Enoch Powell's speech, the 1960s and early 1970s, finance was comparatively plentiful and yet the increase of facilities for care of the mentally ill in the community was slow and haphazard. Now, at a time when finance is scarce and welfare cuts are the order of the day, the fear is that closure of hospitals is really about saving health authorities money and not about improving the home life of the people who have spent those million and a half years in hospital. We shall return to this argument later.

If fear that community care is to be 'a cheap option' is one reason for pessimism, a second and equally fundamental one is the track record of community care planning over the last quarter of a century. Questions like the amount and types of accommodation that will be required still need workable answers. Just a glance at the practitioner journals with articles titled, 'Mental health hostels - a waste of money?' (Garioch, 1978), 'Group homes - a success?' (Thornicroft, 1979), 'Special housing?' (Murray, 1978), 'What future for the mentally ill?' (Pritlove, 1978), and 'Where to from a "halfway" hostel?' (Smith, 1980) indicates the questioning, doubt and confusion that surrounds this area. These articles all pose the question of how scarce resources should be spent; whether on expensive staffed hostels, on cheaper unstaffed group homes, on supporting landladies, or on adapting ordinary housing. The consequence of the failure to work out an adequate answer to this question is not an academic one, it has immediate implications for those who have suffered from psychiatric illness and are trying to build some stability for themselves within the system of community care, and for the people who work with them. Set against the background of the imminent closure of the big psychiatric hospitals, for too many still the final safety-net, the failure to answer the question raises those terrifying possibilities of homelessness, loneliness and abandonment.

In this chapter we are concerned with the accommodation or home needs of the mentally ill. We will discuss what we believe to be some of the most important issues that will determine whether the closure of the mental hospitals will result in positive or negative experiences for those who have suffered from or are suffering from disabling psychiatric illness. By drawing on the experience of the last 25 years we aim to emphasise some of the lessons that should have been learned, some of the dilemmas that remain and some of the questions that are unanswered.

PLANNING FOR CHANGE

Major changes in the system of mental health care have not always followed a rational and careful planning process.

The obvious example where planning did not take place was in Ronald Reagan's California where there was a massive close-down of the state's mental institutions with the discharge of 32000 of the 37000 inpatients. The 'success' of the programme was seen simply in terms of the massive savings to the State's budget without any attempt to reinvest this money in community facilities (Ramon, 1985). Indeed there is considerable evidence from America that the emphasis on community care programmes in the last 20 years has had more to do with the prospect of saving money than concern for the quality of care for the mentally ill itself (Scull, 1977).

In this country it can be said that planning for community care has been piecemeal and reactive, rather than integrated and proactive. Recent contributions from MIND (MIND, 1983) and the Kings Fund (Towell and McAusland, 1984) have suggested ways in which a more orderly process could be introduced, and some of the worst aspects of unplanned development be avoided.

Very recently, however, the pace of change has quickened, although it is perhaps unlikely that this change is caused by a rational assesssment of newly available strategies or ideas. Indeed, both the urgings of central Government (DHSS, 1975a, 1976 and 1981b) and the literature available (for example, MIND, 1983; Shepherd, 1984; Reed and Lomas, 1984) demonstrate that the principal new element is a monetarist government determined to limit the growth of public spending and, specifically, review the role of the welfare state. The central idea of a community-based integrated mental health service, moving away from institutional care is not new (see Curtis Committee, 1946; Mental Health Act 1959; Cawley and McLachlan, 1973). Few would dissent from the central position stated succinctly by the DHSS itself (DHSS, 1981a):

> Most people who need long term care can and

> should be looked after in the community. This is what most of them want for themselves and those responsible for their care believe to be best. There are many people in hospital who would not need to be there if appropriate community services were available.

The disagreements largely focus upon how best to provide these community services, what they might look like and, principally, the suspicion that despite a lot of contrary evidence (DHSS, 1981b; Short, 1985) community care is seen as a cheap option. Mrs Short's committee put the contrary view succinctly: 'It (community care) cannot and must not be done on the cheap ... It is no good imagining that community care will save money' (Short, 1985). It is unlikely, however, that Sheffield is unique among health authorities in the assumption made in the 1984-85 round of decennial strategic plans required by the DHSS. Sheffield's plan envisages a major reorientation towards a community-based mental health service, and anticipates that this service can be more effective than the current, hospital bed-orientated, service at 90 per cent of the cost, in real terms (Sheffield Health Authority, 1985). Bamford (1984) refers to current social policy, which advocates increasing local authority responsibility for service provision yet severely restricts local authority expenditure, as an 'Alice in Wonderland policy'.

In the area of residential care, providing alternatives to the discredited hospital bed inevitably means, in part, at least, non-health service care also. This might be contested by the trade unions, as David Williams of COHSE did in his minority report to the Jay Report (Jay, 1979), but the evidence still seems to support the view that health staffed hostels are the least likely to implement community and normality orientated policies and practices (Ryan, 1979; Heron, 1981). This is not the place to discuss in detail the concept of mental illness itself, over which controversy has raged throughout the century. However, it has frequently been pointed out that demand for mental health services is a function of what is available (see, for example, Freeman, 1983), and attempts at quantification may be as sterile as attempts to number the mentally ill. This is particularly true as the focus moves from the 'old long stay' in the traditional mental hospitals, towards a less institutionalised, younger client group. One short-stay hostel for the mentally ill typically described this change from its opening in 1974, 'the hostel worked through older long-stay hospital residents in its first 4ä years, when some 41 per cent of people admitted had been in hospital for over a year. Latterly, the intake has been younger and less institutionalised, and the average length of stay has been kept well under a year' (Crine, 1982). It is not always evident how the blueprints for the residential component of a community service are arrived at (DHSS, 1975a; Ryan, 1979; Morris, 1981, MIND, 1983), beyond the Maoist principle that a hundred flowers should be allowed to bloom (Mao, 1966). Bradshaws' useful taxonomy (Bradshaw, 1972) identifies four categories of need:

(1) normative need, that is, as defined by professional groups or statute;
(2) comparative need, that is, as evidenced by comparing services available to meet similar difficulties elsewhere;
(3) expressed need, that is, the active demand for a service;
(4) felt need, that is, that which reflects the perception of the individuals concerned.

The principal source for normative need remains the White Paper *Better Service for the Mentally Ill* (DHSS, 1975a). Ryan estimated that by 1979 only 43 per cent of the residential resources recommended by the White Paper were in fact available (Ryan, 1979), and in any event increased ambitions in the community care lobby might suggest a greater need in this area as the number of hospital beds falls below that advocated in the same document. Statute does not tread such thorny ground; the Mental Health Act 1983 contents itself with generalities when resanctioning the provision of non-hospital residential accommodation.

The King's Fund Centre, Good Practices in Mental Health, and MIND have all played an important role in collecting and disseminating information as to the varied ways in which different communities are attempting to meet this need.

The expressed needs are particularly difficult to assess. As argued above, it is difficult to isolate these needs from services available. Not only in the mental health field, but in all health and social services, demand is clearly in large part moulded by what is seen to be provided. It may be a matter of inability to conceptualise the possibility of an unknown service - of which community mental health centres may be an example (Hargreaves, 1984). This could be regarded as the psychiatric counterpart to demand for well-woman clinics. Alternatively this might reflect the withdrawal of a previous service, principally long-term psychiatric hospital care.

Finally, there is a welcome increase in studies which seek the views of consumers themselves (Raphael and Peers, 1972; Creer and Wing, 1974; Brandon, 1981) as well as, specifically in this area, the incorporation of their views in studies of psychiatric residential care (Ryan and Hewett, 1976, MacAndrew, Overton and White, 1980; Pritlove, 1985). Pritlove suggests that residents in a group home principally looked for independence and a sense of being at home. The group home studied fell down in respect of 'homeliness' but 'most residents, however, wanted to stay: that is the acid test' (Pritlove, 1985).

The Italian experiment promoted by Psichiatria Democratica (PD) took seriously the proposition that the provision of alternatives was primarily a matter of making unavailable the traditional, accepted solutions, and challenging established attitudes (Ramon, 1983). The details of PD have become well known and a matter of some controversy (Jones and Poletti, 1984). However the controversy is largely about the extent and adequacy of change throughout Italy, than the real advantages offered to patients by developing multidisciplinary, non-institutional alternatives to '<u>L'Instituzione Negata</u>' (Basaglia <u>et al</u>., 1968). What is clear is that a new pattern of service can be developed given the commitment of service providers, but the political context is important and assuming the old institutions are capable of change may be illusory. On the latter score, Basaglia did not share the optimism of his UK mentors, Maxwell Jones, R.D. Laing or Dennis Martin. An illustration of the necessary commitment is the personal account of one Italian psychiatrist pioneering a community mental health centre based on Southern Italy who took a cut of half his salary to do so. Shulamit Ramon herself argues (Ramon, 1983) that PD cannot be simply imported to another country, and would accept that Italy started from a very much more backward system than obtains in the United Kingdom. Ramon's own reflections on a visit to California reinforce the warnings of personal misery and degradation that can result from failing to provide realistic alternatives to the mental hospital (Ramon, 1985).

The dangers of an institutional mental illness service have been well documented (Goffman, 1961; Wing and Brown, 1970; Rosenhan, 1973); by contrast the benefits of a community-based, multidisciplinary mental health service are less well documented, although valuable evidence is accumulating (Stein and Test, 1980; Braun et al., 1981).

In the final analysis, even careful and thorough planning of future patterns of service, however inspired, can be of no account without 'some real increase over a period of years in expenditure on service' (Short, 1985).

CREATING CHOICE AND DIVERSITY

A decade ago the DHSS report, Better Services for the Mentally Ill (DHSS, 1975a) expressed the need for a range of housing and residential services to be provided by different organisations, both statutory and voluntary, for those with both short-term and long-term needs. The range included the following.

Hospital Hostels

These units were seen as offering care for 'new' long-stay patients. It was stated that they were likely to be 'fairly large houses reasonably close to the general hospital psychiatric unit, with the patients being cared for in a domestic atmosphere but with night nursing supervision'.

Hostels

These were envisaged as small units, with around 10 or 15 places, offering short-term care and rehabilitation. It was stated, 'Their basic purpose is to provide intensive care and rehabilitation on a relatively short-term basis'.

Staffed Homes

These units were distinguished from hostels in that they were for people with longer-term needs. They were to be 'a form of accommodation offering continuing support, and, in which, whilst rehabilitation remains an important element, the emphasis is on providing a home'.

Group Homes and Clustered Bedsitters
'Unstaffed accommodation,' it was stated, 'can be used to meet both long-term and short-term needs for shelter, but without the same degree of support as in a staffed home.' It was suggested there was scope for experimentation in this area, although group homes and bedsitters, possibly clustered around a staffed hostel, were discussed in particular.

Supervised Lodgings
This was described as a 'rather different form of long-term support', where 'the landlady represents the first line of support' and thus would herself need considerable advice and support.

Ordinary Housing
In another chapter of the report different situations were described where 'what is required is essentially ordinary housing rather than any special form of residential accommodation, and it is right to look to local housing authorities, working together with social services departments to find ways of solving these problems'.

In short, it was stated, that what was needed was 'a range of accommodation, from the purpose-built staffed hostel to the ordinary council house with only occasional social work support' (DHSS, 1975a). What was questionable about Better Services for the Mentally Ill was the calculations about how much of each resource was needed. It is also possible to quibble with some of its categories, one example being the strict distinction between a 'hostel' and a 'staffed home'. However, it is perhaps a sad comment on the state of community care that it remains unparalleled in its attempt to describe the range of residential and accommodation resources needed by the mentally ill. Other writers since 1975 have discussed parts of the range needed (Ryan, 1979; Wing and Morris, 1981), but nowhere is there a more complete list.

This lack of a systematic analysis of the accommodation needs of the mentally ill has characterised the development of alternatives to hospital in the postwar period. In retrospect, it is possible to see the recent history of the development of community care in terms of two distinct periods, both of which threw up different 'answers' to the question of how to accommodate the mentally ill and then found these answers to be inadequate.

In the first period, up to around 1970, the main alternative to hospital was seen as the hostel or the staffed home, originally the province of voluntary organisations but increasingly provided by local authorities in response to the 1959 Mental Health Act. In 1970 a DHSS census showed that of 2689 residential places for the mentally ill provided by local authorities and voluntary organisations, 2584 were in staffed homes and just 105 in unstaffed accommodation (DHSS, 1975b). In a major piece of research in the 1960s, Apte (1968) found that the hostels he studied were characterised by confusion, lack of purpose, lack of understanding of aims and objectives, and that they were, in effect, often little more than mini-institutions in the community. He even found that some hostels put more restrictions on their residents than the hospital wards from which they had come.

Apte's recommendation was that hostels should be run more actively along the lines of 'a halfway house' by 'providing transitional social environments between hospitals and the community' and that this would result in 'an efficient turnover of population'. The view that to succeed hostels have to have a rapid turnover of residents remains influential, as exemplified by a more recent article in which a hostel warden wrote of 'the danger' of residents staying above 12 months and of 'the great care' which 'has to be taken to avoid this happening' (Smith, 1980).

However, further research into hostels in the 1970s showed that while regimes in hostels had greatly improved in terms of clearer aims and objectives and a decrease in restrictions, residents continued to stay for lengthy periods, and indeed that a rapid turnover of residents was not necessarily a desirable aim (Hewett and Ryan, 1975; Hewett, Ryan and Wing, 1975; Ryan and Hewett, 1976; Hewett, 1979; Ryan and Wing, 1979).

In the second period, associated with the 1970s, unstaffed accommodation came to be seen as the main alternative to hospital. One writer summed up the change in this way (Pritlove, 1978):

> If the 1960s was the decade of transitional care, the 1970s seem likely to be labelled the decade of compensatory care ... The typical form of accommodation here is not the short-term staffed hostel but the small group home with no resident staff.

Compared to the purpose-built hostel, the advantages of group homes, bedsitters and lodgings were thought huge; they were cheaper to run, they relied on ordinary housing stock and they offered long-term solutions. They were the obvious answer when the high demand for places in the community was being highlighted. One survey, for example, concluded:

> National figures show that there are only 4500 hostel beds in England and Wales for the mentally ill. The government estimates that at least 11000 places are needed to meet immediate needs for accommodation (Knight and Murray, 1976).

Thus, in the late 1970s the journals were full of articles by writers who were involved in one scheme or another to provide immediate accommodation for ex-patients in the community, exhorting their merits so that others would take them up; accommodation in group homes (Leopoldt and Hurn, 1976; Pritlove, 1976, 1978; Garioch, 1978), lodgings (Anstee, 1978) and clustered bedsitters (Thornicroft, 1979). In these articles the argument was put that for the chronically ill the mainstay of community provision should be unstaffed accommodation, supplemented by a small number of hostels which should be used only for short-term, rehabilitative purposes.

However, more recently the limitations of unstaffed accommodation as an alternative for hospital patients have been realised. It has become clear that for many ex-patients life in a group home or bedsit can be more lonely and more 'impoverished' than in a large hospital (Thornicroft, 1979; Ryan and Wing, 1979). Moreover, the evidence from research into the needs of long-stay patients, both the 'old long-stay' (Christie Brown, Ebringer and Freedman, 1977; Pryce, 1977a and b) and the 'new long-stay' (Mann and Cree, 1976) was that many of these people would need well-staffed accommodation if they were to survive outside hospital. As one writer put it (Paykel, 1978):

> There is no doubt that group homes without resident staff have been very successful, particularly for discharge of some old long-stay,

but he added:

> In the future we must also cope in the community with more severe schizophrenics, showing impaired social function and liability to occasional episodes of disturbed behaviour.

Thus, ten years of experience since the publication of Better Services for the Mentally Ill has merely emphasised the point it originally made, that if community care is to succeed a range of services from well-staffed hostel and homes to unstaffed accommodation is needed and that it is not possible to emphasise one 'solution' over another, whether that 'solution' be a well-functioning halfway house or a successful group home or lodgings scheme. What is always cause for concern, however, is that the more expensive end of the range will be sacrificed even if units can prove their success. Thus, for example, hospital hostels have been shown to enrich the lives of chronically ill patients (Acker, Wykes and Wing, 1979), but because of their expense units like Cranberry Terrace in Southampton are unlikely to be repeated up and down the country (BBC, 1985).

At the same time, what is needed is not just a range of accommodation, but an adequate level of provision within that range. Thus, even in a city like Sheffield, which is regarded by the government as a 'high spending authority', and where its policy-makers are committed to the provision of a range of accommodation for the mentally ill (Sheffield District Labour Party, 1984), the level of service remains inadequate despite considerable expansion in recent years. In 1973 the Authority had just 48 places in residential care (MIND, 1973); 12 years later it has 38 places in traditional hostels, a further 60 places in 'care and cluster schemes' (staffed units with clustered flats and group homes), a supported landladies scheme, and it also makes a significant contribution towards the running costs of two hostels and three group homes within the voluntary sector. Yet despite this, the growth of private and commercial ventures and the increasing numbers of mentally ill people in local establishments for the single homeless indicates the extent of the inadequacy of the present provision. Many local authorities will have considerably worse provisions than this. It is possible, however, to underestimate the gains made over the last two decades. If at times there may have been too close an adherence to one fashion or another, the net outcome has been considerable experience and knowledge about the usefulness and limitations of different forms of supported accommodation for the mentally ill as alternatives to hospital. If, and it is a big 'if', the political will were there to provide the necessary funding, we could indeed look forward with some optimism towards the closure of the hospitals and towards the rehabilitation of those people who live or have lived within them.

POSITIVE REHABILITATION

The concept of 'rehabilitation', like that of 'community care', is much used. It is perhaps comforting for professionals to know that, if they cannot cure people who have had a serious psychiatric illness, they can at least help by rehabilitating them. When research offered hard evidence (Wing and Brown, 1970) for what others had already described (Goffman, 1961), that spending years in a psychiatric hospital could actually increase the handicaps of mental illness, the impetus behind rehabilitation programmes was increased. Few psychiatric hospitals now will not have their 'rehab' units alongside their 'acute' units. Workers in social services are also keen on rehabilitation. How often, when a person is being considered for a place in a hostel or day centre, is the question put as to whether he or she is 'rehabilitative material'? It seems to be a truism that there is more job satisfaction in working with people who can be 'rehabilitated' than with people who have a need for continuing care.

What then do we mean by 'rehabilitation' in this context? One clear statement about this is contained in the concept of the 'halfway house' (Apte, 1968). A halfway house or rehabilitative hostel offers a person a limited period, often one year, in which he or she can be helped from a state of dependence (on a psychiatric ward or with his or her family) to a state of comparative independence so that he or she can manage on his or her own (Apte, 1968; Durkin, 1971; Leopoldt and Hurn, 1976; Smith, 1980).

Rehabilitation, in this sense, has obvious appeal. It means that resources can be offered to a person for a limited time only, so that in the long term money can be saved when that person is independent. It is a view well summed up by two researchers of small hostels for alcoholics where the expectation was that residents:

> make rapid rehabilitative progress along a

smooth upward path towards a planned and orderly departure, followed by re-entry to the approved non-marginal world of social and occupational stability (Otto and Orford, 1978).

An obvious attempt to turn this concept into bricks and mortar is that of the purpose-built rehabilitative hostel that has two or three wings, representing stages towards independence through which the resident has physically to move. Whilst this sort of rehabilitation may work for some, its limitations for others, in particular those with chronic handicaps, has fortunately been recognised. In particular it has been realised that too strict an adherence to a transitional philosophy can perpetuate instability, and increase pressures towards psychiatric breakdown (Ryan and Hewett, 1976; Wing, 1980). Further evidence for this has come from the research into expressed emotion and life events as triggering factors behind schizophrenic breakdowns (Brown and Birley, 1970; Vaughn and Leff, 1976; Leff and Vaughn, 1980). One psychiatrist has described the person who suffers from schizophrenia as having to walk a 'tightrope', where either too much or too little social pressure can lead to breakdown (Wing, 1978).

A more sensitive concept of rehabilitation has been developed by those concerned with social psychiatry (Early, 1965; Wing, 1980). A major proponent of this approach is J.K. Wing who has described rehabilitation as 'the process of minimising psychiatric impairments' and 'of providing options which allows the disabled person a realistic choice so that he or she can make a free decision as to how to act' (Wing, 1980). It is the provision of a range of accommodation and services to allow choice which surely is crucial to a person-centred concept of rehabilitation. In the same article, Wing (1980), when describing the sort of range needed, used the metaphor of a ladder in which the rungs are close together. People who have suffered from mental illness need help and support to climb back up the social ladder but at their pace and not at a pace imposed upon them. Another metaphor used is that of the escalator, stressing that an ex-patient will only want to get on to the escalator if there are safe and frequent places to get off at.

Again, therefore, the experience of community care and the research associated particularly with social psychiatry over the last two decades have led to a more sensitive understanding of the needs of people who have suffered or are suffering from serious mental illness when their rehabilitation is under consideration. The problem remains, however, of how far sensitivity towards the rehabilitation needs of the mentally ill can be maintained in practice when community services are overburdened and under resourced. Will it be possible to plan for the right level of support and accommodation for the large numbers of patients to be discharged from hospitals and, indeed, for those with mental illness already living in the community (Bennett, 1978), when the hospitals are closed down? or will attempts at any meaningful rehabilitation be jettisoned as the need for any sort of accommodation to avoid homelessness becomes paramount?

Increasingly, too, accommodation for the mentally ill is being provided by the private sector, where the first motive is profit. What happens to the rehabilitation of the mentally ill in this situation? It is perhaps too early to assess the full consequences but it is difficult to see how profit-making organisations will want to encourage people to move up the rehabilitative ladder and dispense with their services. Surely the more likely consequence is that of the image portrayed in a recent television programme when a large number of men were seen sitting blankly around a large room handing over their DHSS payments to the proprietor (BBC, 1985).

ROLE OF THE COMMUNITY

Many writers have pointed out how woolly the image of the term community has become in the context of the provision of welfare and health services (see, for example, Bell and Newby, 1971; Abrams, 1977; Walker, 1982). This woolliness is perhaps most clearly exemplified in the DHSS's (1977) document, The Way Forward:

> In this document, the term 'community' covers a whole range of provision, including hospitals, hostels, day hospitals, residential homes, day centres and domiciliary support. The term 'community care' embraces primary health care and all the above services, whether provided by health authorities, local authorities, independent contractors, voluntary bodies, community self-help or family and friends.

In such a context clearly no change is required;

hospital care is community care. However, the phrase in its usual meanings perhaps emphasises several key principles which differentiate the two.

First, community care is seen as rejecting institutional care in favour of models which are small scale, informal and geared to individual freedom and choice. Pritlove (1985) notes the growth of specialist mental health accommodation which is without resident staff, 17.1 per cent of the total in 1973 to 38.1 per cent in 1982, although his study demonstrates that not only large institutions inhibit independence. Second, the use of ordinary facilities and opportunities is advocated rather than principally those which are segregated and specialist. This would tend to disapprove of multipurpose, multirole accommodation as the traditional asylums have become in favour of the same separation of residence, work, education and leisure that 'ordinary' members of the community experience. This is an important element of the normalisation principle (Wolfensberger, 1972). Third, the role of informal networks - family and neighbours, and the contribution of both organised and informal volunteering, are recognised as an important component in a multifaceted service. It is perhaps this aspect of the policy that would ensure it was care 'of' and 'by' the community, rather than merely care 'in' the community. Finally, the policy has a central orientation towards rehabilitation, and the restoration of full membership of ordinary society and access to roles and opportunities taken for granted by those who are not disabled.

The group homes described by Pritlove (1985) are representative of the non-institutional focus of community care, which 'have been tested and tried for over 15 years' (Morris, 1981). What is clear from Pritlove's study is the variety of experiences encompassed by this term. Key variables were the power exercised by supervisors, the objectives of the group home, the disability of the residents and interactions of the resident group itself. Pritlove's conclusions would be described as guardedly optimistic. Residents showed dependence on staff but were able to assert themselves.

> The home did not significantly increase residents' independence, as measured in terms of the 'official' objectives. However, residents enjoyed a quality of life which was varied and valued by them. The home coped with a very considerable amount of handicap and

> illness, with a relatively low rate of readmission to hospital ... Residents themselves rated the home, like the curate's egg, 'good in parts' (Pritlove, 1985).

MacAndrew and his colleagues painted a similar picture of relative success in their survey of Prestwich Hospital Group Homes (MacAndrew, Overton and White, 1980). While they noted some cost in diet and living conditions, on the whole the residents are portrayed as very content, becoming well established with their local community and 'the cost is surely balanced by the advantages which accrue from giving people the independence and freedom to manage their own affairs. In fact, it is a great achievement that, after so many years of living in the safety and dependence of hospital, so many of the ex-patients have managed to look after themselves adequately' (MacAndrew, Overton and White, 1980).

Our own experience would urge some caution in expecting too much of group homes. Two such homes were established in Sheffield over ten years ago, and initially very much supervised by nursing staff from the large hospital where they had spent many years. Both homes have required substantial assistance with basic household management. The links with the hospital have been important in social terms also, the residents having developed few other opportunities for leisure or social contact. Only recently has each house developed a close link with a neighbour to provide informal support and a friendly watchful eye. On the whole the life in the house has been unstimulating in terms of daily activity, and rehabilitative in only the most passive sense.

While no formal research has been undertaken in the style of MacAndrew or Pritlove, impressions are that realistically such group homes may achieve only limited goals. These may still on balance be positive for the residents, but it is important that honest recognition of the costs is also given: the loss of the stimulation and opportunities offered by a large, albeit enclosed, hospital community; the wider social network left behind; the enforced interdependence with others the resident may have had little real say in choosing. Without being cynical, it has to be noted that so many of the glowing reports received by such developments have been researched and written by those in positions of authority in the home: Pritlove (group home supervisor), MacAndrew, Overton and White (psychiatrists and nursing officer). The lessons we are learning is that community in the moral sense, Tönnies' gemeinschaft (Tönnies, 1957), may or may not exist in the residential area and in the hospital. Slogans are no substitute for the careful matching of available resources and individual need.

The criticisms of the policy of community care are substantial, particularly as it is in danger of being implemented, both from theoretical (Scull, 1977; Walker, 1982) and practical (Short, 1985) perspectives. One issue that could be highlighted here is the role of women. Recent surveys (Equal Opportunities Commission, 1980; Levin, Sinclair and Gorbach, 1982; Jones and Vetter, 1984; Jones, 1985) have confirmed the well-known but under-recognised fact that care in the community means care by women - about four in five cases. Wilson (1977 and 1982) discusses the issues raised by this in detail. There is no doubt that the existence of the'reserve army of labour' distorts the demand for, and provision of, welfare services in the community. Dee Jones (1985) noted, for instance, 'it has in some areas become policy that if a female lives with or near her dependent then home helps should not be provided'. These carers 'are supporting their ... dependants at enormous costs to themselves' (Jones, 1985). It is equally likely that it is, disproportionately, women whose jobs will go with the closing hospitals and women who will take on the added burden of dependent mentally ill people living in the community, both their relatives and neighbours.

The findings of research conducted by Hirsch, Leff, and Vaughn are of considerable importance in any discussion of non-institutional modes of care for those suffering from schizophrenia (see Hirsch and Leff, 1975; Vaughn and Leff, 1976; Kuipers, 1979). Inspired by the influential speculations of the sociocultural theorists of schizophrenia (Clare, 1980) substantial work has been done on the interaction between life events, emotional environment and schizophrenic relapse. The critical role of expressed emotion, as Vaughn and Leff describe it, for the wellbeing of psychotic patients is accentuated; in effect this means immediate personal relationships, particularly with kin. Whether or not this is evidence for arousal theories of schizophrenia causation is not germane to our concerns. The important lesson is that highly charged atmospheres, be they of warmth or antipathy, are likely to be deleterious to the stability of the schizophrenia sufferer. The emotional neutrality or 'lack of solidarity' (Pritlove, 1985) found by surveys of mental illness residential care such as Ryan and Hewett (1976) or Pritlove (1985) or MacAndrew, Overton and White (1980) might on the evidence constitute one of their strengths for this group of residents and attempts to increase the level of emotional interaction and interdependence might prove counterproductive. A neighbourhood attitude of benign indifference might in certain respects be what is required of a caring community in these circumstances.

It has become fashionable to say that the community does not care, and pursuit of this policy will lead to community neglect. What urgently needs consideration is the prior question: what sort of care are we asking of the community? The answers are not at all clearcut.

CONCLUSIONS

The challenge facing those involved in planning a new mental health service is the challenge of quality. Whatever pattern of services replaces our current heavy reliance on hospital beds, it must offer an improved service, and above all, access to an enhanced quality of life to those reliant on psychiatric services.

The force for change has been gathering impetus in recent years throughout the country. There is now the opportunity to plan carefully the changes that are to be made, in the hope of avoiding the unplanned concomitants of which Ramon (1985) warns. This will require a newly forged partnership between the statutory health and local authority services as well as voluntary organisations - and the 'informal sector'. The concept of joint planning, though youthful, is not a new one, and most areas will be used to a structure of joint consultative committees with joint care planning teams looking at specialist areas like mental health. Representatives of the voluntary sector and also primary health care have only last year been formally included in this process. In relation to mental handicap services, Heron (1981) warns us that joint planning structures are still much easier to set up and describe than to make work effectively. Many health and local authorities have still to grapple effectively with the task of establishing a planning process that involves the spectrum of interested parties and agencies including, crucially, the consumers of these services and their families. The sensitivity and goodwill of these planning mechanisms will be crucial to developing a high quality, community-orientated mental health service, which caters fully for all accommodation needs. It should, of course, be remembered that 'housing' in a mental health service is not just about meeting accommodation needs of those defined as mentally ill, but looking to the preventive potential of housing provision which gives priority to maintaining the emotional health of the population at large. Initiatives such as the White City project in Hammersmith, and Mental Health on Hyde Park scheme in Sheffield have usefully begun to establish their links.

While we have chosen to emphasise the importance of being able to offer a range of services and resources, it should not be forgotten that the aspirations of those with mental health problems are in large measure much as those of all our community. We need to devise strategies to be more sensitive to these aspirations and respond to them more effectively. The principles of normalisation helpfully ask us to justify very carefully separate and specialist facilities. Asylum has become a very unpopular concept, closely identified with the negative effects of institutions. If the experience of history is any guide, there have always been those who for short or even longer periods require refuge and a higher level of support and insulation from social pressures than many of the community resources envisaged will provide. Perhaps such a concept will require articulation in any comprehensive range of services.

We have suggested that a more flexible and individually tailored concept of rehabilitation is required. Each residential facility should see rehabilitation as one of its central functions in so far as it means encouraging the return of skills for daily living. If it is a separate, specialised function, the dangers are that it will only be offered to some. They will be invited onto a treadmill moving at a predetermined speed, in a predicted direction, throwing them off at a fixed point. In such a system many will very quickly find themselves back where they started. Others - particularly Douglas Bennett's HOUND (the humble, old, unattractive, non-verbal and distressed) (Bennett, 1983 in a paper to the MIND annual conference) may never be offered opportunities for moving on. Who will be surprised when all the most skilled, best trained and paid staff gravitate to work in rehabilitative settings.

A continuing theme in this chapter has to be that of resources. Attempting to promote these changes always at less cost than the existing service will lead to cynicism and probably failure. While there is accumulating evidence, pointed out in this chapter (p.257), that supposedly 'low cost' options can for many offer more appropriate accommodation than high cost institutions, this is not the end of the matter. Community-based services provided by social workers, general practitioners, community nurses, will inevitably be asked to do more. Families and neighbours will come under increasing pressure to cope with difficult situations. Who would argue that they are adequately supported now? Private provision has received encouragement from government since 1979, and is likely to be increasingly evident. The failure to resource recent legislation (HMSO, 1984) designed to control and monitor these private residential facilities, is not evidence of a commitment to a high quality service.

As the hospitals close, providing alternative accommodation will be central to the policy of community care. In this chapter we have argued that there is a lot to be learnt from the experience of the last 25 years about the sort of accommodation that could enhance the quality of life of those who suffer from mental illness, and make community care a success. Whether policy-makers choose to learn from this experience remains an important question. Whatever happens, the commitment towards offering those who have lived in hospitals the basic human requirement of a home will be a good indicator as to how community care is seen - a way of enhancing quality of life or a method of saving money.

REFERENCES

Abrams, P. (1977) Community Care - Some Research Problems and Priorities, Policy and Politics, 6, 125-51

Acker, C., Wykes, T. and Wing, J.K. (1979) A High-dependency Hospital-Hostel for New Longstay In-patients, unpublished

Anstee, B.H. (1978) 'An Alternative to Group Homes', British Journal of Psychiatry, 132, 356-60

Apte, R.Z. (1968) Halfway Houses (Bell, London)

Bamford, T. (1984) 'The Mirage of Community Care', Community Care, 15 November

Basaglia, F. et al. (1968) L'Instituzione Negata (Einaudi, Milan)

Bell, C. and Newby, H. (1971) Community Studies (Allen and Unwin, London)

Bennett, D. (1978) 'Community Psychiatry', British Journal of Psychiatry, 132, 209-20

Bradshaw, J.A. (1972) 'Taxonomy of Social Need', in G. McLachlan (ed.) Problems and Progress in Medical Care: Essays on Current Research, 7th series, (Oxford University Press, for Nuffield Provincial Hospitals Trust, London)

Brandon, D. (1981) Voices of Experience - Consumer Perspectives of Psychiatric Treatment (MIND, London)

Braun, P. et al. (1981) 'An Overview: De-institutionalisation of Psychiatric Patients: A Critical Review of Outcome Studies', in American Journal of Psychiatry, 138 (6), 736-49

BBC (1985) 'No Asylum', Panorama programme, BBC Television

Brown, G.W. and Birley, J.L.T. (1970) 'Social Precipitants of Severe Psychiatric Disorders', in E.H. Hare and J.K. Wing, Psychiatric Epidemiology (Oxford University Press, London)

Cawley, R.H. and McLachlan, G. (eds) (1973) Policy for Action: A Symposium on the Planning of a Long-term District Psychiatric Service (Oxford University Press, Oxford)

Christie Brown, R.W., Ebringer, L. and Freedman, L.S. (1977) 'A Survey of Long-stay Psychiatric Populations: Implications for Community Services', Psychological Medicine, 7, 113-26

Clare, A. (1980) Psychiatry in Dissent, 2nd edn (Tavistock, London)

Creer, C. and Wing, J.K. (1974) Schizophrenia at Home (National Schizophrenia Fellowship, Surbiton)

Crine, A. (1982) 'Breaking the Vicious Circle', Community Care, 8 July

Curtis Committee (1946) Report of the Care of Children Committee (HMSO, London)

DHSS (1975a) Better Services for the Mentally Ill (HMSO, London)

DHSS, Welsh Office (1975b) The Census of Residential Accommodation 1970 - II Residential Accommodation for the Mentally Ill and for the Mentally Handicapped (HMSO,

London)
DHSS (1976) Priorities for Health and Personal Social Services in England (HMSO, London)
DHSS (1977) The Way Forward (HMSO, London)
DHSS (1981a) Care in Action (HMSO, London)
DHSS (1981b) Care in the Community (DHSS, London)
Durkin, E. (1971) Hostels for the Mentally Disordered (Young Fabian Pamphlet no. 24, London)
Early, D. (1965) 'Domestic Resettlement', in H.L. Freeman (ed.) Psychiatric Hospital Care (Bailliere, Tindall and Cassell, London)
Equal Opportunities Commission (1980) The Experience of Caring for Elderly and Handicapped Dependents (Survey Report, London)
Freeman, H. (1983) 'Concepts of Community Psychiatry', British Journal of Hospital Medicine, 30, 90-6
Garioch, G. (1978) 'Mental Health Hostels - A Waste of Money?' Social Work Today, 9 (42), 26-8
Goffman, E. (1961) Asylums: Essays on the Social Situation of Mental Patients and other Inmates (Penguin, Harmondsworth)
Hargreaves, R. (1984) 'Brindle House: A Community Mental Health Service in Practice', in J. Reed and G. Lomas (eds) Psychiatric Services in the Community - Developments and Innovations (Croom Helm, London)
Heron, A. (1981) Service for the Mentally Handicapped in Sheffield - Final Report of the Director (ERG Reports, University of Sheffield)
Hewett, S. (1979) 'Somewhere to Live: A Pilot Study of Hostel Care', in M.R. Olsen, The Care of the Mentally Disordered, (BASW, Birmingham)
Hewett, S. and Ryan, P. (1975) 'Alternatives to Living in Psychiatric Hospitals - A Pilot Project', British Journal of Hospital Medicine, 14 (July), 65-70
Hewett, S., Ryan, P. and Wing, J.K. (1975) 'Living Without the Mental Hospitals', Journal of Social Policy, 4 (4), 391-404
HMSO (1959) Mental Health Act 1959 7 and 8 Eliz. II, ch. 72
HMSO (1984) Registered Home Act 1984 Eliz. II ch.23
Hirsch, S.R. and Leff, J.P. (1975) Abnormalities in Parents of Schizophrenics: A Review of the Literature and an Investigation of Communication Aspects and Deviances (Oxford University Press, London)
Jay Committee (1979) Report of the Committee of Enquiry into Mental Handicap Nursing and Care, Cmnd 7468 (HMSO, London)
Jones, D. (1985) 'A Carers' Work is Never Done', Community Care, 4 July
Jones, D.A. and Vetter, N.J. (1984) 'A Survey of Those who Care for the Elderly at Home: Their Problems and Their Needs', Social Science and Medicine, London
Jones, K. and Poletti, A. (1984) 'Mirage of Reform', New Society, 4 October

Knight, L. and Murray, J. (1976) 'Ready to Leave' Community Care, 23 June, 16-24
Kuipers, L. (1979) 'Schizophrenia and the Family' in J.K. Wing and M.R. Olsen, Community Care of the Mentally Disabled (Oxford University Press, Oxford)
Leff, J.P. and Vaughn, C. (1980) 'The Interaction of Life Events and Relatives' Expressed Emotion in Schizophrenia and Depressive Neurosis', British Journal of Psychiatry, 136, 146-53
Leopoldt, H. and Hurn, R.J. (1976) 'Sheltered Accommodation for the Mentally Ill', Nursing Mirror, 22 January, 57-9
Levin, E., Sinclair, I. and Gorbach, P. (1982) The Supporters of Confused Elderly Persons at Home (National Institute for Social Work Research Unit, London)
MacAndrew, C.H., Overton, N.K. and White, M. (1980) Life in the Community: A Survey of the Prestwich Hospital Group Homes, Occasional Paper no. 5 (Psychiatric Rehabilitation Association, London)
Mann, S. and Cree, W.(1976) 'New Long-stay Psychiatric Patients: A National Sample of Fifteen Mental Hospitals in England and Wales 1972/3', Psychological Medicine, 6, 603-16
Mao Tse-Tung (1966) Quotation from Chairman Mao Tse-Tung, (Foreign Language Press, Peking)
Meacher, M. (1976) 'After One and Half Million Years in Hospital ...', Social Work Today, 7 (6), 162-3
MIND (1961) Report of the Annual Conference (London)
MIND (1973) Community Care Provisions for Mentally Ill and Mentally Handicapped Men and Women, MIND Report no. 11 (London)
MIND (1983) Common Concern - MIND's Manifesto for a New Mental Health Service (London)
Morris, B. (1981) 'Residential Units', in J.K. Wing and B. Morris, Handbook of Psychiatric Rehabilitation Practice (Oxford University Press, Oxford)
Murray, J. (1978) Special Housing, MIND Report No. 19 (London)
Otto, S. and Orford, J. (1978) Not Quite Like Home (John Wiley, London)
Paykel, E.S. (1978) 'Meeting the Needs of Mental Disorder', Health and Hygiene, 1, 193-6
Pritlove, J.H. (1976) 'Evaluating a Group Home: Problems and Results', British Journal of Social Work, 16 (3), 353-76
Pritlove, J.H. (1978) 'What Future for the Mentally Ill?', Community Care, 12 April, 20-2
Pritlove, J.H. (1985) Group Homes - An Inside Story, Social Service Monographs (Joint Unit for Social Service Research, University of Sheffield)
Pryce, I.G. (1977a) 'The Effects of Social Changes in Chronic Schizophrenia: A Study of Forty Patients transferred from Hospital to Residential Home', Psychological Medicine, 7, 127-39

Pryce, I.G. (1977b) 'The Selection of Long-stay Hospital Patients for Hostels: A Study of Patients Selected for an Experimental Hostel and for Local Authority Hostels', Psychological Medicine, 7, 331-43

Ramon, S. (1983) 'Psichiatria Democratica: A Case Study of an Italian Community Mental Health Service', International Journal of Health Services, 13 (2) Baywood, USA

Ramon, S. (1985) 'Out in the Cold in the Sunshine State', Community Care, 9 May, 17-20

Raphael, W. and Peers, V. (1972) Psychiatric Hospitals Viewed by their Patients (King Edward's Hospital Fund, London)

Reed, J. and Lomas, G. (1984) Psychiatric Services in the Community (Croom Helm, London)

Rosenhan, D.I. (1973) 'On Being Sane in Insane Places', Science, 179, 250-8

Ryan, P. (1979) 'Residential Care for the Mentally Disabled', in J.K. Wing and M.R. Olsen (eds) Community Care for the Mentally Disabled (Oxford University Press, Oxford)

Ryan, P. and Hewett, S. (1976) 'A Pilot Study of Hostels for the Mentally Ill', Social Work Today, 4 (25), 774-8

Ryan, P. and Wing, J.K. (1979) 'Patterns of Residential Care', in M.R. Olsen, The Care of the Mentally Disordered (BASW, Birmingham)

Scull, A.T. (1977) Decarceration (Prentice-Hall, Englewood Cliffs, New Jersey)

Shepherd, G. (1984) Institutional Care and Rehabilitation (Longman, London)

Sheffield District Labour Party (1984) Services in Sheffield, (Central Policy Unit, Sheffield)

Sheffield Health Authority (1985) Strategic Plan for Health Services in Sheffield 1984-1994 (Sheffield Health Authority, Sheffield)

Short, R. (1985) Community Care, volume 1, Second Report from Social Services Committee (HMSO, London)

Smith, L. (1980) 'Where to from a 'Halfway' Hostel?', Social Work Today, 11 (25), 14-15

Stein, L. and Test, M.A. (1980) 'Alternatives to Mental Hospital Treatment', Archives of General Psychiatry, 37, 392-7

Thornicroft, G. (1979) 'Group Homes - A Success?', Nursing Times, 75(2), 514-15

Tönnies, F. (1957) Community and Society: Gemeinschaft und Gesellschaft (Michigan State University Press, Ann Arbor)

Towell, D. and McAusland, T. et al. (1984) 'Managing Psychiatric Services in Transition', Health and Social Services Journal, 25 October

Vaughn, C.E. and Leff, J.P. (1976) 'The Influence of Family and Social Factors on the Course of Psychiatric Illness', British Journal of Psychiatry, 129, 125-37

Walker, A. (ed.) (1982) Community Care - The Family, the State and Social Policy (Basil Blackwell and Martin Robertson,

Oxford)
Wilson, E. (1977) Women and the Welfare State (Tavistock, London)
Wilson, E. (1982) 'Women, the 'Community' and the 'Family' in Walker, A. Community Care - the Family, the State and Social Policy (Basil Blackwell and Martin Robertson, Oxford)
Wing, J.K. (1978) Reasoning about Madness (Oxford University Press, Oxford)
Wing, J.K. (1980) 'Innovations in Social Psychiatry', Psychological Medicine, 10, 219-30
Wing, J.K. and Brown, G.W. (1970) Institutionalisation and Schizophrenia (Cambridge University Press, London)
Wing, J.K. and Morris, B. (eds) (1981) Handbook of Psychiatric Rehabilitation Practice (Oxford University Press, Oxford)
Wolfensberger, W. (1972) The Principle of Normalisation in Human Services (National Institute on Mental Retardation (NIMR), Toronto)

Chapter Twelve

GROUP HOME/LANDLADY SCHEMES: A CASE STUDY

Larraine Eastwood

In 1979 the local social services department embarked upon an experimental project, embracing the philosophy of community care for mentally handicapped people. The basic concept was that the more able handicapped person should be cared for in a 'normal' environment with minimal supervision provided on a landlady/supervisor scheme.

For this scheme the social services acquired two semidetached houses from the local authority housing department. The houses were situated next door to each other on a local housing estate. The majority of occupants of the estate were of the mining fraternity. In close proximity to the houses were an assortment of shops, a launderette, and a post office. The town centre was approximately one mile (1.6 km) from the estate and offered the usual amenities. Both houses had three bedrooms, bathroom, through-lounge, kitchen and gas central heating, with large gardens to front and rear.

The landlady/supervisor lived in one of the houses with her family, and by way of remuneration the social services department paid the rent. The landlady was responsible for all the usual household bills incurred, and furnishing of her own accommodation. The department also paid the landlady telephone rental, and £1 each quarter for calls.

In return for the services of the landlady each resident paid £10.00 per week from the weekly DHSS benefits. The residents were also responsible for their rent, gas, electric, food, replacement items for their home, and any other bills incurred.

It was envisaged by the department that the landlady would work on a part-time basis (no more than 20 hours per week), and that her services would be of a supervisory nature only, helping no more than four residents to budget, plan menus, shop, etc. and cope generally with a more independent lifestyle.

Initially the house which was to accommodate the residents contained a wardrobe and some net curtains, and it was expected that the landlady would take on the responsibility of selecting and the purchasing of furniture from a total budget of £800 donated by the RSMHCA.

Table 12.1 is a list of purchases made from the donation given by the RSMHCA.

Table 12.1: List of Purchases

Carpets	395.00
Table and chairs	95.00
Bedding	37.00
Wardrobes	120.00
Curtains	40.00
Crockery	23.00
Iron and board	14.00
TV Aerial	19.00
	£743.00

The remainder was spent on sundries, that is, buckets, mops, wastebin, lampshades, plugs, etc.

The department did supply various items from their store; however, on arrival most were unsuitable for use - chipped crockery, badly stained pillows and cot sheets, dressing tables stained and broken, etc.

As the budget would not meet the price of a three-piece suite and fridge the local hostel provided them on loan.

The residents selected for this scheme were all ladies from the local mental handicap hostel. Prior to selection the ladies had been occupying a bungalow within the hostel grounds; however, the occupancy was more a sleeping arrangement, and the ladies still relied on the hostel for the provision of meals, laundry, and other day-to-day requirements. During the day two of the ladies attended the adult training centre (ATC), while the third remained at the hostel.

The criteria on which these three ladies were chosen was:

(1) they all had good self-help skills;
(2) they appeared to get on well as a group;
(3) it was thought that they would present less problems for the landlady than any other candidates.

As the ladies were familiar with the hostel it

was agreed that, should the landlady experience any difficulties, the hostel would act as a back-up service offering support and practical help if necessary.

Other agencies involved were as follows:

(1) Social workers, both generic and specialist
(2) Adult training centre (ATC)
(3) Daycare officer
(4) Primary health care team
(5) Community nursing services (mental handicap)
(6) Voluntary agencies
(7) Police
(8) DHSS

These agencies are discussed below.

It was agreed that the department would take on full responsibility for the home and its occupants while the landlady was on holiday, providing that adequate notice was offered. It was also agreed that the department would take on full responsibility for the home and its occupants in the event of illness of the landlady.

Initially the department asked the landlady to sign a contract stating that she would accept full responsibility for the home, its contents, residents and their belongings. However, this was totally unacceptable and the landlady refused. It was some two years later before a contract was drawn up acceptable to both the landlady and the department.

THE REALITIES OF THE LANDLADY'S EXPERIENCE

Before I took over the houses there was a lot of opposition to the proposal to house people who were mentally handicapped in the neighbourhood. The myth was prevalent that they would be noisy, dirty, unsightly and, in the view of a few people, downright dangerous.

Fortunately the neighbours on either side of the houses were not of this opinion and due to this active opposition died away. When I conversed with an immediate neighbour she stated that:

> Prior to anyone moving into the houses the social services did nothing to endear themselves to the local population; while the houses were empty they refused to do any maintenance on the gardens or take any measure to prevent vandalism. As a result the gardens

> were left to run wild, and the weeds spread into my garden. The public made a footpath through the property inviting undesirables, and I was afraid to go out into my own back yard after dark.

Another lady told me that:

> There was a lot of vandalism in the area and we repeatedly asked the social services to fence the property, but this was not done. The windows only remained intact due to the constant vigilance of the immediate neighbours going out several times a day to clear the gardens of gangs of children. This went on for over a year. The gardens then began to be used as a rubbish dump; this led to vermin, and at one time after an overpowering smell had hung around the houses for several days, the sanitary department had to be called in to remove a very dead cat.

During the period in which the houses were standing empty, they were left to deteriorate until they looked like slums, dirty and neglected. In the end a mechanical shovel had to be brought in to clear several lorry loads of accumulated rubbish.

In a scheme of this kind the relationships with the local community are of vital importance. In this instance the local community was not only ignored, but appeared to be openly antagonised.

Initially, the selection of three residents was made before the selection of the landlady; consequently the landlady relied on the verbal and written information available.

Personal Comment

The information available I found misleading, and within hours of arrival it was obvious that the ladies had little experience of coping in the home environment. The most simple tasks required full and close supervision.

Self-help skills were not as good as suggested, and as a group the ladies could not function. Due to the discord within the group, the problems became insurmountable, and as a result one lady had to return to the hostel.

The selection of a further two residents was made quickly. The criteria on this occasion was that 'the two ladies got on well together and were close friends'.

The agreed 'back-up' service from the hostel proved to be totally ineffective. The first occasion on which I sought assistance was when one of the ladies reacted violently to her new environment, which happened only days after the arrival of the residents. It was explained by the hostel that they could not offer the help required as their beds were fully occupied. It took a further four weeks to resolve this crisis and necessitated me living and sleeping in the house to ensure the safety of the other residents.

On a later occasion, the response was so slow that the situation could not be contained any longer in the home environment; consequently an emergency admission to the mental handicap hospital resulted.

Realising the impracticalities of this system I approached the department suggesting that a more efficient service be sought. The department, however, did not agree, and argued that with the agencies involved every eventuality was catered for.

Experiencing the inadequacies I accepted isolation as part of my position and learned to deal with other problems with little or no support from these areas.

AGENCIES INVOLVED

Social Workers Generic/Specialist

The input from this area was varied. Two social workers visited on a regular basis every four to six weeks; this offered some continuity and stability to both myself and the residents. The remaining four workers, however, offered a poor service, proving elusive and difficult to track down in times of need.

Specialist workers were approached by myself, but declined to become involved as their generic counterparts were already involved.

Adult Training Centre

Support offered from this area was practical but short-term; however, it was gratefully accepted. Occasionally bedding could be washed and the ladies taught simple tasks.

Daycare Officer

The daycare officer visited quite frequently to discuss problems, and, if possible, help solve them. Unfortunately very little was ever solved in these visits and I came to view them more as a token gesture.

Later the department suggested that because I felt so isolated I could benefit from a regular visit from someone from their office. Consequently, every few weeks a lady would arrive to offer a sympathetic shoulder to cry on. Although this lady offered no practical assistance, establishing herself as a sounding board proved extremely useful to myself.

Primary Health Care Team

General Practitioners. Initially the local general practitioner understood little about the home and my role as landlady. However, after several months of close communication with their receptionists a good working relationship developed.

Health Visitor. The health officer offered short talks to the residents on personal hygiene and dietary needs.

District Nurse. The district nurse visited regularly to administer injections to a resident.

Midwife. The midwife became involved when one of the ladies was pregnant. Due to complications her visits were very frequent.

Community Nursing Service (Mental Handicap)

Regular and frequent visits from the team were very useful and an excellent source of support. Through this team's input, appointments were made for a resident to see a psychiatrist, and short-term care offered for the more problematic resident.

Voluntary Agencies

These offered to visit the ladies regularly; however, after a brief visit decided against any future visiting. Despite this, voluntary agencies proved to be very helpful when the residents moved into the community, offering soft furnishings, etc.

Police

Initially the police understood little of the home.

However, after two rape cases and one assault, they became familiar with both the residents and the landlady. This resulted in a good working relationship. The police did expect the landlady to have a reasonable knowledge of the Mental Health Act, and, on the occasions mentioned, sought some guidance. During the landlady's absence the police checked the home and the resident's wellbeing quite regularly.

DHSS

Money was problematic during the early months. The residents were in receipt of NCIP, supplementary benefit, and a discretionary payment for special board and lodging. Each resident, however, received payments on different days of the week which made budgeting difficult. On occasions pension books would run out and it was weeks before a new book was issued. This problem was only solved after several months, and many hours of waiting in the DHSS offices, until contact was made with the manager.

MISCELLANEOUS RESPONSIBILITIES

Holidays and Sickness

Holiday. I can only relate to the one short holiday taken, and although two weeks notice was offered the department considered this unreasonable. Consequently, I arranged cover for the duration, which resulted in a colleague moving into my home.

Sickness. On the two occasions I was confined to bed for a few days due to minor illnesses, I found that bedrest was totally impossible as the residents still required my assistance, although I felt it was not so much assistance they needed as security. Each time I tried to sleep the perpetual knocking started on the door. When they received no answer, they would then open the door, walk in and start shouting for me. The answer, of course, would have been to lock the door, but unfortunately this was not possible as my children needed access. The residents knew that I was ill, but this knowledge seemed only to encourage more visits.

On a later occasion when exhaustion necessitated my removal from the home for a period of three weeks the true inadequacies of the department's earlier arrangements were revealed.

The cover during my absence arranged by the department was that someone from the hostel should call on a daily basis to ensure that the residents had their daily requirements. These visits were brief and the remainder of the time the residents were left alone to cope. As a result gangs of children invaded the home removing several items belonging to the ladies and their home. Several police visits were made, but the ladies did not think to report the children, or the missing items. On my return I was faced with total chaos within the home. Community relations had become inflamed, and hostile actions were directed towards the residents, my family, and myself.

A TYPICAL WEEK

In the following I have opened my diary at a time three months after the arrival of the residents. It shows very clearly how difficult those early months were, and the impracticalities of the department's expected role of the landlady.

Monday

Crawled from my bed feeling numb and tired at 6.00 a.m. Enjoyed a coffee in the quiet of my own home before running next door. The path was frozen this morning, and so my feet stayed dry!

Wished the ladies a cheery 'good morning' before observing them wash. Lucy requires a lot of supervision in this area, but this must be done gently as she appears to resent my intrusion and growls at me - cannot blame her really, I would not like it either!

Emma refused to rise and needed coaxing from her bed; however, once up copes well, although she does tend to put dirty clothes back on, including her knickers.

Doris copes well and offers no problems - she is a love.

May was reluctant to rise, only because she dresses before going to bed, a habit I am trying to break.

Lucy set the table this morning; on it she placed a milk bottle, cups (no saucers), plates, a packet of sugar, a spoon, and a packet of butter, complete with a knife in upright position.

Emma helped her to reset the table.

Doris made a pot of tea, but forgot to boil the

kettle.

May requested a cup of tea whilst sitting on the toilet - constipated again!

Ran back home to call my children for school at 7.30 a.m.

7.45 a.m. Returned to the ladies with the drug box, and taking each lady in turn allowed them to open their own bottles, and take their medications. I never realised taking a couple of pills could be so time consuming!

8.15 a.m. Doris washed the dishes, Emma and Lucy dried, and May disappeared to the toilet.

8.30 a.m. Walked the ladies half way to the Training Centre to escort them across the busy road.

Emma and Lucy cope well with the crossing of roads; Doris, however, relies on them. Perhaps she is deaf!

9.00 a.m. May still in the toilet but complains of the housework and shopping.

9.15 a.m. Found a note from my husband asking me to collect the children from school.

9.30 a.m. Organised May and the housework. I did not think that dusting and using a hoover could be such hard work! Escorted May to the shop and helped her prepare some lunch.

12.00 p.m. Returned to make some lunch for myself.

1.00 p.m. Washed the ladies clothes, had to do this in my own home as there is no washing machine next door.

3.00 p.m. Returned to May - she complains of toothache, her teeth are in an appalling state.

3.15 pm. Rang the dentist to make May an appointment (Wednesday 10.30 a.m).

3.30 p.m. Picked the children up from school and made them some tea.

4.00 p.m. Met the ladies from the Centre to see them across the road - they seemed pleased to see me.

4.45 p.m. Helped them to prepare the dinner. More truthfully - they helped me!

6.00 p.m. Observed medications.

6.15 p.m. Observed Lucy wash the dinner pots, what a mess - water everywhere! Lucy resented being asked to clean up afterwards but I stood firm.

7.00 p.m. Returned to be with my own kith and kin.

9.00 p.m. Raised voices from next door. Lucy and Emma do not appear to get on too well. Lucy stormed from the house. Emma refuses to talk with me.

9.15 p.m. I put my shoes on to go and find Lucy. It's cold outside and she left without her coat.

9.30 p.m. Returned with Lucy. Emma had gone to bed, probably without washing. I went to Emma's bedroom to say 'good night' but she did not reply. Because she is epileptic I switched on the light to make sure she was all right. My actions were met with verbal abuse and we had firm words.

10.00 p.m. Bathed May (her frame is so fragile) and tucked her in bed.

10.30 p.m. With the ladies safely in their beds I returned home, kissed my children as they slept, and retired at midnight.

Tuesday
Slept in this morning rising at 7.30 a.m. Called my husband and children before running next door. There is snow on the path today but it is pleasant.

8.00 a.m. Everyone was still in their beds. Emma was still very annoyed about last night and we had words again! May must have dressed after I left last night - she rose fully clothed. I made her remove her clothes, wash and redress in clean. Hurried the ladies through breakfast. Doris set the table and did very well. I feel that she is really bright but lacks confidence.

8.30 a.m. Observed medications.

8.45 a.m. Walked the ladies across the busy road before returning to May and the breakfast dishes.

9.15 a.m. May had made no attempt to clear the pots or the table. I asked her again before returning to collect my diary.

9.30 a.m. Had a coffee with May and listened to her endless list of complaints, headache, constipation, etc. While she talked I noticed that her body continually moved. After consulting my diary I realised that the district nurse was due to administer a medicate injection. Left May to finish the washing up whilst I ran to the shop. It would have been so easy to collect May's pension, but felt that May would come to expect it of me on a permanent basis.

11.30 a.m. May had just finished the dishes. As I gave her the pension book she asked if Lucy could collect it for her later. Reluctantly May put her coat and shoes on and left.

12.00 p.m. Received a telephone call from the local shopkeeper. May had called for her cigarettes and left her pension book and purse on the counter.

12.15 p.m. May returned to collect her belongings from the shop. However, on this occasion left her gloves.

1.00 p.m. Rang the DHSS regarding Emma's pension book - now two weeks overdue. They do not seem to understand that she needs that money to meet her commitments.

1.30 p.m. The daycare officer called to check that all was well. I pointed out once more that this was no part-time occupation, but just as the discussion got going he had to leave.

2.00 p.m. Checked that May was all right and had washed her lunch pots before enjoying a quiet afternoon.

3.30 p.m. Walked down the road to meet the ladies from the training centre. Emma was a little more sociable.

4.15 p.m. Spent a little time with my children. My daughters informed me that some other children had been calling them names, and asked if they liked living in the looney bin. When I asked what they had said my eldest replied 'Nothing, we hit them'.

5.00 p.m. As the children left to play with their friends I returned to the ladies. Lucy was peeling potatoes - what a mess, but she was showing initiative.

5.45 p.m. Left the ladies to enjoy their dinner.

6.15 p.m. Observed medications. Doris washed the dishes. Emma began knitting. May settled in front of the television. Lucy, however, was thumbing through a book obviously wanting some help. I spent some time with Lucy listening to her read - she does very well. I promised her that I would try and find someone from adult literacy to help her.

Doris made everyone a cup of tea and it was

warm!

7.00 p.m. Returned to my own home.

10.00 p.m. Observed bedtime routines. Told May firmly that if she dressed after I left, and got into bed, she would have to strip and wash again in the morning.

10.30 p.m. Wished everyone 'goodnight'.

Wednesday
Rose at 6.45 a.m. and had a coffee before running across the snowy path to next door. Called the ladies and wished them 'good morning'. May had not dressed after I left last night, and we both smiled with achievement. While upstairs helping May, Lucy had begun breakfast preparations, and Doris set the table.

Shouts from the kitchen brought me dashing down stairs - Lucy has set the frying pan on fire. Fortunately I was able to show Lucy what to do without any mishaps. This really shook Lucy and she now approaches the frying pan with the respect it deserves.

7.30 a.m. Ran back to my own home to call everybody, although this was unnecessary. As I walked through the door my husband handed me a coffee.

8.00 a.m. Checked my diary for appointments. May's dental appointment was for 10.30 a.m.

8.15 a.m. Returned to the ladies with their medications and went through the usual routine.

8.40 a.m. Saw the ladies across the busy road before driving the children to school.

9.00 a.m. Hurried May through the washing up of the breakfast pots.

9.30 a.m. The training centre telephoned to inform me that Emma was unwell and asked if she could return home.

10.00 a.m. Emma returned, but did not appear ill. I explained to her that I had to take May to the dentist. This annoyed Emma and she complained saying that she was ill and that I should look after her as that was my job! It was difficult explaining to Emma that nursemaiding her was not my job. I was there to help her stand on her own two feet. Emma saw me as an uncaring person; that hurt - however I gave her a cuddle which seemed to make her feel better.

10.40 a.m. Arrived at the dentist late and offered my apologies. May is to have all her teeth out on Monday at 9.30 a.m.

11.00 a.m. Returned home with May. Emma had cleaned up and done a very thorough job - this pleased May. Talked to the ladies over a coffee and discovered that May had been a tramp for many years (perhaps that explains the sleeping in clothes?)

12.00 p.m. Observed lunch being prepared. Emma is methodical and enjoys preparing food.

1.00 p.m. Lucy's father called to see his daughter. May made him a cup of tea and he stayed until Lucy returned from the ATC.

4.00 p.m. Emma assisted with the dinner whilst Lucy talked to her father. Emma was annoyed that Lucy had a visitor.

5.00 p.m. Lucy's father left. Emma served her culinary delight and Lucy tucked in as if this was to be her last meal. Emma was close to tears until I explained that Lucy was really enjoying her cooking.

6.00 p.m. Observed medications.

6.15 p.m. Returned to my own home to prepare dinner, and met my husband on the doorstep. We enjoyed seeing each other!

7.30 p.m. A loud crash from next door disturbed our peaceful evening. On investigation Emma had smashed the dinner set in a temper about Lucy's visitor. I made her clean it up - this was the first real battle I had encountered with Emma. As she swept the pieces of broken crockery up, she muttered about dental appointments, Lucy's visitor, and other occasions when she had not been directly involved. Emma then refused to talk with me.

8.30 p.m. As I talked with the other ladies about their day, Emma threw a chair across the room. This was the last straw and I became very annoyed at her childish outburst. I escorted her to her bedroom with the words 'If you are going to act like a child, then I will treat you as one'. The negative reinforcer became the positive - she had won!

9.00 p.m. Returned to my own home to talk to my husband. I was annoyed with myself for not handling the situation better.

10.00 p.m. Observed the bedtime routines and made sure that May undressed before getting into her bed.

Thursday
Rose at 7.00 a.m. The path was muddy today.

7.30 a.m. Eureka! May rose in her night clothes. Emma greeted me coolly. There was an appalling smell in her bedroom. After bathing Emma, organised the breakfast which went reasonably smoothly.

8.30 a.m. Observed medications. Emma was difficult this morning, pretending that she did not know which were her tablets and how many to take.

8.45 a.m. Observed the ladies across the road - it would have been easier to escort them.

<u>**9.30 a.m.**</u> Rang the ATC to check that Emma was all right, and suggested that I called in later that morning to discuss individual programmes.

<u>**10.00 a.m.**</u> Checked that May had done some housework, but found her sleeping in the chair - I also noticed a cigarette burn in her skirt.

<u>**11.00 a.m.**</u> Called at the ATC and we agreed that the ladies could benefit from half a day a week individual attention from myself in the home. I would have liked a full day, however, this would have resulted in the loss of their incentive payment.

<u>**12.00 a.m.**</u> Organised May's lunch.

<u>**1.00 p.m.**</u> Cleaned out Emma's room and found an assortment of rotting fruit.

<u>**1.30 p.m.**</u> Called into the DHSS office to try and sort out Emma's pension book. Made an appointment to see the Manager for next Thursday afternoon, 2.30 p.m.

<u>**2.00 p.m.**</u> Called in on May before returning to my own home, and the lunch pots still awaited their dip in warm soapy water!

<u>**2.30 p.m.**</u> Received a telephone call from Emma's social worker saying that she would visit tomorrow at 5.00 p.m.

<u>**3.00 p.m.**</u> Grabbed a cup of tea before collecting the children from school.

<u>**3.45 p.m.**</u> Met the ladies, but they had already crossed the road under Lucy's supervision.

<u>**4.00 p.m.**</u> Made the children some tea.

<u>**5.00 p.m.**</u> Helped the ladies prepare stew and

dumplings for their dinner. Lucy poured a whole box of salt in the meat whilst I talked with Emma, this remained undiscovered until I tasted the gravy. I asked Lucy to taste it also, so that she could experience her mistake. Lucy did not flinch and took another spoonful just to be absolutely certain about its taste. After swallowing another good mouthful she turned and said 'short on pepper'. It is moments like those when one appreciates the 'person'.

5.30 p.m. Left the ladies to eat their bacon and eggs and returned to my own home.

6.30 p.m. After observing medications we planned next week's menu. Whilst planning menus there were many suggestions forthcoming, although tripe and black puddings were not everyone's favourite meal, much to May's disappointment. Once the menu was complete we then went on to prepare the shopping list. Lucy made the first suggestion - a packet of salt!

8.15 p.m. Left the ladies watching television and returned home.

9.45 p.m. Called in to observe bedtime routine and found that Doris had already retired. Emma had decided to tidy her bedroom and was busy throwing out accumulated rubbish. May said that she was taking a bath and I could hear her splashing water, however as I opened the door offering to wash her back I found her fully clothed sitting on the edge of the bath flicking the water with her fingertips. After bathing May and ensuring that she was safely in bed I joined Lucy for a short while. She asked if she could watch the television a little longer, and was really pleased when I gave her the responsibility of switching off the set, and locking the back door. However, I did have to stress that she must remove the door key so that I could get in in the morning.

12.00 a.m. Crept next door to check that Lucy had understood - she had - and I was delighted.

12.15 a.m. I retired.

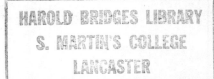

Friday
Got up at 6.30 a.m. The path remains muddy today.

7.00 a.m. Called the ladies; May rose fully clothed - just when I thought I was winning! I fell over Emma's accumulated rubbish left on the landing which caused her to laugh. Emma was in a very cheerful mood today, and was excited about her social worker's visit later in the day.

Breakfast was chaos - Lucy dropped a pint of milk on the kitchen floor. There was milk and glass everywhere, made worse by Lucy and her attempts to clean it up.

8.15 a.m. Medications taken.

8.40 a.m. Walked the ladies to the road. Lucy was only too willing to show me her skills in this area, and taking Doris by the arm, marched her across.

9.00 a.m. Returned to coax May into clearing the breakfast pots and hoovering up.

10.00 a.m. Coffee time in the quiet of my own home. May, however, had different ideas and, following me, moaned constantly about her usual ailments.

10.15 a.m. Asked May to leave after promising to make a doctor's appointment. A good physical for May would not go amiss.

10.40 a.m. Rang the opticians to make an appointment for Doris as I feel that her eyesight may be defective.

11.00 a.m. Went into town to do some shopping and find a cheap dinner service - the next one Emma will buy from her savings.

12.00 p.m. Helped May to prepare her lunch. She is really pleased about the doctor's appointment; but is concerned about getting there - after all she may have to walk!

1.00 p.m. Lunch time for myself and bookwork to catch up on.

3.30 p.m. Collected the children from school, and met the ladies. Found that the lollypop lady often stops the traffic to ensure that the ladies are across safely. Although this is helpful, Lucy becomes angry, insisting that she is 'not a kid'.

5.00 p.m. Emma's social worker called to see me before seeing Emma. We discussed Emma's childish behaviour and she revealed a lot of helpful information.

5.30 p.m. Before escorting the ladies shopping we enjoyed a drink and a biscuit. With medications taken, we left.

Shopping is exhausting work and individual programmes need urgently sorting out.

8.00 p.m. Returned with the shopping, everything had to be logged and priced before items can be put away. This is not 'normal', but necesary in order to keep control of finances. It also serves as a good learning exercise for all - myself included.

8.30 p.m. Lucy offered to go to the fish and chip shop instead of making dinner.

9.00 p.m. Left the ladies to eat their dinner - not before I had pinched a couple of chips!

10.00 p.m. Ensured that all was well with the ladies and observed bedtime routines.

10.45 p.m. Wished everyone a 'goodnight' and dragged myself home.

Saturday
Slept until 8.00 a.m. and hurried next door through a sea of mud. The only person up and dressed was Doris, and I helped her to prepare a simple breakfast. With no one else around, and feeling uneasy about leaving Doris alone I asked her to join me next door. Doris was really pleased about the invite, and enjoyed a coffee with the children.

9.00 a.m. Returned to check the ladies while my husband watched Doris. Lucy was preparing some hot milk for her cereals. She asked if she could visit her father today. I hesitated as it entailed a bus journey. Lucy found this highly amusing, telling me that she had done the journey several times before. Fortunately her father arrived to visit her before we set off to the bus station.

9.30 a.m. May appeared in her dressing gown and asked whether she should dress or not. Initially, I tried to leave the decision to her, but May needed a more positive directive.

Called Emma for breakfast and medications.

10.00 a.m. Returned to my own home to find that Doris had dusted the lounge and swept the kitchen floor.

12.00 p.m. Helped the ladies to prepare their lunch.

1.00 p.m. Left the ladies to enjoy their lunch and returned to my home to eat my lunch prepared by my husband.

2.00 p.m. Doris came round to my home to ask if she could wash up. When I said 'no' she appeared to be hurt, and I felt dreadful, consequently Doris washed up and I still felt dreadful!

4.00 p.m. Lucy and her father returned from their shopping trip; Emma was sociable and charming and willingly helped to prepare dinner.

5.00 p.m. Left the ladies and Lucy's father to eat

their meal.

6.30 p.m. Medications observed. Lucy's father left.

7.30 p.m. Visited the local pub with the ladies. May got 'tipsy' on two snowballs and needed helping home.

9.00 p.m. The ladies settled down to watch television for the remainder of the evening.

10.00 p.m. Observed bedtime routines and tucked May in her bed.

11.00 p.m. Said 'goodnight' to everyone, leaving Lucy to watch the late film.

12.30 a.m. Checked that Lucy had unplugged the television before retiring.

Sunday
Rose at 8.00 a.m. The path was frozen, but the sun shone this morning.

8.30 a.m. Doris accompanied me next door, and we had a coffee and a chat, strictly onesided, perhaps one day she will talk to me!

9.00 a.m. Doris and I went to see if anyone else had got up next door. We found May and Lucy eating burnt toast and Emma in the bathroom.

9.30 a.m. Medications taken.

10.00 a.m. Organised the ladies' morning. Recreational activities are difficult to suggest, however Lucy practises her writing skills. Emma knits a scarf, and May watches the morning service on television. Doris finds concentrating difficult and so she tends to potter around the home doing domestic tasks.

__10.30 a.m.__ Returned to my own home to try and relax.

__12.00 p.m.__ Helped Lucy to prepare lunch - much to Emma's annoyance.

__1.30 p.m.__ Doris washed up the pots and cleared away.

__2.30 p.m.__ Observed Emma prepare the vegetables for dinner before returning to my own home.

__4.30 p.m.__ Returned to instruct Emma on the cooking of vegetables.

__5.30 p.m.__ The ladies sat down to enjoy their evening meal.

__7.30 p.m.__ Called to check that all was well next door. Doris had cleared the dishes and washed up. I suggested that perhaps a rota system could be introduced for the dishes, explaining the unfairness of allowing one person to do them continually. My suggestion was unacceptable on the grounds that during the week others have to do them.

__8.00 p.m.__ Returned to my own home.

__10.00 p.m.__ Observed bedtime routines.

__11.00 p.m.__ Said 'goodnight' and left to recharge my own batteries for the following week.

VIGNETTES

__Lucy__

Lucy digging in the garden, moving through the soil with the ease of a plough horse, but going the wrong way, so that she stood on the row she had just dug in order to dig the next.

Lucy trying to open a drawer that was stuck and breaking it in pieces.

Lucy trying to open the fridge door when it got

stuck and removing it completely.

Me trying to get a urine specimen from her for the doctor and meeting with no success after various attempts. Finally having to hold a bucket under while she peed up my arm.

A neighbour, with his head under his car bonnet, bending over the engine. Lucy walking up behind him with a cheery 'hello' and butting him with her stomach. Neighbour catapulted upsidedown into his engine with a lump on his head and seeing stars not knowing whether to laugh or be cross.

Lucy standing foursquare to the world, feet sturdily apart, arms akimbo, saying 'I don't want nowt to do with men, all they are after is me body'.

Doris

Doris, putting her knickers to soak in the bathroom washbasin and leaving the taps running, then sitting in the bath, deafly oblivious to the sound of running water while it overflowed from the basin behind her, through the floor into the striplight in the kitchen below, then overflowing along the edges of the striplight - turning it into a very good imitation of 'Mother Shipton's Dropping Well', and flooding the kitchen to the depth of a good 5cm.

Doris, after getting her new glasses, standing at my kitchen sink peeping into the next door neighbour's lighted kitchen window with a look of wonderment on her face.

Doris's maddening habit of twiddling every knob in sight, turning an oven left on 'low' to 'high' and burning the dinner to a cinder, or turning the heating full on in the middle of summer and completely off on a freezing cold day in the middle of winter.

Doris stunning everyone by ordering the dog to go to her basket. The dog, equally stunned, obeying.

Doris spitting on the carpet and rubbing it in with her foot.

When Doris wanted a new floor cloth I went up into the airing cupboard and tore up a piece of old sheet, kept for that purpose. Next time Doris wanted a new floor cloth she knew what to do, she went up and helped herself ... to my best embroidered pillowcases.

May

May standing in the garden pegging clothes on the line, giving a perfect imitation of a slow motion video replay. Holding a pair of knickers on the line with one hand and then dropping the peg. Still holding the knickers on the line and looking at the peg on the floor, unmoving, for several minutes and finally solving the problem by dropping the knickers on the floor too.

Going in to find May with a duster in her hand trying to look busy, the telltale red finger marks glowing on her cheek, giving away the fact that she had been fast asleep, head on hand, until the noise of the back door opening woke her up.

May back from the dentist sneezing her new bloody teeth out.

My husband putting them back for her.

Leaving May vacuuming the living room carpet - hearing from my own home the continuous hum of the hoover for the next hour and going back to tell her that an hour should be long enough - only to find May still doing the same bit of carpet!

Emma

Emma in a paddy smashing the dinner service.

Emma falling down stairs and laying there with a broken bone in her foot, 100kg of collapsed blubber with 40kg me and 40kg May trying to move her.

Emma back from the hospital with a pot on her foot, standing at the bottom of the stairs thinking that my husband would be quite able to take her in his arms and carry her up the stairs.

Cleaning Emma's room and finding every nook and cranny crammed with food - apples, oranges, bananas, bags of sugar, biscuits, chocolate, etc.

THE EVENTS LEADING TO BREAKDOWN AND CLOSURE

After two years of continual hard work, the ladies became quite independent, and approached the objective for which the project was designed - taking their place in the community.

The progress made by Lucy was such that she decided to move from the home and live totally independently in a one-bedroom flat.

As the home finances were dependent upon the number of residents, Lucy's move necessitated the selection of another candidate. The department did contribute one-quarter of the rent to make up the deficiency, but no contribution was made towards other bills, or the landlady's salary.

The selection of the new resident was made by

the hostel with little consideration towards the established residents, and what appeared to be a total lack of sensitivity towards the landlady's position.

The new resident, who shall be called Kate, sparked off a series of events which led to the home's closure in 1982.

The initial problem was that of rejection. The established group refused to accept Kate. This led to constant heated arguments between the ladies. Their resentment only deepened when it was realised that whenever Kate's family visited the home, several items disappeared, including the housekeeping purse. Due to this discovery personal effects and money could no longer be left unattended, consequently a state of dependency re-emerged.

The second problem for Kate came to light only two months after her arrival when she was confirmed as being well advanced into a pregnancy. Throughout the pregnancy Kate was very ill which placed extra demands on the residents and the landlady.

The effect the pregnancy had upon the established ladies was extraordinary. Emma presented behavioural problems unlike any previously experienced, she began urinating anywhere in her bedroom, refused to use protection when menstruating, hoarding food, and appeared to suffer from epileptic-type seizures. As the time for Kate's confinement approached Emma became aggressive towards the other group members, and as a result an emergency admission had to be sought to the mental handicap hospital.

The department's reaction to this situation was to suggest that the objectives of the home should be reviewed, and that the landlady should offer a more basic care. It was also suggested that the social worker should take on more responsibility to ensure that Kate attended her antenatal appointments. However, due to Kate's ill-health this was almost impossible to arrange as visits to clinics and doctors became an almost daily occurrence.

Kate was confined and delivered of a son, but unfortunately the child was extremely ill. Kate returned home childless and in a distressed state requiring full and close supervision. Emma also returned to the home with little improvement in her behaviour.

The demands now being made became excessive, and as a result exhaustion necessitated the landlady's removal from the home, the consequences of which are outlined on pages 279 and 280.

Despite the events leading to its closure the house was the ladies' home, and their different personalities echoed throughout its four walls; Emma's knitting occupied an armchair, Doris's ornaments cluttered the polished surfaces, Lucy's homemade buns could always be found uneaten on a plate, May's false teeth occasionally decorated the draining board, and Kate's baby clothes continually aired ready for use.

The home accumulated an assortment of pets which the ladies learned to take care of and respect. Indeed, the home attained a great measure of 'normality' within which the ladies developed.

As landlady I was always very proud of the achievements made by each lady, and in spite of the occasional turmoil within the home, the ladies demonstrated their abilities and coped admirably.

When the ladies finally left I watched with sadness from a neighbour's window. I strongly felt that had more practical support been available, and more responsibility shown by the support agencies, the ladies could have continued and perhaps accomplished a life of their own.

SUMMARY

Many of the difficulties encountered could have been eliminated with foresight and planning.

Before the project began the houses had been empty for almost two years, this resulted in the local community speculating as to their use. These speculations led to the home being viewed as 'special' by the neighbourhood, and my initial task was to dispel local rumours, which incidentally ranged from a home for battered wives to Yorkshire's first legalised brothel!

It was obvious that, previous to their move, the ladies had received very little help on how to cope in a home environment. This lack of planning extended to the ladies' personal thoughts, and it took several months for them to act more responsibly towards their home. They would carelessly damage equipment and expect immediate replacements, or leave fires on to keep a room warm while they went out. Consequently, when the first fuel bills arrived the ladies had to withdraw from their savings accounts to subsidise the amount already set aside for this purpose.

On arrival the ladies had several physical complaints - nothing serious - but appointments for doctors, dentist and optician were required which I felt should have been attended to prior to their move.

Despite assurance that careful planning and assessments had been carried out on the group and that they were ready for the move into the community it did not take more than a few hours to realise that this was not found to be so. The group could not live together compatibly which necessitated the removal of one lady. I felt that the choice of a further two residents was made in the same slapdash manner, as was the replacement for Lucy. As the choice of residents is one of the most important lynchpins it is imperative that a responsible attitude is taken by all people concerned, and the final selection should not be left to one person. If one person is to have the final word surely it should be the landlady. It is her who is taking the responsibility.

The experience shows very clearly that a person who may not be regarded as a 'problem' in a large group can present a huge problem in a smaller group.

As individuals some people will blossom in this type of environment while others will undoubtedly fail. By failure, I mean that the individual continues to perform at their previous level and does not show any indication of responding to the immediate environment. Surprisingly, the people chosen for this scheme, who were considered totally unacceptable by those who knew them prior to their move, but had no involvement in selection, developed beyond expectations, conversely those who were considered 'ideal' candidates failed.

The residents coped well. However, the personality conflict between Emma and Kate was problematic in that it hindered their personal growth, and prevented each from attaining their full potential. With the passing of time the conflict became more intense which affected the other group members and, as a result, regression ensued.

CONCLUSIONS

A home of this type certainly has a great deal to offer. It caters for the individual's needs at their level, and offers an opportunity for personal development in areas often excluded in hostels or larger institutions. However, I do feel that the landlady and residents are both open to exploitation if great care is not taken in the planning of such a scheme.

Although the time spent with the ladies was

unremitting hard work for myself and my family, the satisfaction derived from observing four individuals exercise their rights as people was such that I would not hesitate to do it all again.

Chapter Thirteen

INDEPENDENT LIVING ARRANGEMENTS FOR ADULTS WHO ARE MENTALLY HANDICAPPED

Margaret Flynn

> From time to time anxieties are expressed concerning people discharged from hospitals into poor quality accommodation in city centres or seaside towns, but we know almost nothing about how many people are involved, where they come from, or what becomes of them (Tyne, 1982, p.144)

For almost three years I have been studying the lives and circumstances of 88 people who are currently living in their own homes in north-west England. In association with these people and their keyworkers in social services departments, a great deal of information has been gathered regarding this population's residential careers and their experiences in their own homes.

In the section that follows I shall describe how the study has been carried out, and then I shall outline the living arrangements of the study population. This will be followed by five detailed case studies that are presented for two reasons: (1) they demonstrate the existence and variety of the lifestyles and circumstances of the study populations; and (2) they shed light on some of the difficulties that bear upon the practicalities of living independently for adults who are mentally handicapped. In the final section I shall point to a number of issues that must be addressed by service providers. It is hoped that they will invite the debate that they deserve.

METHOD OF STUDY

During the first year of the study I contacted eight areas in the north west which were represented in the

DHSS Personal Social Services Local Authority Statistics (1976-82) as having unstaffed accommodation for adults who are mentally handicapped. Of the six areas which finally took part in the study, the personnel working with adults living independently were willing to cooperate and they maintained case records for each of their clients.

The existence of case records was critical as in the first year, I read the case records of people living independently in three areas. This was to gather an impression of the sorts of tasks in which social workers were engaged. I also visited 15 people who had lived independently for at least two years.

At the end of the first year four measures were devised:

(1) The information from case records measure organises and categorises the information generally available in case records about a client's history and current living circumstances. This is initially completed by me and is subsequently checked and amended by the keyworker.

(2) The information from keyworkers measure gathers details about the frequency and type of contact with the client; the client's skills, activities and income. It also gives the keyworker an opportunity to rate the success of the placement.

(3) The house environs and living facilities measure is completed following a visit to a clients home. It notes the type of housing, home ownership, the existence of household durables and facilities, and the rateable value.

(4) The interview schedule attempts to establish whether individuals can manage alone in particular skill areas, and further, whether they are satisfied with such aspects of their lives and environs as their daily activities and neighbourhoods for example.

Keyworkers were asked about the most appropriate way of contacting their clients. Generally, letters telling people about the study and asking if they wanted to be involved were sent. Dates and times of visits were suggested in the letters and people were assured that their involvement was voluntary. Many keyworkers approached their clients beforehand, told them about the study and asked if they wanted to take part. If a person said that she or he did not wish to be interviewed, then no attempt was made to encourage reconsideration. Further, during interviews people were reminded that they did not have to answer any question if they did not wish to do so.

Gathering information from case records and from keyworkers occupied over two years, the interviews with the study population taking the first 18 months of the study. The remaining months of the study were spent analysing the information gathered on all of the measures.

THE LIVING ARRANGEMENTS OF THE STUDY POPULATION

The majority of the study population live in their own homes/tenancies for two reasons: (1) their local authorities are committed to establishing community based alternatives for people currently cared for in hospitals and hostels; and (2) the individuals themselves appeared to have a high probability of successfully adjusting. It is noteworthy that a small number of the study population has never resided in any form of specialist provision. These people have continued to live in former family homes following the death of a parent.

In the main, this population live in council-rented accommodation. A small number live in housing association property or property rented from social services departments. Two people live in their own homes.

Table 13.1: Living Arrangements of the Study Population

	Males	Females	Total
Living alone	17	9	26
Living with somebody else:			
marriage partner/cohabitee	9	9	18
sister/brother	2	2	4
parent/child	2	-	2
friends	6	7	13
Living with two others	4	6	10
Living with three others	8	4	12
Living with more than three others	2	1	3
Total	50	38	88

It will be seen from Table 13.1 that 26 people live alone, 37 people live with one other person, and

25 people live with two or more than two others. It should be pointed out that the living arrangements of some of the study population do not correspond entirely to current suggestions for living arrangements for adults who are mentally handicapped (British Association of Social Workers, 1984). For example there are two men who are living with somebody else categorised in Table 13.1 as 'parent/child'. One of these men lives with an elderly father who is an invalid. This man has assumed responsiblity for the full-time care of his father who is frail and dependent on a wheelchair for mobility. The second man has been divorced for two years and he has the custody of his six-year-old child. Of the three people categorised as 'living with more than three others' two men live in a coresidency with a non-handicapped family. The woman has a bedsit in a block of bedsits for people who are elderly.

It should be noted that this is not a static picture. Even at the time of writing changes for some individuals are in the air. Peoples' living arrangements change over time and the reasons for change may include in isolation or combination: the poor repair of a tenancy; hostility from a neighbourhood/interpersonal difficulties; and/or preference to live elsewhere/with somebody else.

FIVE CASE STUDIES

This section gives a three-dimensional picture of the lives of five people: one person who lives alone; one person who lives in a bedsit in a block for people who are elderly; two people who live as a couple; and one person who lives with three other people. It will be recalled from the initial section that the case studies have been selected for two reasons: (1) they demonstrate the variety of lifestyles and circumstances of the study population; and (2) they shed light on some of the difficulties that bear on the practicalities of living independently. Although the case studies are accurate, names have been changed.

Mr Dawson

Mr Dawson is 54 years old. He is a very slightly built man whose appearance resembles that of a Victorian male will full and sweeping sideburns. He lives alone in a council rented terraced house in a street adjoining one in which his brother lives. In addition to being described as a man who is 'mildly mentally handicapped', Mr Dawson has a speech impairment that renders his conversation difficult to follow. His face contorts in attempts to make himself understood and he uses an imaginative, if idiosyncratic signing system. Over a number of years Mr Dawson's drinking has been a matter of concern.

Mr Dawson remained in his parent's former home when they had died. Although he was supported largely by his brother's family, recurrence of management difficulties associated with drinking resulted in his placement in a hostel at the age of 46. He remained in the hostel for eight years.

During his residence in the hostel, Mr Dawson presented management difficulties that resulted from drinking; he experienced interpersonal problems with staff and residents and on occasions, he was physically and verbally abusive:

> Unfortunately Jeff's proclivity concerning alcohol and the resultant effect of irresponsible behaviour, has always marred his social relationships both within and without the hostel.

Mr Dawson has been living in his own tenancy for almost three years. As a consequence of intimidation from local children, it required three visits to his home before he allowed me to come in. It transpired that Mr Dawson's brother had been unable to be present for the other visits and the latter had advised his brother not to let anybody in unless he too was present.

Mr Dawson's brother explained that he was present as it would otherwise be very difficult for me to understand Jeff without his assistance. This became evident as the interview progressed. It emerged that in respect of Mr Dawson's household skills, he remains largely dependent on his brother and his social worker:

> (Food preparation)
> I do bacon and eggs, tinned meat, sausage, mince, pork chops. I do it myself. Get a meal at work - have dinner ...
>
> (Laundry)
> Go to brother's - give it to our Bill and he does it. Puts it in machine. Only lives down the road ...

> (Cleaning)
> Myself. Got a hoover on Saturday ...

Mr Dawson's brother frequently interjected to temper any favourable impression I might otherwise gather:

> He's got into arrears so the social worker is arranging for the bills to be paid weekly ... He still likes a pint ... The social worker comes to make sure he's done his buying in - for food - but if you look in now you won't find any ...

Mr Dawson had no fond memories of his years in the hostel, saying of his home: '(It is) best here, see my brother, play darts ...' Mr Dawson's brother has been instrumental in eliminating the intimidation Jeff experienced from teenagers and the callousness of a neighbour when he moved into his home:

> He used to have a bit of a bad do with the kids banging on his windows and his doors. We used to get the police. They were all about 15. In the end I sorted them out with a couple of lads from work ... Also the bloke next door had a key. He pinched his brand new telly. He wouldn't tackle me. He's gone now. I know who it was. That's the trouble when you're on your own and at work ...

When Mr Dawson was placed in his tenancy it was acknowledged that he could not function without support:

> I believe that a degree of supervision will always be necessary if Jeff is to function adequately in the community.

Mr Dawson continues to have periods of heavy drinking. Unsupervised, his weekly salary of around £60 is largely spent in the pub. Friday afternoon visits from his social worker have reduced this tendency. His social worker either checks Mr Dawson's shopping or does this with him. He consults him regarding the implications of spending his money in the pub; he assists with household tasks; and monitors the cleanliness of his home. Mr Dawson's social worker acknowledges that his client needs help in managing his finances, making everyday decisions, managing time and planning activities and paying his bills. He also appreciates that Mr Dawson is lonely and that he enjoys the conviviality of a pub. In addition to weekly visits from his social worker, Mr Dawson has intermittent assistance from a home help and regular help from his family. Although Mr Dawson's social worker describes his client as 'moderately successful', Mr Dawson's brother has reservations:

> (tapping his forehead) I've had it up to here. I preferred it when he was in the hostel. He drinks his money and he's round at our place for meals. I've had him all me life ...

Miss Spencer

Miss Clara Spencer is 61 years old and is retired. She is a very slight woman who takes great care of her appearance. Miss Spencer lives in a very comfortable bedsit in a two-storey block of bedsits for elderly people. The warden resides in a nearby bungalow. Miss Spencer is houseproud and her bedsit is very homely and attractive. She is an extremely engaging woman and she nods and smiles throughout conversation.

Miss Spencer has moved home seven times. When her mother died she went to live in an old people's home, and from there was transferred to a private residential home. Due to a series of illnesses associated with poor early nutrition, she was transferred to a general hospital. Next, Miss Spencer moved to a hostel for people with mental handicaps. During the latter stage of her 14 years in the hostel, Miss Spencer moved to the rehabilitation section of the hostel and from here she transferred to a tenancy for three women. She was unhappy during her two years' residency in this tenancy, so she moved, and for the last two years she has been living in her own bedsit.

During her residence in staffed accommodation Miss Spencer presented no problems. However, general deterioration characterised Miss Spencer's initial unstaffed placement. As a result of interpersonal difficulties (which they had initially sought to conceal) the women began to neglect their hygiene and the condition of their home. Miss Spencer started to remain out of her home and was taken home by the police on one occasion. During this period Miss Spencer was observed to be physically and verbally abusive.

This placement confronted the social services with considerable difficulties. Miss Spencer's problems with money management were compounded with exploitation by a coresident. She was being compelled to undertake more than her share of the household tasks and her attendance at the ATC became intermittent. Irrespective of frequent and regular visits from social services personnel, it was very clear that the incompatibility of the group could not be overcome. Of the woman who was the source of the difficulties in the house and their departures Miss Spencer said:

> Really, I used to like the house and then like, we had another girl living with us and she couldn't help it like, bless her, she like went funny, so we got split up.

In contrast, Miss Spencer views her current home and lifestyle with a great deal of enthusiasm.

> I never let meself get poorly and down. I used to cry a lot, Simon (home carer) will tell you - but I'm loads better now - I'm happy - see like now I've landed in here. I'm really like, set up about it. Yes, they were worried about me at first but yer see, that's all like, gone now ...
>
> (In the day) I vac and dust and polish. There's me little iron, I enjoy doing that you know. Don't worry me if it's touching the ceiling - I love doing ironing ... and otherwise, I'm out for an hour, you know, going to friends. I had Sally and Peter here on Sunday. Now isn't it kind of them - at Christmas, sometime, I'll be up there. That's a nice break for me and I really look forward to it you know.
>
> (In the evenings) I'm not TV mad ... but I do like the TV now, I enjoy a good comedy - otherwise I might sit and put a nice letter together to someone that I really know. At night sometimes I go to bed early - sometimes I don't ... I've got Lovely (a budgie). He's a little love and oh - he's company.

While Miss Spencer is very reassured by the presence of a warden, she does not associate with people in the other bedsits a great deal.

> You're supposed to like, battle on yourself, you know, carry on if it's possible like. But if they like, see that someone needs any attention, they're supposed to like, see to it. (The

> warden) She comes every day practically, and if she can't come we get these mobile people calling - what they call 'mobile wardens'. See that thing over the bed? Like, well you can press that if anything's the matter ... and someone comes along. I've never been in anything like this beforehand and it were all strange to me. You can imagine what I felt like. There is a place (communal living room) where we can all communicate. I never go down. Sometimes there's people in looking at magazines and reading - nothing like great exciting. But sometimes we have do's there ... I really enjoy it.

Miss Spencer has weekly visits from her home carer and two weekly visits from a home help. They help her with some household tasks and encourage her to use skills about which she is apprehensive. They discuss how she is to spend her time during the following week and they also assist with any official correspondence:

> Simon comes along and he'll say 'Is there anything we must know about?' He'll never miss. So I put things on a file - that letter thing and he comes along and gives me a bit of help with it. There are some things, but not much what I wouldn't understand proper. If it was really particular therefore like, they help me. That's why they help because like it means a great lot to me.

Although it is a source of concern that Miss Spencer 'always values peoples advice and therefore restricts her decision making and competence', her social worker rates this placement as 'successful'.

Miss Finney and Mr White

Miss Finney and Mr White are in their early 30s and they live together in a flat on a council estate of multistorey buildings. Miss Janet Finney lived with her family until her late teens when her mother's ability to control her lessened and she requested placement in a hostel. Miss Finney met Mr Paul White in the hostel. Mr White had moved there following the death of his mother. Although the hostel staff discouraged the relationship between Miss Finney and Mr White, their efforts failed. Staff were anxious that Miss Finney would adopt some of Mr White's antisocial behaviours, in particular stealing.

Miss Finney and Mr White have lived independently for six years. During this period they have moved five times, the moves being prompted by hostility from neighbours; vandalism; burglaries; and problems with the repair of their flats.

Both Miss Finney and Mr White have pronounced speech impediments. Only Miss Finney is able to understand Mr White and consequently he says little in the presence of others. Miss Finney attributes most of their difficulties to their speech:

> He can't talk properly Paul. It's his speech. There's nobody to teach him to talk or read or write ... he needs a woman to teach him to read, write and talk properly. They don't understand. Sometimes I stutter a bit 'cause I got asthma. Makes me can't get words out properly. I could do with a woman to teach me as well. A speech woman ... I stutter sometimes. It's like a kid's talk. Everybody treats me like a kid instead of a woman you see ... Just me speech. I need someone to teach me how to talk ...

Residence in all of their tenancies has been characterised by particularly harrowing styles of abuse, mostly from youngsters.

Of the youngsters Miss Finney's observations reflect her intense dissatisfaction with the area in which she lives:

> I'm not happy with the children. They can't understand me, that's why they do this to me. They throw all muck on me windows, smashing me windows every night, causing trouble, sending me up. They're naughty children they are - little ones and big ones ... They make a big mess on me windows. They give me hassle. I shouldn't be here. It's a very bad place. A bad place for me. I been knocked about. I hate it. The place itself would be alright if you got rid of the children - all the bullies. I hate it. You're all by yourself you're all alone. I'd be better of by meself, going back with me mum ...

It is not surprising that Miss Finney is compelled to think about the advantages of being separate from Mr White. Although she did not discuss difficulties in their relationship, her social worker is concerned about the violence that Miss Finney is subject to from her partner. His behaviour apparently oscillates between violence and affection. The violence brings him into frequent contact with the police.

Money management is the particular focus of Mr White's and Miss Finney's social worker. She frankly acknowledges that it is an uphill, even impossible task at present. Their joint weekly income is £57.00 and on receipt of this, their social worker's attentions are unwelcome. They invariably call for her assistance when after three or four days they have no money left. The social worker observes:

> Janet and Paul have been exposed to rather ruthless members of the community who have taken advantage of their handicaps to manipulate their finances to their own advantage - often leaving them with insufficient reserves to purchase food and pay bills ... because of their handicap they have great difficulty in forward planning and as soon as they have any money they reject any positive help and this usually means that they must be disciplined over what they buy.

Miss Finney regrets that they no longer receive the assistance they have had in the past:

> See I had a homemaker to help me one time, but they won't let me have a homemaker. She used to help me with curtains, cooker and shopping like. See, people have me money here. The DHS is not helping me any more. And there's another one, social services don't seem to be doing nothing for me any more. I could do with somebody to help me. I can do the shopping alright. I'm not handicapped. I can count money sometimes. I look after meself the best way I can. You got to in this world ...

Inability or reluctance to avoid the company of unscrupulous individuals who gradually milk them of their money results in debts and sometimes unrealistic expectations regarding the role of neighbours:

> I've got no food in today, nothing in. I'm starving. The neighbours won't help me, they're nasty ... Mind you I keep to meself round here mind you. I don't like to get involved with the neighbours. They're very good with the dog, they're good with Spot, but they don't feed me an' him you see. We're starving ...

Some of Miss Finney's frustration regarding finances originates from the fact that benefits are paid directly to Mr White. Given that his communication skills are extremely limited, that he assumes the major responsibility for the money (because he believes it to be his), and that he will not accept any advice on its management, it is clear that he is unequal to the task of being financially solvent:

> I'd prefer to have me own money and everything. They've taken things away from us you know. The telly, bill, gas fires. I don't seem to get on with anybody you know. It's 'cause I can't talk properly you know ... I've been to the DHS and tell them I've got no money. They don't seem to care ...

Miss Finney and Mr White have lived in their current tenancy for 12 months. Invariably it is a similar pattern of incidents that has resulted in their removal from the four preceding tenancies: they fail to budget adequately and they refuse assistance from social workers; they get into debt; they have 'friends' who manage to part them from most of their weekly income; their windows are smashed and replacements are not prompt; they are frightened of youngsters who also take money from them; they neglect to look after their flat and their personal standards of hygiene deteriorate. Consistently, they have lived in 'hard-to-let' tenancies on large estates close to schools. They appear to excite the attentions of unscrupulous and ruthless youngsters and adults within weeks. They become frightened of the locality and so they remain in their flat and their relationship suffers. Miss Finney fondly recalls the two years she spent in a hostel when she attended an ATC:

> I was in a hostel a long while ... I need a woman in charge of me. I asked the social worker if I could go back to the hostel last time. See, she won't listen. You see you get money there ... See when I first went in the hostel I had no trouble and no worries. They got me a job (at the ATC) and everything ... Unemployment is terrible ... There's no job and no work you know. You can't get a job and they think you're lazy.

In spite of Miss Finney's reflection that she

would be better off with her mother or in a hostel she said very deliberately:

> I like being together. We've always been together in hostels and things ... I supply all the fight and the fun. It's great fun after a while. I won all the fights. When you're together it's alright. But you can't get out because of the kids and the children ...

It is noteworthy that Miss Finney did not include Mr White in her wishes to return either to her mother or to the hostel.

During their total of seven years' residence in the hostel Miss Finney and Mr White were trained in self-help, social, academic and vocational skills. It is clear, however, that they are ill-equipped to manage in their present and former tenancies. Inevitably their social worker rates their placement as 'not successful' and suggests that the reasons are: 'problems with vandals and youngsters who get money from them (thus) they are at risk ...'. Of the future, the social worker comments:

> It is difficult at this stage to predict what degree of success we will be able to achieve as both parties are suspicious over any efforts to advise them how to manage their finances. Much will depend on the level of cooperation we can develop with them ...

Miss Burns

Miss Dorothy Burns is 59 years old. She is a small and very slightly built woman whose mobility is limited due to gross motor spasticity. She walks with the aid of sticks.

Miss Burns has lived in a group home for eleven years. Her coresidents are three women friends and they all met in a hospital for people who are mentally handicapped. Miss Burns lived in the hospital for 49 years, and two of her coresidents lived there for 39 years and 32 years respectively. (It is not known for how long the remaining woman lived there.) Miss Burns said of the hospital:

> I wouldn't go back ... I didn't want to come out though. I was there nearly 50 years - 49 years and 11 months ....

Although it is known that Miss Burns originated

from the south, little else is known of her early life. Her mother died during her residence in the hospital and, unlike her friends who have no contact with relatives, she sees her relatives occasionally.

Miss Burns is the oldest member of the household, the ages of her coresidents being 43, 44 and 55. The group became friendly living on the same hospital ward. As they are a very able and highly skilled group of people their roles in hospital frequently blurred between those of patients and nursing assistants. They all enjoyed working on the babies and children's ward and their pleasure in the company of the (former) nursing staff continues:

> Our friends come to see us ... like the nurses who used to be at the hospital, they help us. They come to see us, Nurse Watkins and Sister Wilkinson come and see us. They used to work with us on B7, the babies ward. And Sister Baily. Dave (social worker) comes down too and Miss Curran, she used to be a Guide Leader. She used to have us in the guides when we were small. On Wednesday and Sunday she still comes.

Although Miss Burns requires some assistance (provided by coresidents) with dressing, cooking, washing and shopping as a result of her physical limitations, she is focal to the routine household tasks. She shops twice a week with one of her coresidents and she does the washing for everybody:

> I do the machining, bedding and that ... Got to keep yourself clean haven't you?
>
> (Coresident)
> ... and I put it (the washing) outside for her, peg it out. No one needs to help us. We're all right.

Their household tasks are shared and the housework is routinised:

> Liz cleans on Friday, polishing and that and Dorothy does the dusting. I scrubbed the carpet today with some stuff and I scrubbed the two carpets upstairs on Tuesday. Sally cooks every night and when she goes to pottery Dorothy does it.

Miss Burns assumes responsibilty for a large part of the running of the household as she is mostly at home during the day. Two women work in pubs on a part-time basis and the third attends a college of further education. They are a very active and talented group of people and their home is a monument to their varied skills and interests, that is, pottery, knitting, painting, lampshade-making, rugmaking, gardening and household plants. When they purchase seeds or bulbs Miss Burns reads the instructions as her friends are unable to do so:

> In the day I go out. We go visiting anybody what we know. We go to the British Legion on a Monday, go to St Gregory's club once a month and we go to church on Sundays ... We go out a lot - we go by taxi. When it's light we walk it.

They all take great pride in their newly decorated home. Within a mile of their former home, it is a large semidetached house in an attractive area and it is rented from the social services department. The women were very keen to hear my impressions of their home, and I was given a guided tour within minutes of arriving. It was easy to be very positive and to share their enthusiasm. Of their neighbours, one woman said:

> We've got very good neighbours, they don't bother us. If they want to use the phone, like Mrs Hall next door, she's a bit crippled and she can't go far, so we let her use the phone.

Their social worker describes these women as 'successful'. They receive 'general supervision by the home carer' who joins them for coffee one evening a week and chats to them about any difficulties that may have arisen in the preceding week. They generally have assistance with bills:

> If we want anything important like letters or cheques and like that ... the girl comes to see us on Tuesday from Social Services. It's Fran what comes.

I met Fran briefly and she had nothing but praise for her clients: 'They're very easy and incredibly nice. I love coming here.'

THE DIFFICULTIES OF INDEPENDENT LIVING

The individuals described here exhibit a wide range

of lifestyles. As with the remainder of the study population their lives are varied and complex and they change over time. Although the analysis of the information gathered continues, a few observations are in order. These concern some of the difficulties of independent living for the individuals described and for the study population in general.

Firstly, money management is a recurring theme for people who are living independently and it is a major preoccupation of keyworkers (Flynn, 1985). The majority of the study population are in receipt of supplementary benefits, but the complexity of this fragmented income support means that very few people can manage their finances without help from keyworkers. Most people required assistance both in liaising with the DHSS, in the completion of DHSS forms, and paying of bills (see, for example, Miss Spencer and Miss Burns).

A further dimension of money management relates to the actual income. The range of incomes for the people described here is from £28.50 to £60.00 per week. Given that people who are mentally handicapped have problems with abstract thinking, it is to be expected that budgeting difficulties will result for many people. This is especially the case when incomes are so limited. People living in groups, such as Miss Burns and friends are financially better off, as they can pool their money. Atkinson (1980) has elaborated upon the issue of poverty:

> One problem is that, almost always these days, we discharge people into poverty, a subsistence level of living with few, if any extras ... And we discharge people into the cold - people used to a warm environment then face prohibitive costs, inefficient central heating systems and the draughts of council houses ... There is probably little or no money for 'extras' such as hairdressing, outings, holidays, nice clothes ...

The experience of Miss Finney's and Mr White's keyworker is not atypical. Her clients choose to exclude her from their budgeting with the result that she regularly reprimands them for giving away their money and for making non-essential purchases. While there are no easy solutions to the chaotic handling of finances, the accumulation of debts means that: incomes are regularly eroded until the debts are paid; clients' lifestyles are even further restricted; and, most importantly, a question-mark hangs over the continuation of independent living.

A further difficulty experienced by some adults living in their own homes/tenancies is that of victimisation. This takes many forms, but focusing specifically on the people described: Mr Dawson had his TV stolen and youngsters teased him until his brother intervened; Miss Finney and Mr White are subject to physical and verbal abuse from youngsters and they are regularly financially milked. Arguably also, victimisation is more likely to occur when people are placed in hard-to-let tenancies as with Miss Finney and Mr White. Residence in such depressed places is affected by crime. It is conspicuous that all three people have pronounced speech impediments. This appears to serve as a cue to youngsters and others that they are different.

There is no evidence to suggest that the experience of being victimised is less harrowing for people who are mentally handicapped than anybody else (Fischer, 1984, p.166):

> Being criminally victimised is a disruption of daily routine. It is a disruption that compels one, despite personal resistance, to face one's fellow as a predator and oneself as prey ... one experiences vulnerability, separateness and helplessness in the face of the callous, insensitive often anonymous enemy ... As life goes on, the victim finds him/herself pervasively attuned to the possibility of victimisation ... through recollections of the crime, imagination of even worse outcomes, vigilant suspiciousness of others ... and desires to make sense of it all ... One begins to get back on top of the situation through considering or taking precautions against crime, usually by restricting one's range of activities so as not to fall prey again ...

Clearly there is merit in reflecting carefully upon the choice of (or existing) living arrangement and area. There are no advantages from placements in 'hard-to-let' tenancies and these should be avoided:

> ... when complexes built to high standards lie vandalised, demoralised and boarded up (they are) no place for anyone, let alone those with disabilities and other difficulties (Purkis and Hodson, 1982, p.33)

An area that can be a minefield for personnel

supporting people in independent living arrangements is that of group compatibility. Miss Burns and her friends have known each other for many years. They opted to share a house together and this has resulted in a successful living arrangement and in the continuation of their friendship. Heller (1984, p.142) underlines the importance of the continuity of friendships:

> ... disruption of friendship networks is a key factor leading to poor relocation adjustment. The fact that broken friendships could adversely affect transferred residents is often ignored in placement decision ...

Miss Spencer's first experience in independent living was extremely distressing. Their incompatibility gradually became apparent and resulted in their general deterioration. This could not be ameliorated by regular visits from social services personnel. Miss Spencer's current living circumstances bear no relation to her past experience. She is now extremely happy since the powerful influences of incompatibility and resulting stress are gone.

Miss Finney's and Mr White's association continues in spite of their dire living circumstances. Miss Finney is physically abused by her partner, and when she thinks about how problematic and frightening their circumstances are, she considers returning to the hostel or to her mother. While separation from Mr White may prove advantageous, it should not be forgotten that Miss Finney said 'I like being together'. Further their relationship is tested and strained by their particularly adverse circumstances.

CONCLUSIONS

The people whose lives are described here are not unique in the difficulties they experience. Nor are the difficulties outlined the only ones which affect their lives. Although many others spring to mind, I have chosen to stress three particularly vexing issues for keyworkers as they are relevant to the lives of many of their clients.

Independent living arrangements for adults who are mentally handicapped entail risks of both exploitation and victimisation, and to relationships.

In the preceding section some broad

prescriptions have been suggested, for example, hard-to-let tenancies should be avoided for adults who are mentally handicapped; and friendship networks should not be disrupted in the placement process. The features of successful placements continue to be investigated. While successful placements will not inevitably result from observing these recommendations alone, minimally they will ensure that people are not poorly served by the commitment to close institutions.

ACKNOWLEDGEMENT

The research on which this chapter is based was supported by the Economic and Social Research Council (1983-86).

REFERENCES

Atkinson, D. (1980) 'Moving Out of Mental Handicap Hospitals', APEX Journal of the British Institute of Mental Handicap, 8 (3), 76-8

British Association of Social Workers (1984) Evidence to the House of Commons Social Services Committee Inquiring into Community Care for Adult Mentally Ill and Mentally Handicapped People (BASW Publications, Birmingham)

DHSS Personal Social Services Local Authority Statistics (1976-82) Homes and Hostels for the Mentally Ill and Mentally Handicapped at 31 March 1976-82, England (seven vols), A/F77/11-A/F83/11

Fischer, C.T. (1984) 'A Phenomenological Study of Being Criminally Victimised: Contribution and Constraints of Qualitative Research', Journal of Social Issues, 40 (1), 161-78

Flynn, M.C. (1985) 'Objectives and Prognoses Recorded in the Case Records of Mentally Handicapped Adults Living in their Own Homes', British Journal of Social Work, 15, 519-24

Heller, T. (1984) 'Issues in Adjustment of Mentally Retarded Individuals to Residential Relocation', in N.R. Ellis and N.W. Bray (eds) International Review of Research in Mental Retardation, vol. 12 (Academic Press, London)

Purkis, A. and Hodson, P. (1982) Housing and Community Care (National Council for Voluntary Organisations: Bedford Square Press, London)

Tyne, A. (1982) 'Community Care and Mentally Handicapped People', in A. Walker (ed.) Community Care: The Family, the State and Social Policy (Basil Blackwell and Martin Robertson, Oxford)

Chapter Fourteen

PUBLIC ATTITUDES TOWARDS PROVIDING COMMUNITY CARE

Sheila Manning

INTRODUCTION

Historically, it can be stated, institutions and asylums became necessary because of general public attitudes. These were, firstly, a feeling that society must be protected from people with mental handicaps or illness; and secondly, that people with mental problems must be cared for in a safe and secure environment for their own good. It appeared that the public were humane and sympathetic and wanted to shield the unfortunate people who were of no use to society, from evil and exploitation, but at the same time ensure law-abiding, 'normal' citizens freedom from the violence, abuse and embarrassment which this type of person could create. Is there any reason to believe that these attitudes have changed?

People working in the field of mental handicap (a minority group) find it difficult to understand and sometimes hard to accept that people may still consider institutionalisation the kindest, most caring way to look after people with mental handicaps. What has been done to find out whether or not this viewpoint has remained the same or altered to any degree?

Literature on any in-depth probing into the attitudes of the general public towards mental handicap is limited. The few reports available relate to specific localities and usually to specific situations such as the reaction of the public to a new hostel. This does not give any indication of whether or not the modern philosophies and ideology for the future of people with mental handicaps are acceptable to the general public. It is very alarming when the success or failure of people with mental handicaps actually becoming part of society <u>depends on</u> being accepted by the public.

The study by D. Locker et al. (1979) suggests that mental handicap as a terminology is poorly understood by the public but there is little evidence to suggest that it needs to be for the public to accept people who have a mental handicap. The suggestion that knowledge regarding mental handicap is not related to attitudes is particularly interesting. If it is not 'knowledge of' that influences acceptance and attitudes then what does and is it possible to find out and do something about it? Locker concludes that there is little understanding of the concept of community care. This is not surprising when many people working in the field find it difficult to define and have differing views themselves!

The Dalgleish (1979) study reporting on attitudes to purpose-built units for people with mental handicaps states 'it appeared that the more a unit resembled local housing the better it was liked'. This suggests that the public are more tolerant of buildings in which people with mental handicaps live if they merge with the local scenery. A statement such as this does not give much indication of how the people living in the building will be treated. Will they be accepted if they merge into the background and make no demands but not if they stand out as individuals?

An APMH report (Males, 1980) delved into the attitudes of school children towards people with mental handicaps, with a view to forming appropriate educational programmes. Jeanne Males concludes that 'it remains evident that the community may not be able to care about something if it does not know about it'. This opens up questions related to how much people need to know before they begin to care, or whether it is more likely to be involvement and contact with people with mental handicaps that influence attitudes.

Discussion points are highlighted in a study by Christine Hammonds (1980) who writes about adoption of handicapped children which could be applied to the acceptance (or not) of people with mental handicaps living a more integral life in the community. She states 'it is easy for professional workers to make two basic assumptions

(1) That everyone else is equally aware of the needs of people with mental handicaps.
(2) That despite this knowledge, nobody cares enough to offer help.'

The report goes on to say 'fortunately there is enough evidence to suggest that both assumptions are false and that successfully dealing with the first (the need for knowledge) quickly disproves the second'.

Another reference in the same study says that it is natural that not everyone will want to participate, get involved or help at all, nor should they be expected to. In this case tolerance and some understanding of potential problems is all that is required and people can be helped towards tolerance by the example of others. It is, however, vitally important that there is an attitude of acceptance and a recognition of the rights which people with mental handicaps have as fellow citizens.

Better Services for the Mentally Handicapped (DHSS, 1971) lists as one of its basic principles - 'understanding and help from friends and neighbours and from the community at large are needed to help the family to maintain a normal social life and to give the handicapped person as near normal life as his handicaps permit'. This is a commendable statement, but practical advice and suggestions as to whether this can be achieved and how to go about initiating this type of acceptance are difficult to find.

Society is a way of life, a culture, a belonging in individual ways to the surrounding community. Each person has, to some degree, a variety of choices and can ideally exercise those choices to develop a place which not only suits their own expectations and needs but also those of people around them. People with mental handicaps have been excluded from society until recently and now need advocates to support and help them find a comfortable and rightful niche within the community and to exercise those democratic rights which a democratic country such as ours offers to its citizens. It is only in this way that people with mental handicaps can begin to lead a meaningful and self-satisfying existence. This as a project will fail without the support of society itself - the general public.

THE REASONS FOR CONDUCTING A SURVEY

From the previous discussion several questions arise.

(1) Is there any reason to believe that the general public attitudes prevalent at the beginning of

the century towards people with mental handicaps have changed?

(2) What is being done to determine whether this viewpoint has remained the same or altered in any way?

(3) Do the general public understand the concept of community care? What is community care?

(4) Does the amount and type of involvement or contact with people with mental handicaps influence attitudes? Is involvement tied up with knowledge of mental handicaps and does having both influence attitudes to a greater degree?

(5) How will people with mental handicaps be treated by neighbours?

(6) Do the general public recognise and accept that people with mental handicaps are fellow citizens and have the same rights as any other person?

(7) What can be done to ensure positive attitudes towards people with mental handicaps? What is the best way to organise and present public relations exercises? Are they beneficial or a waste of time and effort? What alternatives are there?

As progress becomes more commonplace in the field of mental handicap, particularly with the development of core and cluster models, group homes, surrogate families and integration into community activities it may be helpful to investigate the attitudes of the general public to this changing philosophy. Conducting a survey may provide an insight into <u>some of</u> the answers to the questions raised above. It may also make it possible to decide whether or not nature will take a positive course without interference. If people with mental handicaps are introduced slowly into more normal lifestyles without publicity, without discussion and without planned involvement, perhaps a gradual tolerance of 'evolution and change' will develop leading to total acceptance. However, it is far easier to sit back waiting to see whether or not this will happen and hoping it will, than it is to formulate ways and means of encouraging positive attitudes.

Very often when embarking on a new project involving people with mental handicaps, there is a strong feeling that some sort of public relations work is essential. This becomes very controversial once the initial enthusiasm dampens a little, and suggestions for 'roadshows', public talks and open days need to be translated into a practical and organised exercise. The modern philosophy revolves around 'normalisation' and people's rights, and yet public relations exercises usually consist of advertising, selling and 'showing off' a product - in this case it is marketing people! This must be unethical as well as degrading and insulting to the people concerned and is certainly not normal. There is also a great danger that it could do much more harm than good by strengthening fears, apprehension and misgivings people have inherited.

It could even initiate these feelings. Unfortunately, however, the general public have the potential to make life extremely difficult for the people who are disadvantaged (because of their handicaps) with communicating and learning acceptable concepts of social behaviour. It is for this reason that some type of public relations work must have an important role in the advancement of modern trends.

THE SURVEY

A survey to try and find answers to the questions outlined previously has been carried out, its specific aims being twofold:

(1) To aid public relations work in the future, so that it can be focused on specific aspects.
(2) As a public relations exercise in its own right. To stimulate people's thoughts and encourage them to ask questions, pass comment or become interested passively or actively without any pressure.

The survey was conducted in Boston (Lincolnshire) and surrounding villages with a population of approximately 30000. In this locality the social services manage a hostel with 40 residential places and an adjoining adult training centre providing occupation for 100 people with mental handicaps. In addition to these there is a residential home for 12 children with mental handicaps and also a special school for 70 children provided by the Education Authority. There are three group homes in the area which have minimal staff support. There had never been national health facilities for people with mental handicaps in the Boston area until 1982 when a residential unit for 40 people and a day centre for

64 people were built in the same neighbourhood as the hostel and adult training centre. The nearest large, old institutions with which local people may associate are a mental illness hospital with 300 places, 32 km from Boston at Rauceby, and a mental handicap institution at Fleet (26 km away) with 100 places, both being managed by South Lincolnshire Health Authority.

A postal questionnaire was used, 350 being distributed within a 9.6 km radius of Boston town centre. Seven specific areas were chosen and coded representing as wide a sample of the general public as possible. It was felt that this was worth exploring because of the hopefully widening choice of places for people with mental handicaps to live and that the results would provide useful information regarding the attitudes of people already living in the different types of residential areas, but for the purpose of this report these observations have not been included.

RESULTS

Of the 350 questionnaires delivered 91 were returned. Unfortunately 22 of these were devoid of answers and therefore of no use to the survey. The survey is based on 69 questionnaires, a return of 19.7 per cent. Of the total number of respondents 40 per cent were men and 60 per cent women, indicating that more women than men are interested in the subject of mental handicap or are more inclined to fill in questionnaires!

Defining Mental Handicap: What's in a Name?

The aim of the first two questions 'Do you know what mental handicaps are?' followed immediately by 'How would you describe a person with mental handicaps?' was to determine whether or not there is a general understanding of the term 'mental handicap'.

Of the 69 questionnaires three people did not attempt to answer this question. Only three people were prepared to state that they do not know what a mental handicap is. It is interesting that these are all male respondents. In fact the overall analysis between men and women for this question shows that men are much less positive in their replies than women, with only 57.7 per cent of men but 83 per cent of women answering positively to knowing what mental handicaps are.

It was expected that people would find it difficult to describe a person with mental handicaps, but 85.5 per cent of respondents penned a reply. There were very few answers the same, with obvious difficulty or confusion shown regarding the words and terms to use. This resulted in a very wide range of descriptions, and also highlighted some very deliberate thoughts on the meaning of 'mental handicap'. For the purpose of this evaluation the statements were split broadly into three groups - those which obviously related to mental handicap, those obviously descriptive of mental illness and those which could apply to either.

Although 72.5 per cent of people are positive they know what a mental handicap is only 49.3 per cent gave a specific description of mental handicap. It is also interesting that only three people (4.3 per cent) stated that they do not know what a mental handicap is but as many as 14.5 per cent (ten people - seven men and three women), did not give a description. There was an obvious reference to mental illness in 7.3 per cent of the replies which is much lower than anticipated, but a higher proportion (28.9 per cent) of answers could relate to either mental handicap or mental illness. There were 59 replies with several people offering quite a lengthy description containing one or more terms.

An obvious sensitivity emanates from many of the replies and quite a surprising reluctance to use terms such as 'subnormal', 'retarded' and 'backward'. The words 'idiot' and 'lunatic' were not used, with one exception - a man who described a person with mental handicaps as

> a person with limited intelligence and responsibility, but who isn't? Aren't we all mentally limited (handicapped, inadequate) in some way or other? And isn't it for you to say which type you have in mind? A John Clare, the poet, for instance; a Virginia Woolf; a Down's syndrome or brain-damaged victim; a poor unhappy lunatic; idiot or schizophrenic. Even a literary genius can be hopeless at maths.

There are also misconceptions, controversial issues and thought-provoking statements contained amongst the replies. Some examples are as follows:

> An IQ under 50% diagnosed before the age of 18
> A person in a wheelchair
> A human being who has the misfortune, through no

fault of their own to be deprived of living life to the full.

Brain damage was mentioned more often than any other term but usually accompanied by a qualifying statement of the effect the brain damage has on a person. Physical disabilities and intelligence or IQ were also quoted in several cases along with slow learning or learning difficulties. Many people (49 per cent) showed an awareness of the problems which a person with mental handicap may have, and although many descriptions were vague and showed some confusion, there appeared to be a general understanding of the term.

There are several ways in which the general public can be informed about any subject. Articles in newspapers, programmes on television, books and pamphlets are some of the more common sources of knowledge. An attempt was made to find out which of these sources was most likely to pass on information regarding mental handicaps.

It is immediately obvious and perhaps not surprising that programmes about mental handicap on television attract the highest percentage of people, although newspaper articles follow close behind. It is interesting to consider and compare the style and presentation of reports by television and papers. A documentary type programme on television is more liable to be well researched (basically because of the time available in which to do this) than newspaper articles which aim at being topical and if possible exclusive. As a result television will explore more than one aspect or viewpoint and present a broader more sensitive outline to the topic. It is possible during television programmes to raise key issues and to present facts and figures as well as discussions concerning these. More information can be seen and heard in a relatively short period of time than can be read in many pages of literature.

Newspapers are more inclined to present reports which play on human emotions of pity, outrage, shock, etc, and therefore tend to portray a dramatic and sensationalist approach to minority happenings. Very rarely is a newspaper willing to give space to factual information or current trends without an accompanying scandal or drama which will help to sell the newspaper. Unfortunately, this gives an unavoidable bias or exaggeration to newspaper reports or articles, and also political overtones depending on which newspaper secures the story.

People who have read books about mental handicap

amounted to only 17.6 per cent of the total respondents, and a significantly higher proportion were women. It may be that books tend to be very factual and written with a cloistered viewpoint and well-formed opinions. In addition, they are aimed at people already involved in the field and not the general public. Those books which might have a wider appeal, such as Born a Number and Joey, although available in libraries and bookshops, have such competition from the wide range of literature available that they have little chance of becoming best-sellers.

A surprisingly high number of respondents, 44.1 per cent, indicated that they had seen pamphlets about mental handicap. It would be interesting to have more explicit information about the format of these and where they had been displayed or circulated; it is very rare that pamphlets are printed specifically with mental handicap mentioned. A possibility in the Boston area is that one or two booklets have been seen, namely one designed for potential voluntary workers or one giving information about the services offered by the local community unit. These were circulated quite widely, the former to the unemployment worker's centre, job centre, library, women's institutes and churches and the latter to general practitioners' surgeries and health centres. It is heartening to think that in a small way these two booklets may have been read and may be having some degree of positive influence.

The term 'mental handicap' often triggers off a stereotype picture or initiates certain feelings or reactions. The respondents were asked 'What do you think of the term "mental handicap"? to see if reactions could be assessed. The answers to this were subdivided into:

(1) Positive responses indicating that the term is 'appropriate', an 'adequate description', 'fits the bill' and generally acceptable.
(2) Negative responses such as 'not nice', 'can disturb people', 'crude and cruel', 'too medical', 'distressing', etc.
(3) Indifferent responses where it was not possible to determine either negative or positive feelings.

Half of the respondents think that the term 'mental handicap' is acceptable but several comments give the view that a better term could be used. Expressions such as 'adequate description but has odd connotations nowadays', 'describes condition but is too medical' and 'interpreted properly it is all right' were among those classed as accepting the term.

Those who do not like the term 'mental handicap' (38 per cent of respondents) have stronger feelings than those finding it acceptable. Among the reasons given for finding it unacceptable were:

It's like being labelled different.
Gives the impression of madness.
People class it as insane - like in the 1880s.
Frightening description of a disability.

If the analysis of this question is split into male and female replies there is quite a difference in the style of answer. The indifferent replies do not differ significantly, but men definitely seem to find the term 'mental handicap' more acceptable than women.

Following on from this question people were invited to offer an alternative. Of the 22 people who thought 'mental handicap' unacceptable 10 people suggested a different one. The remaining 12 answers, although finding the term 'mental handicap' acceptable expressed reservations and therefore gave an alternative phrase or terminology. Some respondents felt there must be a way of improving the term but could not think of anything suitable.

One person felt that it would be a pointless exercise to change the term as 'any changed term could in time attract the usual associations'. This point is arguable in that having studied the replies closely there is evidence to suggest there is less stigma/ridicule/fear attached to the term 'mental handicap' than there is to that of 'idiot' or 'imbecile'. Perhaps a changed term omitting reference to 'mental' could be a positive move in lessening the stigma further.

Of the suggestions only two still included a reference to mental - 'mental underdevelopment' and 'mentally disabled'. All the others seemed to suggest avoidance of the word 'mental' rather than the word 'handicap'. 'Just disabled' or 'disability' was recommended in four cases, and 'just handicapped', 'genetic handicap' and 'handicap of the mind' again in four cases. Last but not least one respondent suggested 'non-physical handicap'. This terminology is perhaps worth exploring in the sense that if mental handicap can be thought of in the same way as deafness or blindness, then life could be so much easier for many people, including those families who support a relative with a mental handicap at home.

An American study (Hollinger and Jones, 1970) entitled 'What's in a name' has shown that in the locality of the study there was little understanding of either the term 'slow learner' or 'mental retardate', the latter being American analogy of mental handicap in England. However, when the name of a group of people was changed from 'mental retardates' to 'slow learners' the study showed a greater acceptance by the general public of this group of people than a similar 'control' group still referred to as 'mental retardates'.

It was with this study in mind that participants in this survey were asked to differentiate between a slow learner and someone with a mental handicap. There was a high response to this question with the answers being of a very similar nature. From a total of 59 answers 41 were specifically related to a lowered potential ability. This was then clarified by an indication that a slow learner is able to achieve/develop/learn/become independent whereas someone with a mental handicap is not able to progress in any of these areas. Only eight respondents thought there was very little difference with the exception of a time factor; the length of time taken to learn skills being greater for people with mental handicaps than slow learners.

Two questions were asked to determine the amount of contact people already have with relatives, friends or casual acquaintances who have mental handicaps. It is apparent from some of the answers that a small proportion of respondents have included people suffering from mental illness. Reference was made to the respondents themselves - 'only me' - and also to relatives receiving treatment at the local mental illness unit.

Of the 32 people who know someone with a mental handicap 25 people do have some contact with the person, five do not have contact for various reasons such as the person has died or moved away, and the remaining two have no contact at all.

The type of contact differs significantly in that four people have a working relationship with people with mental handicaps, and another four have frequent contact of once a month or more.

The remaining 17 people appear to have much less contact and involvement consisting mainly of visits socially, once or twice a year, infrequently or very occasionally. This indicates that only 12.5 per cent of the total survey population have any significant contact or involvement with people with mental handicaps.

To pursue further the extent of contact people have with mental handicap services the question was asked whether people had ever visited a place where people with mental handicaps live. A total of 35.4 per cent of respondents had visited a range of social services and health authority facilities including large institutions, hostels, community unit and day centre. Several answers quoted Rauceby, a large mental illness hospital in Lincolnshire, adding weight to the apparent confusion there still is between mental illness and mental handicap.

The remaining 64.6 per cent of respondents have never visited residential places for people with mental handicaps, but 38 per cent of these expressed a wish to do so in the future which indicates a certain amount of interest and curiosity. Only 19 per cent of the replies did not state a firm 'yes' or 'no' when asked, but 42 per cent were definite in that they had no desire to visit such places. It is unfortunate that reasons were not given making any investigation into why this is impossible. It may be simply a lack of interest although if people have been stimulated sufficiently to answer the questionnaire it seems unlikely that this is the sole reason. Perhaps a wariness or fear of what they might see, not knowing how to react or even due regard for people's privacy may have been instrumental in these decisions.

People who have made visits were asked to give their opinion of these places to try and gain some idea of how this type of service is viewed. The comments were frequently directed at the staff and buildings, for example, 'staff very caring', 'place clean and well kept', 'dark and dismal'. Of the 23 respondents who gave descriptions 16 used positive comments and seven negative comments.

Where Should People with Mental Handicaps Live?

There was quite a varied response to the question 'Where should people with mental handicaps live?' Of the 61 opinions given 15 (24.5 per cent) contained reference to the '<u>Family home</u>', with nine of these suggesting alternatives if this was not possible or the family could not cope. One respondent included 'daycare support' and one other suggested 'visiting supervision'. A small number of people (five) referred to 'the community', but it seems that the understanding of 'community' differs considerably and that perhaps this word is used when an alternative is difficult to find. The references in these cases indicate residential places in built-up areas as opposed to miles away in the countryside, 'in communities where they can receive the help they require with only limited access to a difficult and non-understanding world'. It may be that those respondents who suggest 'normal homes' with families and 'integration into society' are those referring to the community in the way people working within the mental handicap services understand it. If this ambiguity is not corrected then misunderstandings and misinterpretation may arise and hinder the development of positive public attitudes.

When giving reasons why people should live in the community, normal homes or with families, it is interesting that reference to integration is made by some respondents, such as:

> To relate to normal people and normal lives.
> Possibility of learning from experiences with non-handicapped.
> Surrounded by everyday life and are a part of it.

Not all respondents were so positive in their views as the following quotes show:

> In a home altogether so they feel no different and then it would be better for them.
> I do not agree with the present community placing; surely it is far better to care for these poor people on a person to person basis and not foist them on a generally uncaring public.

Nevertheless some of these statements show a sensitivity and awareness that people with mental handicaps do have feelings and that these should be considered.

A small number of people felt it difficult to be exact without knowing the extent of the handicaps or disability but those who did (34) included institutions, hospital, special homes, hostels, sheltered accommodation and units with professional staff. Medical care, supervision and oversight were also quoted in six replies. The most disappointing observation was that only two people suggested that those involved should make their own choice or have any say in the matter.

When asked 'Who in your view should be

responsible for people with mental handicaps?' only three people did not give an opinion. Of the 66 replies, 25 referred to parents or families but 18 suggested supportive help or alternatives if parents unable to cope. These included local authority, social services, national health service, trained people, home helps and residential facilities.

As many as 64 per cent (41) did not expect families/parents to take responsibility; instead opinions were split. The most popular view (14) stated qualified or trained people. The government was specified in nine instances, national health service in four cases and the Department of Health and Social Security only once. Caring or devoted people were cited by six respondents with a further six placing the responsibility onto the public, everyone or the community.

It would have been interesting to ask the question 'Do you think someone needs to have special training/qualifications to care for people with handicaps?, this being such a controversial issue and when so many of the people caring for or supporting people with mental handicaps are without professional, nursing or social services qualifications.

'Are there any people with mental handicaps living near you?' gave an indication that very few people (11 per cent) actually live near a family with a handicapped member. If this is the case then very few people can have experienced a neighbourly relationship to help them to form opinions or gain knowledge of the lifestyle or problems and difficulties which may face these people and their families. These results are much lower than expected when a local case register indicates that there are people with handicaps living in most of the areas covered by the survey.

'How would you feel about living next door to a person with a mental handicap?' produced the following results:

Total	Strong positive	Positive	Indiff- erent	Don't know	Negative	Strong negative
64	5	34	10	4	9	2
	60.9 per cent		15.6 per cent	6.3 per cent	17.2 per cent	

The majority of people (76.5 per cent) had no reservations about such a situation and ranged from 'no different to living next door to anybody else' to 'perfectly happy' and 'friendly'.

A small proportion of respondents expressed reservations such as 'if not violent' or 'if adequate supervision available'. Some mothers expressed anxiety on behalf of their young children and another was wary of noise or trespass. The results imply that the thought of a single person with a mental handicap is not upsetting/threatening or unacceptable to the majority of people.

'How would you feel about living near an institution for 150 people with mental handicaps?' produced quite different results.

Total	Strong positive	Positive	Indiff-erent	Don't know	Negative	Strong negative
63	1	24	7	3	22	6
	39.7 per cent		11.1 per cent	4.8 per cent	44.4 per cent	

The response showed a marked difference in attitude to that of living near a single person with a mental handicap. Although there were still respondents who did not express reservations (50.8 per cent) a much higher proportion (44.4 per cent) expressed quite strong feelings and worries, and even specified the terms or conditions which should apply (for example, 'adequate supervision', 'situated in own grounds', 'not violent or frightening appearance'). The feelings expressed were 'not keen', 'unhappy', 'I would move', 'sceptical', and 'cautious' amongst others.

The most common emotional response to people with mental handicaps was that of sympathy (81 per cent) with 21.7 per cent adding pity, sorrow or sadness. Apprehension was the second most frequently occurring (33 per cent) followed by fear (21.7 per cent). Confusion was expressed by 15.9 per cent as was uncertainty. Positive feelings such as pleasure and happiness were interspersed with those above, but only by a relatively small percentage of people. Guilt was indicated by 10 per cent of respondents and anger by 5.8 per cent. Indifference was shown by 13 per cent.

When asked 'Should residents be consulted prior to people with mental handicaps moving nearby?' a small majority, 55.6 per cent, thought it unnecessary for people (neighbours) to be consulted, which is encouraging. References were made by some respondents to the rights of people to live where they choose, and not to be vetted or get permission to reside in a particular area.

Those who felt people should be consulted (44.4 per cent) gave various reasons, the most popular being the need to know what to expect and how to help.

It was suggested that support would be more forthcoming if prior consultation took place.

Several people felt that people already living in an area have a <u>right</u> to be considered and involved in the decision. An interesting comment by a respondent who said that consultation should take place was that 'people have a right to live normal, uncomplicated lives'. Another said 'we all have a right to choose our own mode of living' as the reason for being consulted and not wanting people with mental handicaps living nearby. How sad that these definitions of peoples' rights do not include those people with mental handicaps.

An interesting exercise might be to compare, after a period of time, the attitudes of neighbours who had been approached and consulted with those where there had been no special contact or public relations work prior to people with mental handicaps moving into a group home. Unfortunately, as in all these types of exercises, it is impossible to evaluate these situations scientifically because of the inability to create two <u>identical</u> situations and because of the individuality of all the people involved.

An attempt was made to find out what sort of reaction there would be if two people with mental handicaps moved into the respondent's neighbourhood. The response from 39.4 per cent was that they would do nothing with reasons along the lines of 'live and let live', 'it's none of my business' and 'they can live where they choose'.

Those who indicated they would wish to find out more about the people with mental handicaps amounted to 42 per cent (only two of these respondents indicating they would be so opposed to the move as to sign a petition against it). Very few people gave reasons for wanting to know more but those who did suggested it may be easier if they knew what to expect or how they could help, with one person mentioning 'in case violent' and two suggesting their views would depend on the severity of the handicaps the people may have. An inclination to start petitions was given by very few, with four people feeling strongly enough to raise a petition <u>supporting</u> the move but nobody wanting to start one opposing it. A larger proportion would be inclined to sign a petition if asked, with 15 people supporting and four opposing. Those strongly opposed amounted to only 9 per cent, six people either willing to sign a petition against or feeling they would want to move house. The percentage of people wishing to find out more (42 per cent) is very similar to the percentage of respondents who favoured consultation with people already living in the area (44 per cent).

To determine the willingness or otherwise of people to be neighbourly towards people with mental handicaps, several likely responses were listed as indicators. The response to this showed that 70 per cent would help their neighbours (with a mental handicap) if asked. This compares to the lesser number of 40 per cent who would feel able to volunteer help. This point is worth bearing in mind in that there may be many more people available to help if needed than there appears to be initially and a few words of encouragement could promote in certain circumstances a much higher neighbourly goodwill and initiation of involvement.

It was also apparent from the survey result that a high proportion (60 per cent) of people would feel able to visit socially. A rather disappointing finding was that rather fewer people could reciprocate these visits (46.6 per cent) by inviting their neighbours with mental handicaps into their own homes. It was nevertheless encouraging that only 11.6 per cent would not wish to visit, help or be involved in any neighbourly way.

When asked if the relationship people anticipated with their neighbours would differ depending on whether or not the neighbours were handicapped only one person indicated that they would be more inclined to help or be involved with people with handicaps. The majority (82 per cent) said their reactions would be no different with 16.2 per cent indicating a withdrawal of contact. Some of the reasons for this withdrawal were an ability to feel more relaxed, at ease and less awkward if people do not have handicaps.

What Rights Should Mentally Handicapped People Have?

Of the 65 replies to the question asked to determine whether or not people with mental handicaps should be entitled to a list of basic rights, the following positive results were obtained:

A right to		per cent
(1)	Education	92
(2)	Drink in pubs	75
(3)	Normal sex life	67
(4)	Protection from the public	43
(5)	Purpose-built units	69
(6)	Marry	63
(7)	Take part in local social/leisure activities	94
(8)	Work	94
(9)	Have children	28
(10)	Special facilities	77
(11)	Choose where to live	68

This analysis produced some contradictory observations - the same amount of people who thought people with mental handicaps had a right to purpose-built units also thought they should be able to choose where to live. The only three areas from the list which were thought by the majority to be applicable were education, to take part in local social/leisure activities and work. These are probably the areas of most importance in everyone's life with the exception of family life.

A right to a normal sex life, to marry and to have children were in many cases ticked to indicate that a person with mental handicaps has this 'right' but in several cases there was a note to indicate list of conditions, for instance 'Marry - should be allowed if able to function at reasonable level'. In effect it could be argued that the respondents felt that people should <u>not</u> be entitled by right to marry but there may be exceptions 'if able to cope'. This was certainly the case with 'having children' where the most opposition and negative feelings were expressed. A small percentage, 15 per cent, indicated that people with mental handicaps had a right to <u>all</u> the listed items, but because of the controversy between one or two statements (4, 5 and 10) this is more likely to mean a lack of understanding as to the concept of a 'right'. Three people quoted 'Total human rights/the same as everyone'. Very few people listed their own suggestions or ideas of rights people with mental handicaps may have, but those that did included health, pensions and legal rights.

How Involved Should the General Public Be?

The question 'How involved should the general public be?' revealed a definite split in opinions with 47.3 per cent saying firmly that the involvement by the general public should be much more than at present. A similar proportion, 43.6 per cent, said that it must be dependent on the wishes of each individual as to how involved (or not) they wish to be. A very small number, 7.3 per cent, were definite that there should be no involvement from the general public at all. The remaining answers indicated uncertainty ('don't know'), with one exception who felt this would depend on the handicapped person's wishes.

The most interesting point noted in the response to this question was the style of the replies. Very few people gave short direct answers, and many respondents indicated a willingness to discuss the subject and offered personal reasons for their own lack of involvement.

From the 69 returned questionnaires it was possible to determine that 27 people had at some time or another been approached to become involved in one or more ways with people with mental handicaps, or with organisations attached to the mental handicap services.

The type of involvement included fund raising, voluntary work, visiting a residential unit or day centre, attending a talk or visiting/befriending a person with a mental handicap.

An interesting observation is that 63 per cent of people approached had actually followed this through and participated, the most popular area being fund-raising. Unfortunately, fund-raising does not often include any contact with the people for whom the money is being raised. As a result the 'fund-raisers' may be inclined to think of people with mental handicaps as deserving causes and objects of charity work instead of individual people who are more often in need of friends and social relationships than money.

The areas which actually involve contact with individuals such as befriending/visiting people and voluntary work were the subjects of which respondents had been least often approached. <u>All</u> those asked regarding voluntary work followed this through as opposed to 60 per cent of those approached about befriending/visiting people. Of those asked to visit residential places 66 per cent accepted. An immediate conclusion to these observations is that more people should be approached but on reflection this is the approach of salesmen. The more people you contact the more 'sales' you make, and this in turn leads to pressure on and aversion from the 'customers'.

To determine whether people are generally interested in becoming involved a variety of activities were listed and respondents asked to indicate any interest. It appears from the analysis that less than half the respondents would wish to become involved in any direct way. This is a very similar percentage to those who said they had already been approached at one time or another but were not the same respondents. It could, therefore, be anticipated that 15 or 16 of these respondents might follow their expressed interest through.

At the end of the questionnaire those people wishing to talk further on this issue were invited to volunteer their names and addresses. A total of 15 respondents agreed to be contacted again.

REACTIONS TO THE QUESTIONNAIRE

The reactions to the questionnaire produced some comments relating to the difficulty found in answering some of the questions because they 'did not give an indication of the severity of handicaps' and also some expressions of an inability to answer properly because of 'not knowing enough about it'. Very few people felt strongly enough to comment on other aspects of the subject but those that did warrant reproduction.

> I do not wish to be involved, I go out of my way to help friends, family, neighbours, etc, but choose to do so. I feel many facts of life are imposed by 'authority' without consulting the people likely to be involved. I am a great believer in the referendum, but realise that 'authority' dare not institute these as they would not like the results.

> I strongly disagree with the present trend of treating pathetic people in the modern method of community living, it can never be this no matter how hard people try. I see and observe Mencaps every day passing by and bless them they do try to be normal even though they are not. I've answered all the questions from a personal viewpoint with as much honesty as I can. To offer advice to the compiler of these questions would be easy but not productive.

> I am offended by the implication that 'they' are some sort of dirty embarrassment which open-minded survey compilers are not frightened to talk about. Had this survey been on the subject

> of homosexuality, prostitution, blacks, Jews, Irish, etc, etc, would the questions have been all that different? The greatest of prejudice is often unwittingly shown by those purporting to show the greatest concern. Examine <u>your</u> motives.

CONCLUSIONS

The area of public attitudes is far too complicated and personal to achieve conclusive answers through surveys. The general public is composed of individuals all unique in their thoughts and reactions in exactly the same way that people with mental handicaps are. Perhaps the <u>basis</u> of public relations should be to emphasise this very point and to create an atmosphere in which people with mental handicaps are not treated as a separate entity, that is, the general public <u>and</u> people with mental handicaps, but that the general public is made up of <u>all</u> people within a society some of whom happen to have a handicap.

It is a fact of life that people have to earn acceptance within a society, so why should this be any different for people with mental handicaps? Support and advocacy can and should be provided where necessary, but up to now are the 'professionals' guilty of shutting people away from reality and in many ways overprotecting <u>both</u> parties.

People employed as carers or instructors are very guilty of creating a false public image. They show off their 'protegés' to enhance their own public image and lose sight of the effect this has on the general public who visit. Voluntary workers and fund-raisers are encouraged, adding to the image of a charitable organisation which although appears commendable does nothing to get across the modern philosophies.

Groups of non-handicapped people form because of a common interest such as sport, politics, religion, etc, and with the aim of achieving a common goal. People are free to decide with which groups they associate and can change loyalties as and when they choose. Those with mental handicaps are grouped together for other people's convenience and because they are handicapped. The fear, apprehension and aversion felt by the public is not towards one person with a handicap but towards the 'herds', large groups and stereotype images of <u>many</u> people with mental handicaps being kept together. Often, it seems people living with their families are so well known as individuals they are not classed as 'mentally handicapped' by the people who know them.

If normal living, including basic citizen's rights in a democratic society, are to be promoted then the outdated attitudes still portrayed by some of society have to be disregarded. There appears to be little if any understanding of the concept of citizen's rights extending to people with mental handicaps. It seems that if there is any doubt as to a person's capability to exercise their rights then these should be denied the person. Until there is an understanding that rights exist, whether or not they are used, the public will not look upon people with mental handicaps as members of society.

Consultation appears to be important to many people where those with mental handicaps are moving into an area. It seems extremely likely that opposition and hostility will be the reaction from some new neighbours whether or not prior discussion has been organised; in other words, consultation with neighbourhood residents will be a wasted exercise, and will undermine the rights of the people with mental handicaps who are going to live in the area.

Personal involvement and getting to know people over a long period of time has more influence on attitudes than factual information about mental handicaps. The former has the added advantage of dispelling any stereotype images and creating understanding and empathy, but ideally both, hand in hand, will be even more influential. It must not be forgotton that individuals will not all be accepted any more than any member of society if personality traits or social behaviour stray outside the limits of society's toleration or expectations.

Care in the community is <u>not</u> a government-originated policy. It is a promotion of rights started by people very involved with people who have mental handicaps, are mentally ill or are elderly. This was picked up by politicians as a way to provide less costly care. The political overtones now attached to 'community care' are doing more harm than good by building up doubts as to the reasoning behind this move. The publicity which has surrounded this issue has rarely been positive and the public's feeling is one of being 'used' as the government pass on responsibility as a means to an end, that is, to save money. The majority of people with mental handicaps already live in the community and those who have moved from institutional to more normal settings have been able to do so well supported and successfully. These instances will not become widely publicised (nor should they be) to counteract the negative image. But unfortunately, if there is no publicity the immediate feeling is that of suspicion as to what may be covered up or hidden. There does not seem to be an answer to this dilemma.

There is evidence to suggest that a changed term omitting reference to 'mental' would be a positive step. The majority appear to feel that slow learners are able to progress but people with mental handicaps are not - this could be an indication of why people are not particularly interested and are negative when they come across the term mental handicap. It gives the impression of 'nothing to be gained so why bother?'

The general public (groups or individuals) do not have any right to discriminate against people because of their handicaps nor do they have any right to feel their wishes are superior or that they should be instrumental in making decisions which affect the lives of people with mental handicaps, unless by specific request from or by virtue of their commitment to the people affected. Legislation to cover these issues has been suggested and may be the only way to stress the point but unfortunately may serve to deepen any prejudice or hostility already felt.

RECOMMENDATIONS

(1) The rights of people must be promoted by those with mental handicaps and their advocates. It would not take much imagination to create a never ending list but some examples of the ways in which this can be achieved are:

(a) Permission or approval must <u>not</u> be sought in areas where people with mental handicaps may wish to live.

(b) People should not be grouped together because they have handicaps - large outings/holidays/ residential accommodation/leisure and social activities are but a few of the examples where this should apply.

(c) Where discrimination occurs because of a person's handicap then legal action or some form of justice should be pursued to fight the case.

(d) Places where people with mental handicaps live or use daily should not be viewed as places of interest for the public to 'inspect' neither should the people themselves be a spectacle. The prerogative for inviting people lies with those who live or work in an area, not the members of staff employed as carers or instructors.

(2) Voluntary workers should not be discouraged, but an emphasis on one-to-one advocacy should be fostered as an alternative. The term 'voluntary worker' should be dropped. Although extra money is always welcome, fund-raising as an entity in itself should not be encouraged but rather ways of enabling individuals access to greater independent spending power.

(3) People with mental handicaps/advocates should be encouraged to approach neighbours to chat or invite home socially, and know how to ask for help when needed. Where good relationships with neighbours or local people have already been formed these people may be able to offer advice or be willing to discuss sensitive areas with people who have fears or anxieties because their new neighbours have mental handicaps.

(4) Pamphlets such as Myths (from the Campaign for People with Mental Handicap (CMH) 1985) could help to allay fears and should be circulated to public places such as libraries.

(5) The term 'mental' must disappear altogether and whatever term is used instead should follow after 'people' rather than precede as is so often the case with any categorised group: 'people first - disability or category second'.

(6) The National Health Service must make a commitment to reducing the stereotype images that hospital, patients and associated terminology such as inpatient, outpatient, bed-days, etc, create, and make provision throughout the entire system to promote implement and maintain the modern terminology and philosophies.

REFERENCES

Dalgleish, M. (1979) Sheffield Development Project for Mentally Handicapped People: S3 Community Reaction to Local Buildings. Mental Handicap Building Evaluation Programme (HMSO, London)

DHSS (1971) Better Services for the Mentally Handicapped. Cmnd 4683 (HMSO, London)

Hammonds, C. (1980) Family Placements for Mentally Handicapped Children: Workshop Report, Part II, Chapter 7, pp.58-72 (BIMH, Kidderminster)

Hollinger, C. and Jones, R. (1970) 'Community Attitudes Towards Slow Learners and Mental Retardates: What's in a Name'? Mental Retardation, 8, 19

Locker, D. et al. (1979) 'Knowledge of and Attitudes Towards Mental Handicap - Its Implications for Community Care', Community Medicine, 1, 127-36

Males, J. (1980) 'Community Services in Action. Mentally Handicapped Children - Plan for Action', Royal Society of Health Journal, 99(2), 79-81

INDEX